Teacher's Edition

Unit 6
Growing and Changing

Nell Duke • Douglas Clements • Julie Sarama • William Teale

The McGraw-Hill Companies

Authors

Nell Duke
Professor of Teacher Education and Educational Psychology and Co-Director of the Literacy Achievement Research Center Michigan State University, East Lansing, MI

Douglas H. Clements
Professor of Early Childhood and Mathematics Education University at Buffalo, State University of New York, New York

Julie Sarama
Associate Professor of Mathematics Education University at Buffalo, State University of New York, New York

William Teale
Professor of Education University of Illinois at Chicago, Chicago, IL

Contributing Authors

Kim Brenneman, PhD
Assistant Research Professor of Psychology at Rutgers University, National Institute for Early Education Research Rutgers University, New Brunswick, NJ

Peggy Cerna
Early Childhood Consultant Austin, TX

Dan Cieloha
Educator and President of the Partnership for Interactive Learning Oakland, CA

Paula Jones
Early Childhood Consultant Lubbock, TX

Bobbie Sparks
Educator and K-12 Science Consultant Houston, TX

Image Credits: Cover (wheels)felinda/istockphoto, (all other)The McGraw-Hill Companies; **18-19** Frank Krahmer/Getty Images; **19** Royalty-Free/Masterfile; **24** Asia Images Group/Getty Images; **25** The McGraw-Hill Companies/Ken Karp photographer; **26** Mike Wesley; **32** Digital Zoo/Getty Images; **36** John Kurtz; **38** Ingram Publishing/Alamy; **41** Jan Bryan-Hunt; **44** Valeria Cis; **48** Photodisc Collection/Getty Images; **48** Steve Mack; **50** Hector Borlasca; **54** The McGraw-Hill **56-57** Comstock/JupiterImages; **57** Image Source/Getty Images; **62** Radius Images/CORBIS; **63** Takako Kawai/Getty Images; **64** John Kurtz; **70** Kirk Weddle/Photodisc/Getty Images; **76** Getty Images; **80** Steve Mack; **86** C Squared Studios/Getty Images; **92** (t)Ingram Publishing/Alamy, (tc)The McGraw-Hill Companies, Inc., (bc b)C Squared Studios/Getty Images; **94-95 100** Royalty-Free/Masterfile; **101** Creatas/PunchStock; **102** Daniel Griffo; **112** (all)The McGraw-Hill Companies; **113 116** Stockbyte; **118** Mike Wesley; **122** Melissa Iwai; **123** Jose Luis Pelaez/Blend Images/Getty Images; **126** Ryan McVay/Getty Images; **130** Jan Bryan-Hill; **132-133** Don Farrall/Getty Images; **133** Royalty-Free/Masterfile; **138** Ariel Skelley/Blend Images/CORBIS; **139** IT Stock/PunchStock; **144** Enigma/Alamy; **149** Steve Mack; **152** Burke Triolo Productions / Getty Images; **156** Daniel Griffo; **162** Laura Gonzalez; **162** Melissa Iwai; **163** Royalty-Free/CORBIS; **164** Melissa Iwai; **166** Ingram Publishing/Alamy; **168-169** TSI Graphics; **171** (r)The McGraw-Hill Companies, Inc./Ken Cavanagh photographer; **172** Ariel Skelle/Getty Images; **178** D. Berry/PhotoLink/Getty Images; **181** (t)Steve Mack, (c)Ingram Publishing/Alamy, (b)Daniel Griffo; **183** (t)Susan LeVan/Getty Images, (b)Laura Gonzalez; **185** Mike Wesley; **186** (t)The McGraw-Hill Companies, Inc., (b)Eileen Hine; **192** Photodisc Collection/Getty Images; **BackCover** (all wheels)felinda/istockphoto, (pencil)Andy Crawford/Getty Images, (rust wicker)Comstock/CORBIS, (bell)Stockbyte/Getty Images, (webcam)Medioimages/Photodisc/Getty Images, (pencilmirror)Yasuhide Fumoto/Getty Images, (U3roof)Ryan McVay/Getty Images, (elephant)PhotoLink/Getty Images, (looking glass) CMCD/Getty Images, (alligator)Siede Preis/Getty Images, (alligatorbelly)Ryan McVay/Getty Images, (U5traincar)83owl/ Getty Images, (toothbrush)Raimund Koch/Getty Images, (U8traincar)Ryan McVay/Getty Images, (brush)Brand X Pictures/PunchStock, (all other)The McGraw-Hill Companies.

The McGraw·Hill Companies

www.WrightGroup.com

Printed in the United States of America.

Send all inquiries to:
Wright Group/McGraw-Hill
P.O. Box 812960
Chicago, IL 60681

ISBN 978-0-07-658084-2
MHID 0-07-658084-9

2 3 4 5 6 7 8 9 WEB 16 15 14 13 12 11 10

Acknowledgment

Building Blocks was supported in part by the National Science Foundation under Grant No. ESI-9730804, "Building Blocks— Foundations for Mathematical Thinking, Pre-Kindergarten to Grade 2: Research-based Materials Development" to Douglas H. Clements and Julie Sarama. The curriculum was also based partly upon work supported in part by the Institute of Educational Sciences (U.S. Dept. of Education, under the Interagency Education Research Initiative, or IERI, a collaboration of the IES, NSF, and NICHHD) under Grant No. R305K05157, "Scaling Trajectories and Technologies" and by the IERI through a National Science Foundation NSF Grant No. REC-0228440, "Scaling Up the Implementation of a Pre-Kindergarten Mathematics Curricula: Teaching for Understanding with Trajectories and Technologies." Any opinions, findings, and conclusions or recommendations expressed in this material are those of the authors and do not necessarily reflect the views of the funding agencies.

Reviewers

Tonda Brown, *Pre-K Specialist*, Austin ISD; Deanne Colley, *Family Involvement Facilitator*, Northwest ISD; Anita Uphaus, *Retired Early Childhood Director*, Austin ISD; Cathy Ambridge, *Reading Specialist*, Klein ISD; Margaret Jordan, *PreK Special Education Teacher*, McMullen Booth Elementary; Niki Rogers, *Adjunct Professor of Psychology/ Child Development*, Concordia University Wisconsin

Table of Contents

Getting Started

Getting Started with *The DLM Early Childhood Express*

The DLM Early Childhood Express is a holistic, child-centered program that nurtures each child by offering carefully selected and carefully sequenced learning experiences. It provides a wealth of materials and ideas to foster the social-emotional, intellectual, and physical development of children. At the same time, it nurtures the natural curiosity and sense of self that can serve as the foundation for a lifetime of learning.

The lesson format is designed to present information in a way that makes it easy for children to learn. Intelligence is, in large part, our ability to see patterns and build relationships out of those patterns, which is why *DLM* is focused on helping children see the patterns in what they are learning. It builds an understanding of how newly taught material resembles what children already know. Then it takes the differences in the new material and helps the children convert them into new understanding.

Each of the eight Teacher Edition Unit's in *DLM* are centered on an Essential Question relating to the unit's theme. Each week has its own more specific focus question. By focusing on essential questions, children are better able to connect their existing knowledge of the world with the new concepts and ideas they are learning at school. Routines at the beginning and end of each day help children focus on the learning process, reflect on new concepts, and make important connections. The lessons are designed to allow children to apply what they have learned.

Social and Emotional Development

Social-emotional development is addressed everyday through positive reinforcement, interactive activities, and engaging songs.

Language and Communication

All lessons are focused on language acquisition, which includes oral language development and vocabulary activities.

Emergent Literacy: Reading

Children develop literacy skills for reading through exposure to multiple read-aloud selections each day and through daily phonological awareness and letter recognition activities.

Emergent LIteracy: Writing

Children develop writing skills through daily writing activities and during Center Time.

Mathematics

The math strand is based on *Building Blocks,* the result of NSF-funded research, and is designed to develop children's early mathematical knowledge through various individual and group activities.

Science

Children explore scientific concepts and methods during weekly science-focused, large-group activities, and Center Time activities.

Social Studies

Children explore Social Studies concepts during weekly social studies-focused, large-group activities, and Center Time activities.

Fine Arts

Children are exposed to art, dance, and music through a variety of weekly activities and the Creativity Center.

Physical Development

DLM is designed to allow children active time for outdoor play during the day, in addition to daily and weekly movement activities.

Technology Applications

Technology is integrated throughout each week with the use of online math activities, computer time, and other digital resources.

English Language Learners

Today's classrooms are very diverse. *The DLM Early Childhood Express* addresses this diversity by providing lessons in both English and Spanish. The program also offers strategies to assist English Language Learners at multiple levels of proficiency.

Flexible Scheduling

With *The DLM Early Childhood Express*, it's easy to fit lessons into your day.

Typical Full-Day Schedule

10 min	Opening Routines
15 min	Language Time
60-90 min	Center Time
15 min	Snack Time
15 min	Literacy Time
20 min	Active Play (outdoors if possible)
30 min	Lunch
15 min	Math Time
	Rest
15 min	Circle Time: Social and Emotional Development
20 min	Circle Time: Content Connection
30 min	Center Time
25 min	Active Play (outdoors if possible)
15 min	Let's Say Good-Bye

Typical Half-Day Schedule

10 min	Opening Routines
15 min	Language Time
60 min	Center Time
15 min	Snack Time
15 min	Circle Time (Literacy, Math, or Social and Emotional Development)
30 min	Active Play (outdoors if possible)
20 min	Circle Time (Content Connection, Literacy, Math, or Social and Emotional Development)
15 min	Let's Say Good-Bye

Welcome to *The DLM Early Childhood Express.*

Add your own ideas. Mix and match activities. Our program is designed to offer you a variety of activities on which to build a full year of exciting and creative lessons.

Happy learning to you and the children in your care!

Themes and Literature

With *The DLM Early Childhood Express,* children develop concrete skills through experiences with music, art, storytelling, hands-on activities and teacher-directed lessons that, in addition to skills development, emphasize practice and reflection. Every four weeks, children are introduced to a new theme organized around an essential question.

Literature selections and cross-curricular content are linked to the theme to help children reinforce lesson concepts. Children hear and discuss an additional read-aloud selection from the *Teacher Treasure Book* at the beginning and end of each day. At the end of each unit, children take home a *My Theme Library Book* reader of their own.

Unit 1: All About Pre-K
Why is school important?

	Focus Question	Literature
Week 1	What happens at school?	Welcome to School Bienvenidos a la escuela
Week 2	What happens in our classroom?	Yellowbelly and Plum Go to School Barrigota y Pipón van a la escuela
Week 3	What makes a good friend?	Max and Mo's First Day at School Max y Mo van a la escuela
Week 4	How can we play and learn together?	Amelia's Show and Tell Fiesta/Amelia y la fiesta de "muestra y cuenta"
Unit Wrap-Up	My Library Book	How Can I Learn at School? ¿Cómo puedo aprender en la escuela?

Unit 2: All About Me
What makes me special?

	Focus Question	Literature
Week 1	Who am I?	All About Me Todo sobre mí
Week 2	What are my feelings?	Lots of Feelings Montones de sentimientos
Week 3	What do the parts of my body do?	Eyes, Nose, Fingers, and Toes Ojos, nariz, dedos y pies
Week 4	What is a family?	Jonathan and His Mommy Juan y su mamá
Unit Wrap-Up	My Library Book	What Makes Us Special? ¿Qué nos hace especiales?

Unit 3: My Community
What is a community?

	Focus Question	Literature
Week 1	What are the parts of a community?	In the Community En la comunidad
Week 2	Hoe does a community help me?	Rush Hour, Hora pico
Week 3	Who helps the community?	Quinito's Neighborhood
Week 4	How can I help my community?	Flower Garden Un jardín de flores
Unit Wrap-Up	My Library Book	In My Community Mi comunidad

Unit 4: Let's Investigate
How can I learn more about things?

	Focus Question	Literature
Week 1	How can I learn by observing?	Let's Investigate Soy detective
Week 2	How can I use tools to investiagte?	I Like Making Tamales Me gusta hacer tamales
Week 3	How can I compare things?	Nature Spy Espía de la naturaleza
Week 4	How do objects move?	What Do Wheels Do All Day? ¿Qué hacen las ruedas todo el día?
Unit Wrap-Up	My Library Book	How Can We Investigate? ¿Cómo podemos investigar?

Unit 5: Amazing Animals
What is amazing about animals?

	Focus Question	Literature
Week 1	What are animals like?	Amazing Animals Animales asombrosos
Week 2	Where do animals live and what do they eat?	Castles, Caves, and Honeycombs Castillos, cuevas y panales
Week 3	How are animals the same and different?	Who Is the Beast? Quien es la bestia?
Week 4	How do animals move?	Move! ¡A moverse!
Unit Wrap-Up	**My Library Book**	Hello, Animals! ¡Hola, animales!

Unit 6: Growing and Changing
How do living things grow and change?

	Focus Question	Literature
Week 1	How do animals grow and change?	Growing and Changing Creciendo y cambiando
Week 2	How do plants grow and change?	I Am a Peach Yo soy el durazno
Week 3	How do people grow and change?	I'm Growing! Estoy creciendo!
Week 4	How do living things grow and change?	My Garden Mi jardin
Unit Wrap-Up	**My Library Book**	Growing Up Creciendo

Unit 7: The Earth and Sky
What can I learn about the earth and the sky?

	Focus Question	Literature
Week 1	What can I learn about the earth and the sky?	The Earth and Sky La Tierra y el cielo
Week 2	What weather can I observe each day?	Who Likes Rain? ¿A quién le gusta la lluvia?
Week 3	What can I learn about day and night?	Matthew and the Color of the Sky Matias y el color del cielo
Week 4	Why is caring for the earth and sky important?	Ada, Once Again! ¡Otra vez Ada!
Unit Wrap-Up	**My Library Book**	Good Morning, Earth! ¡Buenos días, Tierra!

Unit 8: Healthy Food/Healthy Body
Why is healthy food and exercise good for me?

	Focus Question	Literature
Week 1	What are good healthy habits?	Staying Healthy Mantente sano
Week 2	What kinds of foods are healthy?	Growing Vegetable Soup A sembrar sopa de verduras
Week 3	Why is exercise important?	Rise and Exercise! A ejercitarse, ¡uno, dos, tres!
Week 4	How can I stay healthy?	Jamal's Busy Day El intenso día de Jamal
Unit Wrap-Up	**My Library Book**	Healthy Kids Niños sanos

Tools for Teaching

The DLM Early Childhood Express is packed full of the components you'll need to teach each theme and enrich your classroom. The *Teacher Treasure Package* is the heart of the program, because it contains all the necessary materials. Plus, the *Teacher's Treasure Book* contains all the fun components that you'll love to teach. The *Literature Package* contains all the stories and books you need to support children's developing literacy. You'll find letter tiles, counters, and puppets in the *Manipulative Package* to connect hands-on learning skills with meaningful play.

Teacher Treasure Package

This package contains all the essential tools for the teacher such as the *Teacher's Treasure Book*, *Teacher's Editions*, technology, and other resources no teacher would want to be without!

Alphabet Wall Cards
(English and Spanish)

ABC Picture Cards
(English and Spanish)

Sequence Cards
(English and Spanish)

Oral Language Development Cards
(English and Spanish)

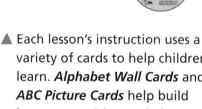

Photo Library
CD-ROM

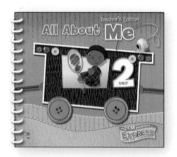

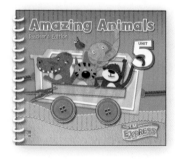
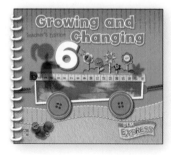

▲ Each lesson's instruction uses a variety of cards to help children learn. **Alphabet Wall Cards** and **ABC Picture Cards** help build letter recognition and phonemic awareness. **Oral Language Development Cards** teach new vocabulary, and are especially helpful when working with English Language Learners. **Sequencing Cards** help children learn how to order events and the vocabulary associated with time and sequence.

▲ There is one bilingual **Teacher's Edition** for each four-week theme. It provides the focus questions for each lesson as well as plans for centers and suggestions for classroom management.

▶ The bilingual **Teacher's Treasure Book** features 500+ pages of the things you love most about teaching Early Childhood, such as songs, traditional read alouds, folk tales, finger plays, and flannelboard stories with patterns.

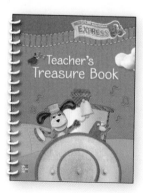

▶ An **ABC Take-Home Book** with blackline masters is provided for each letter of the English and Spanish alphabets.

ABC Take-Home Book
(English and Spanish)

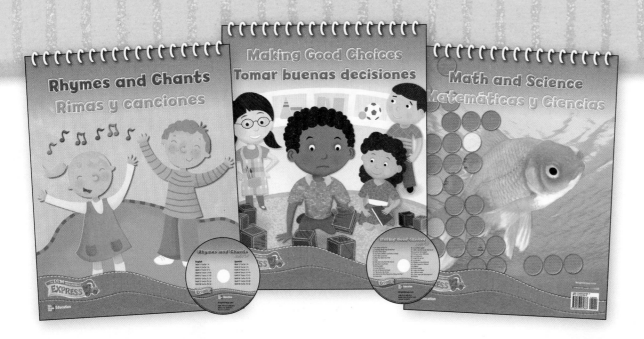

▶ Flip charts and their Audio CDs support the activities in each lesson. Children practice literacy and music skills using the **Rhymes and Chants Flip Chart,** which supports oral language development and phonological awareness in both English and Spanish. An Audio CD is included and provides a recording of every rhyme or chant. The **Making Good Choices Flip Chart** provides illustrations to allow students to explore social and emotional development concepts while facilitating classroom activities and discussion. 15 lively songs recorded in both English and Spanish address key social emotional development themes such as: joining in, helping others, being fair, teasing, bullying, and much more. The **Math and Science Flip Chart** is a demonstration tool that addresses weekly math and science concepts through photos and illustrations.

▶ Other key resources include a **Research & Professional Development Guide,** and a bilingual **Home Connections Resource Guide** which provides weekly letters home and take-home story books.

Building Blocks

Building Blocks, the result of NSF-funded research, develops young children's mathematical thinking using their bodies, manipulatives, paper, and computers.

Building Blocks online management system guides children through research-based learning trajectories. These activities-through-trajectories connect children's informal knowledge to more formal school mathematics. The result is a mathematical curriculum that is not only motivating for children but also comprehensive.

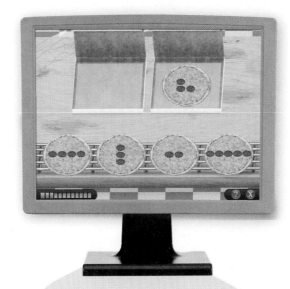

▶ **DLMExpressOnline.com** includes the following:

● e-Books of student and teacher materials

● Audio recordings of the **My Library** and **Literature Books** (Big/Little) in English and Spanish

● Teacher planning tools and assessment support

Tools for Teaching

Literature Package

This package contains the literature referenced in the program. Packages are available in several variations so you can choose the package that best meets the needs of your classroom. The literature used in the program includes expository selections, traditional stories, and emergent readers for students. All literature is available in English or Spanish.

▶ *My Library Books* are take-home readers for children to continue their exploration of unit themes. (English and Spanish)

Los i
obser
cosas
en la
20

den

nest

foxes

elephant

Baby animals need help to grow big and strong. Baby animals need a safe place to live.
20

Concept Big Book 4

7 The Earth and Sky

EXPRESS

Staying Healthy
8

▶ *Concept Big Books* are nonfiction selections that introduce the essential questions for each unit and help children make connections between their background knowledge and unit themes. (English and Spanish)

▶ The *ABC Big Book* helps children develop phonemic awareness and letter recognition. (English and Spanish)

▶ The **Big Books** and **Little Books** reinforce each week's theme and the unit theme. Selections include stories originally written in Spanish, as well as those written in English.

▶ The stories in the **Big Books and Little Books** are recorded on the **Listening Library Audio CDs**. They are available in English and Spanish.

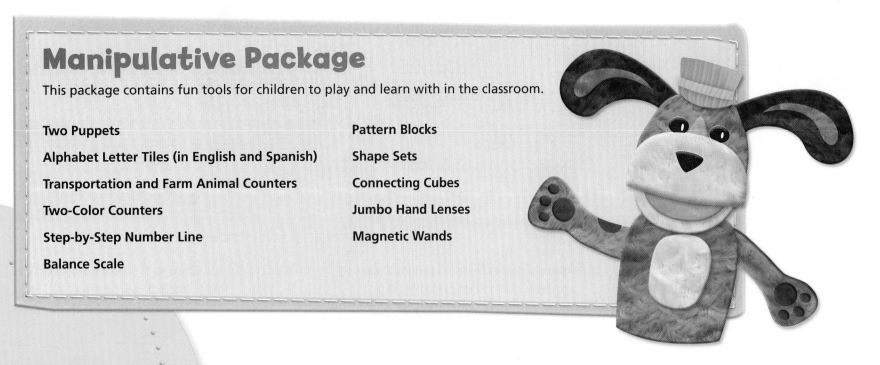

Manipulative Package

This package contains fun tools for children to play and learn with in the classroom.

Two Puppets

Alphabet Letter Tiles (in English and Spanish)

Transportation and Farm Animal Counters

Two-Color Counters

Step-by-Step Number Line

Balance Scale

Pattern Blocks

Shape Sets

Connecting Cubes

Jumbo Hand Lenses

Magnetic Wands

A Typical Weekly Lesson Plan

Each week of *The DLM Early Childhood Express* is organized the same way to provide children with the structure and routines they crave. Each week begins with a weekly opener that introduces the focus question for the week and includes a review of the week's Learning Goals, the Materials and Resources needed for the week, a Daily Planner, and a plan for the Learning Centers children will use throughout the week.

Each day's lesson includes large-group Circle Time and small-group Center Time. Each day includes Literacy, Math, and Social and Emotional Development activities during Circle Time. On Day 1, children explore Science. On Days 2 and 4, they work on more in-depth math lessons. On Day 3, Social Studies is the focus. Fine Art or Music/Movement activities take place during Circle Time on Day 5.

You will find the **Program Materials** and **Other Materials** needed for each day on the Materials and Resources page.

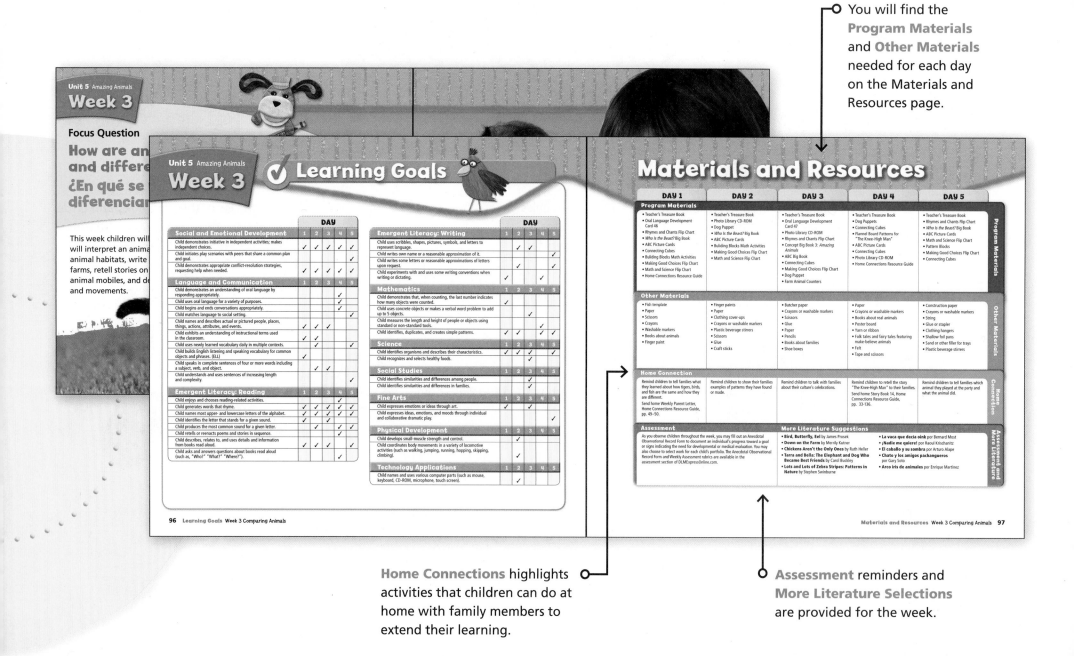

Home Connections highlights activities that children can do at home with family members to extend their learning.

Assessment reminders and **More Literature Selections** are provided for the week.

The **Daily Planner** provides a Week-at-a-Glance view of the daily structure and lesson topics for each week.

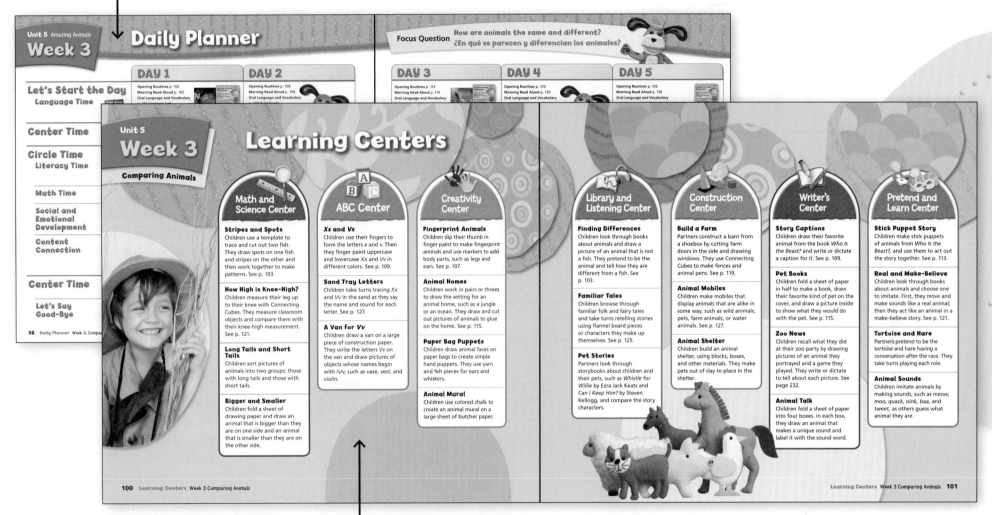

Unit 5 Amazing Animals
Week 3

Daily Planner

Focus Question: How are animals the same and different?
¿En qué se parecen y diferencian los animales?

Let's Start the Day — Language Time	DAY 1	DAY 2	DAY 3	DAY 4	DAY 5
	Opening Routines p. 102	Opening Routines p. 108	Opening Routines p. 114	Opening Routines p. 120	Opening Routines p. 126
	Morning Read Aloud p. 102	Morning Read Aloud p. 108	Morning Read Aloud p. 114	Morning Read Aloud p. 120	Morning Read Aloud p. 126
	Oral Language and Vocabulary	Oral Language and Vocabulary	Oral Language and Vocabulary	Oral Language and Vocabulary	Oral Language and Vocabulary

Center Time

Circle Time
Literacy Time

Math Time

Social and Emotional Development

Content Connection

Center Time

Let's Say Good-Bye

98 Daily Planner Week 3, Compa...

Unit 5 **Week 3**
Comparing Animals

Learning Centers

Math and Science Center

Stripes and Spots
Children use a template to trace and cut out two fish. They draw spots on one fish and stripes on the other and then work together to make patterns. See p. 103.

How High is Knee-High?
Children measure their leg up to their knee with Connecting Cubes. They measure classroom objects and compare them with their knee-high measurement. See p. 121.

Long Tails and Short Tails
Children sort pictures of animals into two groups: those with long tails and those with short tails.

Bigger and Smaller
Children fold a sheet of drawing paper and draw an animal that is bigger than they are on one side and an animal that is smaller than they are on the other side.

ABC Center

Xs and Vs
Children use their fingers to form the letters x and v. Then they finger paint uppercase and lowercase Xx and Vv in different colors. See p. 109.

Sand Tray Letters
Children take turns tracing Xx and Vv in the sand as they say the name and sound for each letter. See p. 127.

A Van for Vv
Children draw a van on a large piece of construction paper. They write the letters Vv on the van and draw pictures of objects whose names begin with /v/v, such as vase, vest, and violin.

Creativity Center

Fingerprint Animals
Children dip their thumb in finger paint to make fingerprint animals and use markers to add body parts, such as legs and ears. See p. 107.

Animal Homes
Children work in pairs or threes to draw the setting for an animal home, such as a jungle or an ocean. They draw and cut out pictures of animals to glue on the home. See p. 115.

Paper Bag Puppets
Children draw animal faces on paper bags to create simple hand puppets. They use yarn and felt pieces for ears and whiskers.

Animal Mural
Children use colored chalk to create an animal mural on a large sheet of butcher paper.

Library and Listening Center

Finding Differences
Children look through books about animals and draw a picture of an animal that is not a fish. They pretend to be the animal and tell how they are different from a fish. See p. 103.

Familiar Tales
Children browse through familiar folk and fairy tales and take turns retelling stories using flannel board pieces or characters they make up themselves. See p. 125.

Pet Stories
Partners look through storybooks about children and their pets, such as Whistle for Willie by Ezra Jack Keats and Can I Keep Him? by Steven Kellogg, and compare the story characters.

Construction Center

Build a Farm
Partners construct a barn from a shoebox by cutting farm doors in the side and drawing windows. They use Connecting Cubes to make fences and animal pens. See p. 119.

Animal Mobiles
Children make mobiles that display animals that are alike in some way, such as wild animals, pets, farm animals, or water animals. See p. 127.

Animal Shelter
Children build an animal shelter, using blocks, boxes, and other materials. They make pets out of clay to place in the shelter.

Writer's Center

Story Captions
Children draw their favorite animal from the book Who Is the Beast? and write or dictate a caption for it. See p. 109.

Pet Books
Children fold a sheet of paper in half to make a book, draw their favorite kind of pet on the cover, and draw a picture inside to show what they would do with the pet. See p. 115.

Zoo News
Children recall what they did at their zoo party by drawing pictures of an animal they portrayed and a game they played. They write or dictate to tell about each picture. See page 232.

Animal Talk
Children fold a sheet of paper into four boxes. In each box, they draw an animal that makes a unique sound and label it with the sound word.

Pretend and Learn Center

Stick Puppet Story
Children make stick puppets of animals from the book Who Is the Beast?, and use them to act out the story together. See p. 113.

Real and Make-Believe
Children look through books about animals and choose one to imitate. First, they move and make sounds like a real animal; then they act like an animal in a make-believe story. See p. 121.

Tortoise and Hare
Partners pretend to be the tortoise and hare having a conversation after the race. They take turns playing each role.

Animal Sounds
Children imitate animals by making sounds, such as meow, moo, quack, oink, baa, and tweet, as others guess what animal they are.

100 Learning Centers Week 3 Comparing Animals

Learning Centers Week 3 Comparing Animals 101

Learning Centers should be used throughout the week during Center Time. This page provides an overview of center activities to set up for children. Additional information about some center activities is provided in the daily lessons. The Learning Centers are intended to remain open for the entire week. These centers provide the opportunity for children to explore a wide range of curricular areas.

Lesson Overview

Our **Teacher's Editions** are organized by theme, week, and day. Each day's lesson is covered in six page spreads. The lessons integrate learning from the skill domain areas of: Social Emotional Development, Language and Communication, Emergent Literacy Reading and Writing, Mathematics, Science, Social Studies, Fine Arts, Physical Development, and Technology.

Each day begins with **Opening Routines** and a **Read Aloud** selection. This structured time helps children settle into their day.

The **Learning Goals** met by the lesson are listed on each page.

Observational Checks at point of use help to focus learning. These informal assessment questions help to ensure children are meeting lesson objectives.

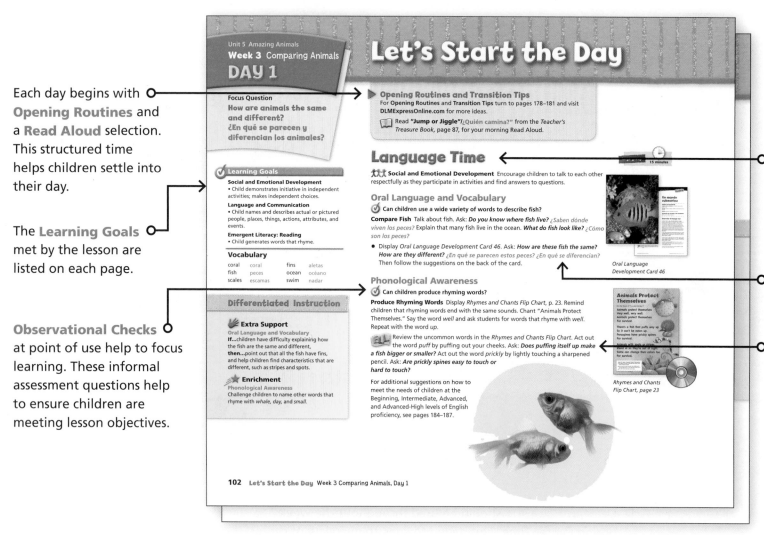

Language Time is the first large-group activity of the day. It includes Oral Language and Vocabulary Development as well as Phonological Awareness activities.

Instructional questions are provided in both **English and Spanish**.

Tips for working with **English Language Learners** are shown at point of use throughout the lessons. Teaching strategies are provided to help children of of all language backgrounds and abilities meet the lesson objectives.

Center Time provides additional information for teacher-guided small-group activities and suggestions for independent activities children will complete during weekly Center Rotation.

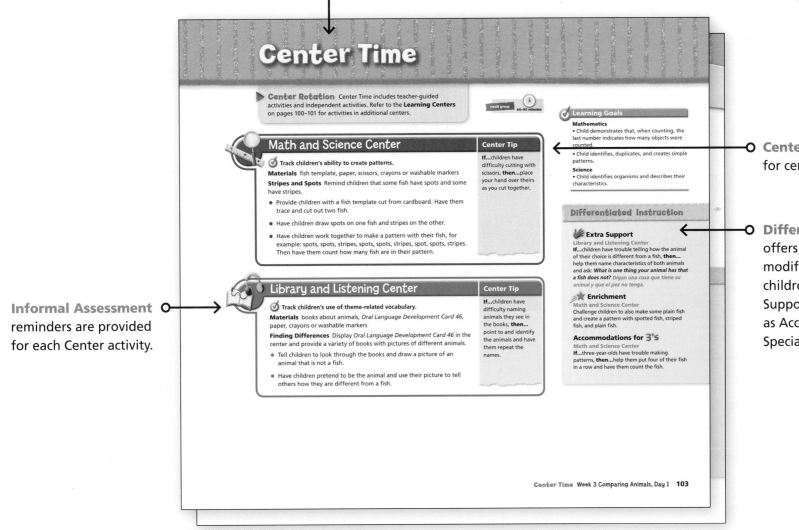

Center Time

▶ **Center Rotation** Center Time includes teacher-guided activities and independent activities. Refer to the **Learning Centers** on pages 100–101 for activities in additional centers.

small group | 60–90 minutes

Math and Science Center

✓ Track children's ability to create patterns.

Materials fish template, paper, scissors, crayons or washable markers

Stripes and Spots Remind children that some fish have spots and some have stripes.

- Provide children with a fish template cut from cardboard. Have them trace and cut out two fish.
- Have children draw spots on one fish and stripes on the other.
- Have children work together to make a pattern with their fish, for example: spots, spots, stripes, spots, spots, stripes, spot, spots, stripes. Then have them count how many fish are in their pattern.

Center Tip
If...children have difficulty cutting with scissors, **then**...place your hand over theirs as you cut together.

Library and Listening Center

✓ Track children's use of theme-related vocabulary.

Materials books about animals, *Oral Language Development Card 46*, paper, crayons or washable markers

Finding Differences Display *Oral Language Development Card 46* in the center and provide a variety of books with pictures of different animals.

- Tell children to look through the books and draw a picture of an animal that is not a fish.
- Have children pretend to be the animal and use their picture to tell others how they are different from a fish.

Center Tip
If...children have difficulty naming animals they see in the books, **then**...point to and identify the animals and have them repeat the names.

Learning Goals

Mathematics
- Child demonstrates that, when counting, the last number indicates how many objects were counted.
- Child identifies, duplicates, and creates simple patterns.

Science
- Child identifies organisms and describes their characteristics.

Differentiated Instruction

✋ **Extra Support**
Library and Listening Center
If...children have trouble telling how the animal of their choice is different from a fish, **then**...help them name characteristics of both animals and ask: *What is one thing your animal has that a fish does not? Digan una cosa que tiene su animal y que el pez no tenga.*

⭐ **Enrichment**
Math and Science Center
Challenge children to also make some plain fish and create a pattern with spotted fish, striped fish, and plain fish.

Accommodations for 3's
Math and Science Center
If...three-year-olds have trouble making patterns, **then**...help them put four of their fish in a row and have them count the fish.

Center Time Week 3 Comparing Animals, Day 1   **103**

Center Tips are provided for center support.

Differentiated Instruction offers suggestions for modifications to activities for children who may need Extra Support or Enrichment, as well as Accommodations for 3's and Special Needs.

Informal Assessment reminders are provided for each Center activity.

Lesson Overview

Children have **Literacy Time** every day. During this time, children listen to and discuss a second Read Aloud from a nonfiction **Concept Big Book** or a **Big Book/Little Book** literature selection

Building Blocks online activities are provided each week during Math Time.

Children work in large groups on 15 minute math activities during daily **Math Time.**

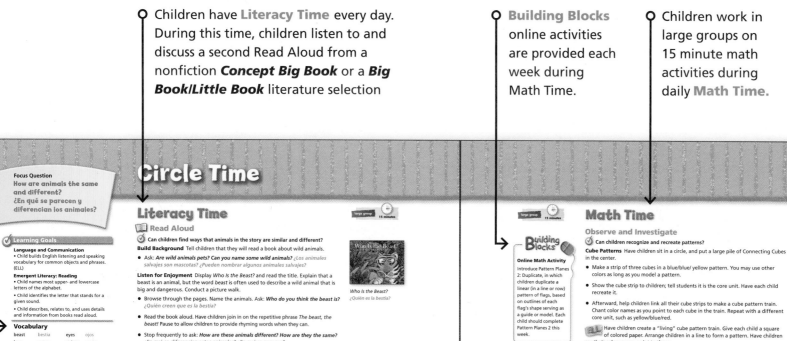

Focus Question
How are animals the same and different?
¿En qué se parecen y diferencian los animales?

Circle Time

Literacy Time

Read Aloud

✓ Can children find ways that animals in the story are similar and different?

Build Background Tell children that they will read a book about wild animals.

- Ask: *Are wild animals pets? Can you name some wild animals?* ¿Los animales salvajes son mascotas? ¿Pueden nombrar algunos animales salvajes?

Listen for Enjoyment Display *Who Is the Beast?* and read the title. Explain that a beast is an animal, but the word *beast* is often used to describe a wild animal that is big and dangerous. Conduct a picture walk.

- Browse through the pages. Name the animals. Ask: *Who do you think the beast is?* ¿Quién creen que es la bestia?
- Read the book aloud. Have children join in on the repetitive phrase *The beast, the beast!* Pause to allow children to provide rhyming words when they can.
- Stop frequently to ask: *How are these animals different? How are they the same?* ¿En qué se diferencian estos animales? ¿En qué se parecen?

Respond to the Story Discuss the story. Ask: *How is the tiger different from the other animals in the story? How is the tiger the same?* ¿En qué se diferencia el tigre de los demás animales del cuento? ¿En qué se parece?

TIP Revisit the illustrations in the book to help children describe how the tiger is different from and similar to the other animals.

ELL As you read aloud, point to details in the illustrations to help children understand words such as *tail, stripes, legs, eyes, whiskers,* and *tracks.* Use gestures and movements for phrases such as *fly by, swing high and low, turn back, buzz along, hide from sight,* and *filled with fear.*

Learn About Letters and Sounds

✓ Can children identify sounds and letters /v/ spelled *Vv* and /ks/ spelled *Xx*?

Identify Letters and Sounds /v/*Vv,* /ks/*Xx* Display the ABC Picture Cards for *Vv* and *Xx.*

- Have children write each letter in the air as they name the letter and say the sound. *What is the letter? What sound does it stand for?* ¿Cómo se llama la letra? ¿Qué sonido tiene?
- Have children write *v* and *x* on index cards. Say: *I will say a letter. Hold up your letter card after I say it.* Yo voy a decir una letra. Levanten la tarjeta con esa letra después de que yo la diga. Say the letter names several times in random order.
- Say: *Now I will say the sounds of the letters. Hold up a letter card for each sound.* Ahora, voy a decir los sonidos de las letras. Levanten una tarjeta de letra por cada sonido que diga. Say /v/ and /ks/ several times in random order.

Who Is the Beast?
¿Quién es la bestia?

Vv violin
Xx x-ray

Learning Goals

Language and Communication
• Child builds English listening and speaking vocabulary for common objects and phrases. (ELL)

Emergent Literacy: Reading
• Child names most upper- and lowercase letters of the alphabet.
• Child identifies the letter that stands for a given sound.
• Child describes, relates to, and uses details and information from books read aloud.

Vocabulary

beast	bestia	eyes	ojos
legs	patas	stripes	rayas
tail	cola	tracks	huellas
whiskers	bigotes		

Differentiated Instruction

Extra Support
Learn About Letters and Sounds
If...children have difficulty remembering letter sounds, then...practice the sounds with them several times as they trace over the letters on the ABC Picture Cards.

Enrichment
Read Aloud
After reading aloud the book once, page through the illustrations and have children take turns telling what happens on each page.

Special Needs
Hearing Impairment
Teach all children the signs for some of the animals you will study this week. Display photographs of each animal, and use the sign when talking about a specific animal.

Math Time

Observe and Investigate

✓ Can children recognize and recreate patterns?

Cube Patterns Have children sit in a circle, and put a large pile of Connecting Cubes in the center.

- Make a strip of three cubes in a blue/blue/ yellow pattern. You may use other colors as long as you model a pattern.
- Show the cube strip to children; tell students it is the core unit. Have each child recreate it.
- Afterward, help children link all their cube strips to make a cube pattern train. Chant color names as you point to each cube in the train. Repeat with a different core unit, such as yellow/blue/red.

ELL Have children create a "living" cube pattern train. Give each child a square of colored paper. Arrange children in a line to form a pattern. Have children say their colors as you point to them.

Building Blocks

Online Math Activity
Introduce Pattern Planes 2: Duplicate, in which children duplicate a linear (in a line or row) pattern of flags, based on outlines of each flag's shape serving as a guide or model. Each child should complete Pattern Planes 2 this week.

👣👣👣 Social and Emotional Development

Making Good Choices

✓ Do children understand how to use problem-solving strategies and seek appropriate help when needed?

Solving Problems Discuss how children can solve problems and find answers to their questions. Display the *Making Good Choices Flip Chart,* page 23. Point to the girl working out with cube patterns.

- Ask: *What problem is the girl trying to solve, or figure out? How might she solve the problem?* ¿Qué problema está intentando resolver la niña? ¿Cómo puede resolverlo?
- Discuss how the girl can try to solve the problem on her own and what she should do if she still needs help.
- Ask: *When is it okay to ask for help? When is it okay to offer to help someone?* ¿Cuándo está bien pedir ayuda? ¿Cuándo está bien ofrecer ayuda a alguien?

Making Good Choices Flip Chart, page 23

Learning Goal

Social and Emotional Development
• Child demonstrates initiative in independent activities; makes independent choices.
• Child demonstrates appropriate conflict-resolution strategies, requesting help when needed.

Mathematics
• Child identifies, duplicates, and creates simple patterns.

Vocabulary

cube	cubo	core unit	unidad
pattern	patrón	problem	problema
solve	solucionar		

Differentiated Instruction

Extra Support
Observe and Investigate
If...children struggle when recreating core units, then...help them name the colors in the core unit you made and have them say the colors with you as they recreate it.

Enrichment
Observe and Investigate
Have partners build a longer core unit pattern, for example: yellow/blue/blue/yellow. Have them link their cubes together and say the color names. Then have them continue adding to the pattern.

Vocabulary is provided in English and Spanish to help expand children's ability to use both languages.

Children learn about **Letters and Sounds** every day. The sound is introduced with the letter. Children also practice letter formation.

Social and Emotional Development concepts are addressed every day to help children better express their emotions and needs, and establish positive relationships.

Circle Time is devoted to longer activities focusing on different cross-curricular concepts each day. Day 1 is Science Time. Days 2 and 4 are Math Time. On Day 3, children have Social Studies Time. Fine arts are covered in Art Time or Music and Movement Time on Day 5.

An end-of-the-day **Writing** activity is provided each day.

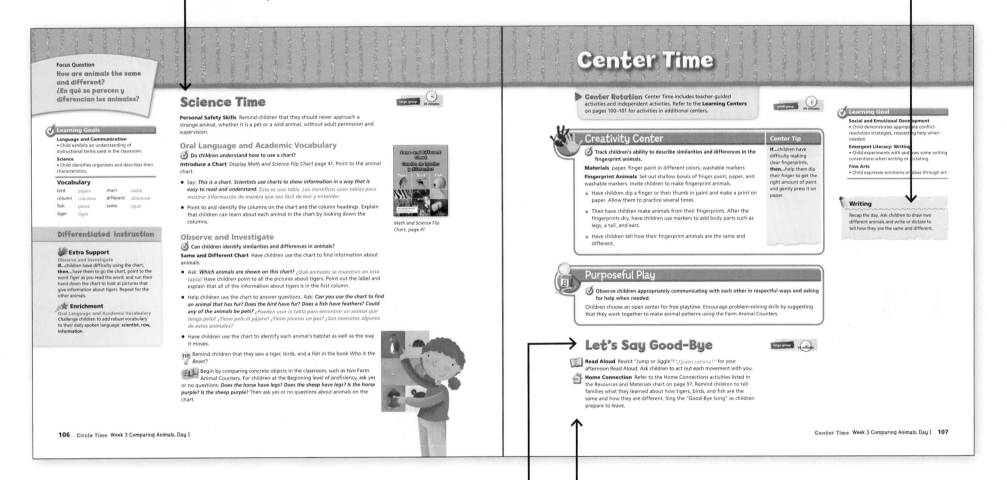

Let's Say Good-Bye includes the closing routines for each day. The Read Aloud from the beginning of the day is revisited with a focus on skills practiced during the day.

Each day provides a **Home Connection**. At the start of each week, a letter is provided to inform families of the weekly focus and offer additional literature suggestions to extend the weekly theme focus.

Week 1

Focus Question

How do animals grow and change?

¿Cómo crecen y cambian los animales?

This week children will learn about animal life cycles. They will compare and contrast adult and baby animals, observe frogs, make sculptures to show life cycle stages, learn about how animals care for their young, and read about animal growth.

✓ Learning Goals

Social and Emotional Development	1	2	3	4	5
Child shows eagerness, curiosity, and confidence while learning new concepts and trying new things.		✓	✓	✓	✓
Child demonstrates appropriate conflict-resolution strategies, requesting help when needed.	✓	✓	✓	✓	✓
Child understands and respects the different ideas, feelings, perspectives, and behaviors of others.				✓	

Language and Communication	1	2	3	4	5
Child follows two- and three-step oral directions.	✓			✓	
Child uses appropriate nonverbal skills during conversations (making eye contact; using facial expressions).			✓		
Child recognizes the difference between similar sounding words (for example, child follows directions without confusion over the words heard; points to the appropriate picture when prompted).				✓	✓
Child experiments with and produces a growing number of sounds in English words. (ELL)	✓		✓	✓	
Child names and describes actual or pictured people, places, things, actions, attributes, and events.		✓		✓	
Child uses complex sentences that include many details, tell about one topic, and communicate meaning clearly.	✓		✓		✓

Emergent Literacy: Reading	1	2	3	4	5
Child generates words that rhyme.	✓	✓	✓	✓	✓
Child names most upper- and lowercase letters of the alphabet.	✓	✓	✓	✓	✓
Child identifies the letter that stands for a given sound.	✓	✓	✓	✓	✓
Child describes, relates to, and uses details and information from books read aloud.	✓	✓	✓	✓	✓
Child asks and answers questions about books read aloud (such as, "Who?" "What?" "Where?").	✓		✓		

Emergent Literacy: Writing	1	2	3	4	5
Child participates in free drawing and writing activities to deliver information.		✓	✓	✓	✓
Child uses scribbles, shapes, pictures, symbols, and letters to represent language.			✓	✓	

Mathematics	1	2	3	4	5
Child understands that objects, or parts thereof, can be counted.					✓
Child recites number words in sequence from one to thirty.		✓		✓	
Child counts 1–10 concrete objects correctly.	✓				✓
Child demonstrates that the numerical counting sequence is always the same.				✓	
Child demonstrates that, when counting, the last number indicates how many objects were counted.			✓		✓
Child understands that objects can be counted in any order.		✓	✓		

Science	1	2	3	4	5
Child identifies organisms and describes their characteristics.	✓	✓	✓		✓
Child understands and describes life cycles of plants and animals.	✓	✓	✓	✓	✓
Child observes, understands, and discusses the relationship of plants and animals to their environments.	✓				✓
Child follows basic health and safety rules.	✓				✓

Social Studies	1	2	3	4	5
Child understands basic concepts of buying, selling, and trading.					✓
Child identifies common areas and features of home, school, and community.			✓		

Fine Arts	1	2	3	4	5
Child uses and experiments with a variety of art materials and tools in various art activities.					✓
Child expresses emotions or ideas through art.			✓		

Materials and Resources

DAY 1	DAY 2	DAY 3	DAY 4	DAY 5

Program Materials

DAY 1	DAY 2	DAY 3	DAY 4	DAY 5
• Teacher's Treasure Book • Concept Big Book 3: *Growing and Changing* • Oral Language Development Cards 51 and 52 • Rhymes and Chants Flip Chart • Making Good Choices Flip Chart • ABC Big Book • ABC Picture Card: *Jj* • Place Counting Cards 1–10 • Math and Science Flip Chart • Home Connections Resource Guide • Building Blocks Online Math Activity	• Teacher's Treasure Book • Concept Big Book 3: *Growing and Changing* • Dog Puppets • Making Good Choices Flip Chart • ABC Big Book • ABC Picture Card: *Hh* • Making Good Choices Flip Chart • Two-Color Counters • Math and Science Flip Chart • Pattern Blocks • Building Blocks Online Math Activity	• Teacher's Treasure Book • Oral Language Development Card 53 • Rhymes and Chants Flip Chart • Making Good Choices Flip Chart • ABC Big Book • ABC Picture Card: *Yy* • Concept Big Book 3: *Growing and Changing* • Photo Library: Structures	• Teacher's Treasure Book • Math and Science Flip Chart • Dog Puppets • ABC Picture Cards: *Hh, Jj, Yy* • Two-Color Counters • Pattern Blocks • Flannel Board Pattern, p. 407–410	• Teacher's Treasure Book • Rhymes and Chants Flip Chart • Making Good Choices Flip Chart • Photo Library: Animals, Home, Structures, Clothing • Concept Big Book 3: *Growing and Changing* • ABC Picture Cards: *Hh. Jj,* and *Yy* • Dinosaur Counters • Sequence Cards: Metamorphosis

Other Materials

DAY 1	DAY 2	DAY 3	DAY 4	DAY 5
• photos or drawings of adult and baby animals • simple picture books • books on frogs and tadpoles • sticky notes • baskets to hold objects	• fake fur fabric pieces • plastic or cardboard beaks • cut out paper animal ears • earmuffs • small paper or plastic bags	• books about birds • pipe cleaners • twigs, feathers, straw • coated wire pieces • labeled drawings • crayons, drawing paper • yarn or tape • play coins, blocks, toy plates • picture books on human homes	• cards with simple words and pictures • sets of four cut-out paper faces • crayons or pencils • Tally sheet	• big bucket • fishing poles with magnets • magnetic letters • toy dinosaurs • play money, toy register • photos of chrysalis, silk, butterfly wings, webbed feet of a frog • clay, coated wire, cotton balls construction paper

Home Connections

DAY 1	DAY 2	DAY 3	DAY 4	DAY 5
Encourage children to tell their families what they learned about the frog life cycle. Send home the Weekly Family Letter, Home Connections Resource Guide, pp. 53-54; ABC Take-Home Book for *Jj*, p. 16 (English), and *Jj*, p. 45 (Spanish).	Encourage children to show their families how they can count to 30. Send home the ABC Take-Home Book for *Hh*, p. 14 (English), and *Hh*, p. 43 (Spanish).	Encourage children to tell their families about different kinds of homes around the world. Send home the ABC Take-Home Book for *Yy*, p. 31 (English), and *Yy*, p. 62 (Spanish).	Encourage children to tell their families they can recognize and make the sounds for all three letters, *Jj, Hh,* and *Yy*. Remind children to tell their families about trying to use problem-solving strategies on their own before turning to an adult for help.	Encourage children to tell their families what they learned this week about how animals change as they grow. Remind children to tell their families how they learned to count to ten using toy dinosaurs and play money.

Assessment

As you observe children throughout the week, you may fill out an Anecdotal Observational Record Form to document an individual's progress toward a goal or signs indicating the need for developmental or medical evaluation. You may also choose to select work for each child's portfolio. The Anecdotal Observational Record Form and Weekly Assessment rubrics are available in the assessment sections of DLMExpressOnline.com.

More Literature Suggestions

- **Diary of a Wombat** by Jackie French
- **The Mixed Up Chameleon** by Eric Carle
- **Fabulous Fishes** by Susan Stockdale
- **Baby Flamingo** by Patricia A. Pingry
- **Count-a-saurus** by Nancy Blumenthal

- **La oruga muy hambrienta** por Eric Carle
- **Las mariposas** por David Cutts
- **El niño pastor** por Kristine L. Franklin
- **Angelita, la ballena pequeñita** por Lolo Rico
- **Soy un oso grande y hermoso** por Janosch

Daily Planner

	DAY 1	DAY 2
Let's Start the Day **Language Time** `large group`	**Opening Routines** p. 26 **Morning Read Aloud** p. 26 **Oral Language and Vocabulary** p. 26 Adult and Baby Animals **Phonological Awareness** p. 26 Produce Rhyming Words 	**Opening Routines** p. 32 **Morning Read Aloud** p. 32 **Oral Language and Vocabulary** p. 32 Baby Animals **Phonological Awareness** p. 32 Produce Rhyming Words 
Center Time `small group`	**Focus On:** **Creativity Center** p. 27 **Library and Listening Center** p. 27	**Focus On:** **ABC Center** p. 33 **Pretend and Learn Center** p. 33
Circle Time **Literacy Time** `large group`	**Read Aloud** Growing and Changing/Creciendo y cambiando p. 28 **Learn About Letters and Sounds:** /j/ p. 28 	**Read Aloud** Growing and Changing/Creciendo y cambiando p. 34 **Learn About Letters and Sounds:** /h/ p. 34 
Math Time `large group`	X-Ray Vision 1 p. 29	Count and Move in Patterns p. 35
Social and Emotional Development `large group`	Solving Problems p. 29 	Solving Problems p. 35 
Content Connection `large group`	**Science:** **Oral Language and Academic Vocabulary** p. 30 Talking About a Frog's Life Cycle **Observe and Investigate** p. 30 Connecting a Frog to a Tadpole 	**Math:** **Talk About Number Words** p. 36
Center Time `small group`	**Focus On:** **Math and Science Center** p. 31 **Purposeful Play** p. 31	**Focus On:** **Math and Science Center** p. 37 **Purposeful Play** p. 37
Let's Say Good-Bye `large group`	**Read Aloud** p. 31 **Writing** p. 31 **Home Connection** p. 31	**Read Aloud** p. 37 **Writing** p. 37 **Home Connection** p. 37

DAY 3

Opening Routines p. 38

Morning Read Aloud p. 38

Oral Language and Vocabulary
p. 38 Adults Care for Babies

Phonological Awareness
p. 38 Produce Rhyming Words

Focus On:

Construction Center p. 39

Writer's Center p. 39

Read Aloud Little Caterpillar/La oruga p. 40
Learn About Letters and Sounds: /y/ p. 40

Knock It Down p. 41

Solving Problems p. 41

Social Studies:

Oral Language and Academic Vocabulary
p. 42 Talking About Where We Live

Understand and Participate
p. 42 Looking at Photos of Structures Around the World

Focus On:

Library and Listening Center p. 43

Purposeful Play p. 43

Read Aloud p. 43

Writing p. 43

Home Connection p. 43

DAY 4

Opening Routines p. 44

Morning Read Aloud p. 44

Oral Language and Vocabulary
p. 44 Stories with Lessons

Phonological Awareness
p. 44 Produce Rhyming Words

Focus On:

Pretend and Learn Center p. 45

Writer's Center p. 45

Read Aloud The Ugly Duckling/
El atito feo p. 46
Learn About Letters and Sounds:
Jj, Hh, Yy p. 46

Count and Move in Patterns p. 47

Solving Problems p. 47

Math:

Oral Language and Academic Vocabulary
p. 48 Talk About Number Worlds

Observe and Investigate
p. 48 Step and Clap to 30

Focus On:

Math and Science Center p. 49

Purposeful Play p. 49

Read Aloud p. 49

Writing p. 49

Home Connection p. 49

DAY 5

Opening Routines p. 50

Morning Read Aloud p. 50

Oral Language and Vocabulary
p. 50 How Animals Change

Phonological Awareness
p. 50 Produce Rhyming Words

Focus On:

ABC Center p. 51

Creativity Center p. 51

Read Aloud
Growing and Changing/Creciendo y cambiando p. 52

Learn About Letters and Sounds: Jj, Hh, Yy p. 52

Dinosaur Shop (Fill Orders) p. 53

Solving Problems p. 53

Art Time:

Oral Language and Academic Vocabulary
p. 54 Animals Change as They Grow

Explore and Express
p. 54 Paint What You See or Feel

Focus On:

Construction Center p. 55

Purposeful Play p. 55

Read Aloud p. 55

Writing p. 55

Home Connection p. 55

Week 1

Animals Change

Math and Science Center

Where Frogs and Tadpoles Live

Children are assigned a label: *eggs, tadpoles, froglets,* and *frogs*. Each group looks through books to learn more about their stage of life and share what they have learned. See p. 31.

It Takes Thirty

Children work in pairs to count to 30 using counters. One partner counts while the other takes one counter out of a bag for each number that is said. See p. 37.

Build It Up

Children build a tower and count how many objects they used. See p. 49.

How Many Rows?

Partners use 30 counters to make arrangements of 5, 6, and 10 counters in a row. After each arrangement, they count the number of rows they see.

ABC Center

Sorting It Out

Children look through four baskets labeled *Jj, Ll, Pp, Tt,* which contain some items whose names begin with the target letter and other items whose names do not. Children sort items by their initial sound and letter. See p. 33.

Fishing for Letters

Partners take turns fishing a letter out of a bucket. They say the name of the letter, the sound it stands for, and a word that begins with that letter. See p. 51.

A Jeep for *Jj*

Children draw a jeep on a large piece of construction paper. They write the letters *Jj* on the jeep and draw pictures of objects whose names begin with /j/, such as *jacket, jar,* and *jump rope.*

Creativity Center

Serious and Silly Books

Children look through sets of animal pictures. For serious books, they match adults with their real babies. For silly books they match adults with the wrong babies. See p. 27.

What If?

Children choose Photo Library pictures of animals, homes, and clothing and use them to create "what if" stories. See p. 51.

Clothespin Animals

Children draw the body of a four-legged animal, such as a deer, cut it out, and color it. Then they clip two clothespins to the body to make legs.

Unusual Animals

Children create a "new" animal from two existing animals, such as a monkey and a tiger. They draw a picture of their animal and make up a name for it.

Library and Listening Center

Making a Match
One partner chooses a picture from a book and says its name. The other partner searches for a picture whose name rhymes with it. See p. 27.

Learn About Homes
Partners browse through books about homes around the world. One child looks for homes that are similar to the ones in his/her town or city. The other child looks for homes that are very different from the ones in his/her town or city. See p. 43.

Caterpillars and Butterflies
Partners look through nonfiction books and storybooks about how caterpillars become butterflies. Then they make up their own story about a caterpillar.

Construction Center

Nesting
Children build nests from materials, such as pipe cleaners, straw, and twigs and explain how birds use their nest. See p. 39.

Construct a Life Cycle Stage
Children use clay and other materials to create a stage in the life cycle of an animal, such as a caterpillar or frog. See p. 55.

Build a Bear's Cave
Children use blocks and fabric to build a bear's cave. They put toy bears in the cave or make bears out of clay.

Writer's Center

Rhyming Booklets
Children use prepared illustrated pages to draw a picture of an object whose name rhymes with the illustrated object. See p. 39.

Characters Have Feelings
Children discuss different feelings that story characters have and label a set of faces with words that describe feelings. See p. 45.

If I Were a Frog
Children draw a picture of something they would like to do if they were a frog. They write or dictate words to complete the sentence frame: *If I were a frog, I would* _____.

Pretend and Learn Center

Baby Animal Care
Partners make up dialogue and act out scenes that show how an adult animal takes care of its baby. See p. 33.

Act Out a Word
One child selects a picture card and acts out the word. His or her partner guesses the word and says a word that rhymes with it. See p. 45.

Fly Away!
Have children take turns role-playing a mother bird helping her babies fly away from the nest.

Rabbit Says
Children play a game like Simon Says, but substitute an animal and its movement. For example, Rabbit says, "Hop like a bunny." Bird says, "Flap your wings."

Focus Question

How do animals grow and change?
¿Cómo crecen y cambian los animales?

Learning Goals

Social and Emotional Development
• Child demonstrates appropriate conflict-resolution strategies, requesting help when needed.

Language and Communication
• Child experiments with and produces a growing number of sounds in English words. (ELL)

Emergent Literacy: Reading
• Child generates words that rhyme.

• Child describes, relates to, and uses details and information from books read aloud.

Vocabulary

beak	pico	chicken	pollo
chicks	pollitos	feathers	plumas
grass	pasto	wings	alas

Differentiated Instruction

 Extra Support

Oral Language and Vocabulary
If...children have difficulty describing differences, **then...**provide a list of adjectives (*big, small*) and a list of comparatives (*bigger, smaller*) and help them to apply the words to classroom objects.

 Enrichment

Phonological Awareness
Challenge children to invent a two-line rhyming couplet about their favorite animal.

 Special Needs

Cognitive Challenges
Plan activities that encourage opportunities to practice a new concept over and over.

Let's Start the Day

 Opening Routines and Transition Tips
For **Opening Routines** and **Transition Tips** turn to pages 178–181 and visit DLMExpressOnline.com for more ideas.

📖 Read **"Mothers and Their Babies"/**"Las mamás y sus bebés" from the *Teacher's Treasure Book*, page 114, for your morning Read Aloud.

 large group 15 minutes

Language Time

👫 **Social and Emotional Development** Remind children to try to work out problems between themselves before asking an adult for help.

Oral Language and Vocabulary

✓ Can children use information they have learned to describe and to compare and contrast?

Adult and Baby Animals Talk about the differences between chicks and chickens. Ask: *What are some changes that happen when a chick grows into a chicken? ¿En qué cambia un pollito cuando se convierte en pollo adulto?*

● Display *Oral Language Development Card 51*. Name the mother chicken and the chicks. Then follow the suggestions on the back of the card.

Oral Language Development Card 51

Phonological Awareness

✓ **Can children produce words that rhyme?**

Produce Rhyming Words Display *Rhymes and Chants Flip Chart*, page 25. Remind children that rhyming words end with the same sounds. Recite "Animals Grow Up." Read the poem a second time, stopping at the end of each stanza. Invite children to identify the two rhyming words in each. Then ask: *What words do you know that rhyme with* small? *Can you tell me some words that rhyme with* bed? *¿Qué palabras que rimen con small conocen? ¿Pueden decirme algunas palabras que rimen con bed?*

Discuss differences as animals grow—for instance, from kittens to cats and from puppies to dogs.

ELL Use the *Rhymes and Chants Flip Chart* to help children generate rhymes. Point to a word in a stanza—such as *big* in the third stanza—that does not rhyme with another. Encourage children to substitute first letters until they hear a rhyming word, such as *wig*. Help them think of as many rhyming words as they can.

Rhymes and Chants Flip Chart, p. 25

Center Time

> **Center Rotation** Center Time includes teacher-guided activities and independent activities. Refer to the **Learning Centers** on pages 24–25 for activities in additional centers.

small group   60–90 minutes

Creativity Center

 Track children's awareness of comparisons among animal changes and characteristics.

Monitor use of oral vocabulary you have focused on.

Materials several scrambled sets of photos or drawings of adult animals and baby animals

Serious and Silly Books Have children look through the sets of animal pictures. Tell them they can choose to make a "serious book" or a "silly book" of these pictures. For the former, they should match each adult with its real baby; for the latter they should pair up any adult with any baby.

- Have children tell you which kind of book they'll make and then select and order the pictures.

- Help them to staple their books together.

- Encourage children to page through their booklets and explain each pairing.

Center Tip

If...children can't decide which kind of book they want to make, **then...**talk through the decision with them and help them make a first pair.

Library and Listening Center

 Track children's ability to recognize and produce rhymes.

 Encourage children to solve problems independently before seeking help.

Materials assortment of simple picture books

Making a Match Have children work in pairs.

- Tell one child to select a book. Have him or her choose one picture in the book and name it.

- Have the other child look through that same book or another book to find a picture of something that rhymes.

- As a bonus, have children hunt together in the classroom for a rhyming object.

Center Tip

If...children have difficulty agreeing on what rhymes, **then...**encourage them to talk together about how they might solve their disagreement before coming to you to resolve it.

Learning Goals

Social and Emotional Development
- Child demonstrates appropriate conflict-resolution strategies, requesting help when needed.

Emergent Literacy: Reading
- Child generates words that rhyme.

- Child describes, relates to, and uses details and information from books read aloud.

Differentiated Instruction

Extra Support
Creativity Center
If...children have difficulty seeing likenesses among adult and baby animal pairs, **then...**help them browse through books that illustrate and describe animals in different stages of maturity.

Enrichment
Library and Listening Center
Challenge children to make up a little story that uses their rhyming words.

Special Needs
Behavioral Social/Emotional
Teach the child to accept natural consequences for his or her actions.

Focus Question
How do animals grow and change?
¿Cómo crecen y cambian los animales?

Learning Goals

Emergent Literacy: Reading
• Child names most upper- and lowercase letters of the alphabet.
• Child identifies the letter that stands for a given sound.
• Child asks and answers questions about books read aloud (such as "Who?" "What?" "Where?").

Science
• Child identifies organisms and describes their characteristics.
• Child understands and describes life cycles of plants and animals.

Vocabulary

adult	adulto	baby	pollito
egg	huevo	hatches	rompe el cascarón
safe	seguro		

Differentiated Instruction

 Extra Support
Learn About Letters and Sounds
If...children have difficulty writing the letter *Jj*, **then...**have them trace the letter using sand and shaving cream or make the letter out of clay.

Enrichment
Learn About Letters and Sounds
Challenge children to come up with a few sentences composed almost exclusively of words that start with the letter *Jj*. (Jeff and Jack jumped.)

Literacy Time

large group 15 minutes

📖 Read Aloud

✓ **Can children use information learned from books to compare and contrast?**

Build Background Tell children that you will be reading a book about how animals change from the time they are born until they're grown and about the needs that baby animals have.

● Ask: *How have the animals in the book changed as they've grown?* *¿Cómo fueron cambiando los animales del libro a medida que crecían?*

Listen for Enjoyment Display *Concept Big Book 3:* Growing and Changing/*Creciendo y cambiando,* page 17, and read the title. Conduct a picture walk.

● Browse through pages 18–21. Invite children to describe the changes they notice as the chick grows into an adult chicken.

● Ask: *What do you think is the biggest difference between the chick and the chicken? How are they most alike?* *¿Cuál creen que es la diferencia más grande entre el pollito y el pollo adulto?*

Respond to the Story Have children describe some ways that baby animals require special care. Ask: *What kinds of care do baby animals need? Why?* *¿Qué tipos de cuidado necesitan las crías de los animales? ¿Por qué?*

TIP Be sure children understand that different animals go through different life cycles and mature at very different rates.

ELL Help students with the questions by providing sentence stems such as, *The baby is _____. The mother is _____. Baby animals need _____.*
For additional suggestions on how to meet the needs of children at the Beginning, Intermediate, Advanced, and Advanced-High levels of English proficiency, see pages 184-187.

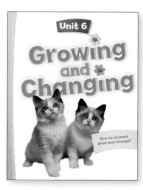

Growing and Changing
Creciendo y cambiando

Learn About Letters and Sounds

✓ **Can children identify the /j/ sound spelled *J*?**

Learn About the Letter *Jj* Page through the *ABC Big Book*, stopping when you get to the letter *Jj*. Point to the photo of the jump rope. Tell children that the word *jump* begins with the /j/ sound. Using either a real or an imaginary jump rope, have children sing "Jump, jump, jump!" in rhythm as they jump through the rope.

● Display the *ABC Picture Card* for upper case letter *J*. Invite children to trace the letter *J* with their fingers.

● Have children pair off and write the letter on each other's backs. Have them say /j/ aloud each time they write the letter.

● Repeat for the lower case *j*. Point out the similarities in the upper case and lower case *Jj*.

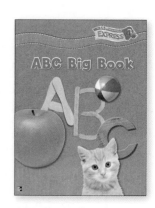

ABC Big Book

Math Time

Observe and Investigate

✓ **Can children count 1–10 items with one count per item?**

X-Ray Vision 1

- Place Counting Cards 1–10 (*Teacher's Treasure Book,* pages 506-507) in numerical order so that children see them in left-to-right order. Count the cards with children. Turn the cards facedown.

- Ask a volunteer to point to any card. Using your "X-ray vision," which is actually you counting from 1 to the chosen card, tell children to which card the volunteer pointed. The volunteer then flips that card to show you are correct and replaces it facedown. Repeat with another volunteer and card.

- Ask children to use their "X-ray vision" after you point to a card. Remind them where 1 is, and then point to 2. Have children spontaneously say what they think the card is, and turn it over to check. Repeat as time allows.

  ELL Have the non-Spanish-speaking child hold up fingers and say the English word for the number. After each number, the Spanish-speaking child does the same, using the Spanish word. Then have the Spanish-speaking child say the number in English and the other child say the Spanish word.

✗✗✗ Social and Emotional Development

Making Good Choices

✓ **Do children use independent problem-solving strategies first and turn to an adult if necessary?**

Solving Problems Display the *Making Good Choices Flip Chart,* page 25. Point to the boy, the spilled juice box, and the teacher in the background.

- Ask: *What is this boy's problem? What should he do first? If that doesn't work, what should he do next?* *¿Cuál es el problema de este niño? ¿Qué debe hacer primero? Si eso no funciona, ¿qué debe hacer después?*

- Discuss the children's suggestions and evaluate as a group which are likely to work at all and, of those, which will work the best. Have children consider how they might know when it's time to ask other students for help and when they might need to ask and adult for help.

large group · 15 minutes

Building Blocks

Online Math Activity

Introduce Dinosaur Shop 2: Children take orders from customers, and fill them by putting toy dinosaurs into a box. Each child should complete Dinosaur Shop 2 this week.

large group · 15 minutes

Making Good Choices Flip Chart, p. 25

Learning Goals

Social and Emotional Development
- Child demonstrates appropriate conflict-resolution strategies, requesting help when needed.

Language and Communication
- Child follows two- and three-step oral directions.

Mathematics
- Child counts 1–10 concrete objects correctly.

Vocabulary

numerical	número	order	orden
vision	visión	x-ray	rayos X

Differentiated Instruction

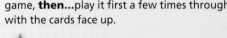

👋 Extra Support

Observe and Investigate

If...children struggle with the X-Ray Vision game, **then...**play it first a few times through with the cards face up.

⭐ Enrichment

Observe and Investigate

Challenge children to play the X-Ray Vision game backward—that is, by starting from the number 10 on the far right and counting backward to the designated card.

Focus Question
How do animals grow and change?
¿Cómo crecen y cambian los animales?

Science Time

 large group 20 minutes

Personal Safety Skills Model how you observe the frog behind the glass and how you do not touch or disturb it. Explain that it is important not to touch or handle an unfamiliar animal unless one has been given permission and been told what the rules are.

Oral Language and Academic Vocabulary

✓ **Can children provide detail, stick to the topic, and communicate their intended meaning clearly?**

Talking About a Frog's Life Cycle Point to the stages of the frog's life cycle shown on the *Math and Science Flip Chart*. Ask: *How many stages do you see altogether? Which is the first stage? Which is the last?* ¿Cuántas etapas ven en total? ¿Cuál es la primera etapa? ¿Cuál es la última?

● Explain that a frog starts life as an egg. Ask: *What other animals start out in egg cases?* ¿Qué otros animales comienzan como huevos?

● Discuss the changes that take place next. Ask: *When does a tadpole start to look like a frog?* ¿En qué momento un renacuajo comienza a verse como una rana?

Observe and Investigate

✓ **Can children use sentences to describe the changes in animals' life cycles?**

Connecting a Frog to a Tadpole Display for children a terrarium that contains a small frog in a suitable environment. Next to or behind the terrarium display several photos or drawings that illustrate the frog's earlier stages. Provide Jumbo Hand Lenses to groups of six children at a time or to pairs.

● Have children observe the frog for several minutes. Say: *Watch especially to see how the frog moves and breathes.* Observen bien a la rana; vean especialmente cómo se mueve y respira.

● Then have children focus on the photos and drawings. Say: *Pay attention to all the details about each animal.* Pongan atención a todos los detalles de cada animal.

● Gather the class to discuss what they observed about the environment and to describe contrasts and comparisons among the different life stages.

Display *Oral Language Development Card 52*. Mention that some kinds of frogs wait until their eggs are hatched, and they care for the tadpoles. Then point to the card and discuss that there are two kinds of penguins shown. Say: *One penguin is much bigger than the other. It is protecting the small one.* Un pingüino es mucho más grande que el otro. Está protegiendo al más pequeño. Ask: *Why does it need to do that?* ¿Por qué debe hacer esto? Then follow the directions on the back of the card.

ELL Help children make connections between Spanish and English vocabulary words by pointing out cognates such as *terrario* (terrarium); *acuario* (aquarium); and *pingüino* (penguin).

Math and Science Flip Chart, p. 45

Oral Language Development Card 52

Center Time

▶ **Center Rotation** Center Time includes teacher-guided activities and independent activities. Refer to the **Learning Centers** on pages 24–25 for activities in additional centers.

  small group 30 minutes

Math and Science Center

	Center Tip
✓ Encourage children to observe and describe the environments and habitats suited to each stage of the frog's life cycle. **Materials** books on frogs and tadpoles **Where Frogs and Tadpoles Live** Divide the class into "Eggs," "Tadpoles," "Froglets," and "Frogs." Tell children that their job is to find out more about what kind of place "their" stage lives in. • Have each group of children browse through the books and place sticky notes on relevant pages. • When they have finished their research, have groups meet to share what their group learned. Remind them to include lots of details.	**If**...children need help finding the part of the book that applies to their stage, **then**...say: *Think about the details that are true of your animal. For example, Does it have legs? What color is it? ¿Piensen en los detalles que aplican a su animal. Por ejemplo, ¿tiene patas? ¿De qué color es?*

Purposeful Play

✓ Observe and informally assess children as they interact and role play.

Children choose an open center for free playtime. Encourage children to solve problems on their own or together as they act out a scene based on the frog's life cycle. The story might show how each stage thinks about itself as it discovers it has changed into a new form.

Let's Say Good-Bye

  large group 15 minutes

 Read Aloud Revisit the story "Mothers and Their Babies"/"Las mamás y sus bebés" for your afternoon Read Aloud. Remind children to think about ways mothers and babies are the same and different as they listen.

 Home Connection Refer to the Home Connections activities listed in the Resources and Materials chart on page 21. Remind children to tell families about the frog life cycle. Sing the "Good-Bye Song"/"Hora de ir casa" as children prepare to leave.

 Learning Goals

Social and Emotional Development
• Child demonstrates appropriate conflict-resolution strategies, requesting help when needed.

Language and Communication
• Child uses complex sentences that include many details, tell about one topic, and communicate meaning clearly.

Science
• Child identifies organisms and describes their characteristics.

• Child understands and describes life cycles of plants and animals.

• Child observes, understands, and discusses the relationship of plants and animals to their environments.

Writing

Recap the day. Invite children to tell what they have learned about how animals change and grow. Record their answers. Read them back as you track the print, and emphasize the correspondence between speech and print.

Focus Question

How do animals grow and change?

¿Cómo crecen y cambian los animales?

 Learning Goals

Social and Emotional Development
• Child demonstrates appropriate conflict-resolution strategies, requesting help when needed.

Emergent Literacy: Reading
• Child generates words that rhyme.
• Child describes, relates to, and uses details and information from books read aloud.

Vocabulary

adult	adulto	den	guarida
egg	huevo	elephant	elefante
foxes	zorros	hatches	romper el cascarón
nest	nido	afe	seguro

Differentiated Instruction

 Extra Support

Oral Language and Vocabulary
If...children have difficulty staying focused on the topic, **then...**help them refocus by repeating the question and emphasizing its main point.

Enrichment

Oral Language and Vocabulary
Challenge children to add robust vocabulary to their spoken language repertoire: **nurture, transform, maturity**.

 Special Needs

Cognitive Challenges
Help everyone who works with the child understand that he or she may not learn something in the same way or as quickly as others, but that he or she can and will learn.

Let's Start the Day

▶ **Opening Routines and Transition Tips**
For **Opening Routines** and **Transition Tips** turn to pages 178–181 and visit **DLMExpressOnline.com** for more ideas.

 Read **"Fuzzy, Wuzzy Caterpillar"/"Linda, linda oruguita"** from the *Teacher's Treasure Book*, page 127, for your morning Read Aloud.

Language Time

large group 15 minutes

Social and Emotional Development Ask: *What should you do when something goes wrong—perhaps someone has grabbed the toy you are playing with? ¿Qué deberían hacer cuando algo anda mal, por ejemplo si alguien toma el juguete con el que están jugando?* Allow discussion. Remind children that they should try to solve the problem on their own. If they cannot, children should ask a friend for help. If they still need assisstance, remind children to go to an adult for help.

Oral Language and Vocabulary

✓ **Can children use information they have learned to compare and contrast?**

Baby Animals Display pages 20-21 of *Concept Big Book 3*, Growing and Changing. Talk about the different kinds of animals shown on these pages. Ask: **What three different animals do you see here?** *¿Cuáles son los tres animales que se muestran aquí?*

• Call on children to describe the scenes on these pages. Ask: **What is the mother elephant doing?** *¿Qué está haciendo la mamá elefante?*

• Encourage children to think about why the baby animals need care. Ask: **Why can't the baby elephant do this by itself** *¿Por qué el bebé elefante no puede hacer esto solo?* Remind children to think about the likenesses and differences between an adult animal and its baby.

Phonological Awareness

✓ **Can children produce a word that rhymes with a given word?**

Produce Rhyming Words Display one of the dog puppets. Tell children that the puppet will say a word. Their job is to think of a word that rhymes with the puppet's word. Explain that if the word rhymes, the puppet will nod his head; if it does not, he will shake his head. Remind children that words rhyme when they have the same ending sounds, like *bat* and *mat*. Have the puppet say these and other words: *day, sad, tin, go, fun*.

ELL Help children respond to questions by encouraging them to use part of the question in their response. For example: If you ask, **What does the baby elephant need?** encourage children to respond, **The baby elephant needs _____.**

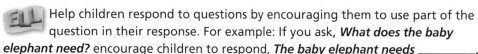

Center Time

Center Rotation Center Time includes teacher-guided activities and independent activities. Refer to the **Learning Centers** on pages 24–25 for activities in additional centers.

 small group 60–90 minutes

ABC Center

☑ **Keep track of the letter-sounds children are beginning to master.**

Materials three or four "letter baskets," each filled with an assortment of objects

Sorting It Out Set up three or four baskets, one labeled with the letter *J* and the others with review letters—for example, *L, P,* and *T.* Place about ten items in each basket, including items that start with the sound of the designated letter and some that don't.

- Have children go through each basket to sort the items according to their initial sounds. Have them say aloud the name of each item as they sort.

- As a variation, suggest that children work with a partner. One partner sorts out the items that begin with the targeted sound and the other sorts out those that do not begin with the targeted sound.

Center Tip

If...children have difficulty agreeing about their sorting decisions, **then...**remind them to try to solve the problem on their own but if necessary to come to you for help.

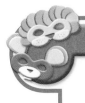

Pretend and Learn Center

☑ **Observe children's ability to understand and interpret animal characteristics and behaviors.**

Materials pairs of simple props such as fake fur fabric pieces, plastic or cardboard beaks, animal ears glued to earmuffs, and so on

Baby Animal Care Tell children that they will use simple props as they make up dialogue and act out brief scenes to show how an adult animal would care for its baby. Have them decide who will be the adult and who will be the baby. Encourage children to act out their scenes for their classmates.

- Point out that the props come in pairs. Say: *If you are a baby bird, your partner will be the mama bird. Which pair of props would you use? Si uno de ustedes es un polluelo, su compañero será la mamá pájaro. ¿Qué par de materiales usarían?* Have partners talk together to figure out the action that will happen in their scene. With a volunteer, model an example scene. For instance, act out a mother bring bringing food to the nest.

Center Tip

If...children have difficulty generating plots for their scenes, **then...**provide basic ideas to get them started.

 Learning Goals

Emergent Literacy: Reading
- Child names most upper- and lowercase letters of the alphabet.
- Child identifies the letter that stands for a given sound.

Science
- Child identifies organisms and describes their characteristics.
- Child understands and describes life cycles of plants and animals.

Differentiated Instruction

 Extra Support

ABC Center
If...children have difficulty connecting a letter with its sound, **then...**provide the ABC Picture Card along with the simple letter name label.

Enrichment

Pretend and Learn Center
Challenge children to create more fully developed dramas that involve additional characters and more elaborate plots.

Focus Question

How do animals grow and change?
¿Cómo crecen y cambian los animales?

Learning Goals

Emergent Literacy: Reading
• Child names most upper- and lowercase letters of the alphabet.
• Child identifies the letter that stands for a given sound.
• Child describes, relates to, and uses details and information from books read aloud.

Science
• Child understands and describes life cycles of plants and animals.

Vocabulary

care	cuidar	describe	describir
nest	nido	feathers	plumas
foxes	zorros	different	diferente
same	igual		

Differentiated Instruction

Extra Support

Learn About Letters and Sounds
If...children have difficulty writing the letter *Hh*, **then...**have them trace the letter using sand and shaving cream or make the letter out of clay.

Enrichment

Learn About Letters and Sounds
Challenge children to think of as many animals as they can that start with the letter *h* and the /h/ sound. Then have them name the animals with *H* names. For example, *Hilda the Horse, Howard the Hog, and Henry the Hippo*.

Literacy Time

 Read Aloud

✓ **Can children use information learned from books to compare and contrast?**

Build Background Tell children that you will be reading about how a chicken grows and about how animals they take care of their babies.

● Ask: *Have you ever seen an adult animal caring for its baby? Where? What did the adult do?* ¿Han visto alguna vez a un animal adulto cuidar a su cría? ¿Dónde? ¿Qué hacía ese animal adulto?

Listen for Understanding Display *Concept Big Book 3:* Growing and Changing, page 17, and read the title. Remind children that this book talks about very different kinds of animals but they all share one thing—they start as babies and grow up.

● Read pages 18–21. Point to the baby animal shown on each page.

● Ask: *In what ways are each of these babies the same? In what ways are they different?* ¿En qué se parecen estas crías? ¿En qué se diferencian?

Respond to the Story Have children discuss what they have learned. Ask: *Why do babies need a safe place to live? What do the adult animals do to take care of their babies?* ¿Por qué las crías de los animales necesitan un lugar seguro para vivir? ¿Qué hacen los animales adultos para cuidar a sus crías?

Can you show me where this story starts? Where it ends? Point to those places. Which is the front [cover] of the book? Back [cover]? ¿Pueden mostrarme dónde comienza el cuento? ¿Y dónde termina? ¿Cuál es el frente [portada] del libro? ¿Cuál es la parte trasera [contraportada]?

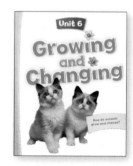

Growing and Changing
Creciendo y cambiando

Learn About Letters and Sounds

✓ **Can children identify the /h/ sound spelled *h*?**

Learn About the Letter *Hh* Invite children to sing the Alphabet Song with you as you page through the *ABC Big Book*. Stop when you get to the letter *Hh*. Point to the photo of the horse. Tell children that the word *horse* begins with the /h/ sound. Invite children to ride an imaginary horse as they sing "Ha, ha, ha, I have a horse!"

● Display the *ABC Picture Card* for upper case letter *H*. Invite children to trace the letter *H* with their fingers. Repeat for the lower case *h*. Point out the similarities in the upper case and lower case *Hh*.

ELL Point out that this week children are learning the letters and sounds for *Jj* and *Hh*. In Spanish, the letter *J* is pronounced as /h/ and the letter *H* is always silent. For additional suggestions on how to meet the needs of children at the Beginning, Intermediate, Advanced, and Advanced-High levels of English proficiency, see pages 184–187.

ABC Big Book

Math Time

Observe and Investigate

 Can children rote count to 30?

Count and Move in Patterns Recall the story of *"Three Billy Goats Gruff."* Explain to children that you are all going to pretend to be goats bounding across a bridge, jumping in groups of 3. Count to 30, or more as appropriate, in patterns of 3, such as 1, 2, 3 (pause), 4, 5, 6, (pause), and so on. Once the goal number is met, have each group hop safely across a run (the "bridge").

Mr. Mixup (Counting)

● Tell children when Mr. Mixup makes a mistake, they need to stop him and correct him. Have Mr. Mixup make the following mistakes: forget to stop when producing (counting out) a certain number (show the numeral 5, ask Mr. Mixup to provide five counters, Mr. Mixup counts out 5, but continues to count out more); track unordered items (place eight to ten counters in a random collection); double count by counting one or more items again; and skip items as they are counted. Add to these by making mistakes children need to practice identifying. Challenge children to count to 20, 30, or more.

● To make the activity easier, exaggerate Mr. Mixup's mistakes; make mistakes with amounts less than 5; have children touch each item counted to keep track. For a challenge, use larger groups in arrangements such as in a circle.

Building Blocks

Online Math Activity

Introduce Pizza Pizzazz 3: Make Number Pizzas (1-10), in which students put toppings on a pizza to match a given number. Each child should complete the activity this week.

⚞ Social and Emotional Development

Making Good Choices

 Do children use independent problem-solving strategies first and turn to an adult if necessary?

Solving Problems Revisit the *Making Good Choices Flip Chart* page 25, "How can he solve his problem?"

● Display one of the dog puppets. Say: *The puppet isn't sure what's happening. Tell what the boy's problem is and how he might solve it.* *El perrito no está seguro de lo que pasa en esta imagen. Díganle cuál es el problema que tiene el niño. Después, díganle algunas de las maneras en que el niño puede resolver su problema.*

● Remind children that everyone faces problems every day. We all need to figure out when we can fix something ourselves and when we need help.

Making Good Choices Flip Chart, p. 25

Learning Goals

Social and Emotional Development
● Child demonstrates appropriate conflict-resolution strategies, requesting help when needed.

Mathematics
● Child recites number words in sequence from one to thirty.

Vocabulary

counters   fichas   numeral   número

Differentiated Instruction

✋ **Extra Support**

Observe and Investigate
If...children have difficulty counting to thirty, **then...**use a Counting Wand game, tapping first one child, who counts 1–5 (or 1–10), then another who counts 6–10 (or 11–20), and so on.

⭐ **Enrichment**

Observe and Investigate
Invite children to choose a favorite animal or item such as a cloud and to draw thirty of these in any configuration they wish.

♥ **Special Needs**

Cognitive Challenges
Use short sentences when explaining something new.

Focus Question
How do animals grow and change?
¿Cómo crecen y cambian los animales?

Learning Goals

Social and Emotional Development
• Child shows eagerness, curiosity, and confidence while learning new concepts and trying new things.

Language and Communication
• Child names and describes actual or pictured people, places, things, actions, attributes, and events.

Mathematics
• Child recites number words in sequence from one to thirty.
• Child understands that objects can be counted in any order.

Vocabulary

all number names up to and including thirty

todos los nombres de los números hasta treinta

count   contar   **pattern**   patrón

Differentiated Instruction

 Extra Support
Observe and Investigate
If...children have difficulty re-creating the full 30-block structure, **then...**have them focus on only the first three or four rows.

 Enrichment
Observe and Investigate
Challenge children to use their Counters to create multiple arrangements that add up to 30. Have them keep a tally of how many patterns they made.

Math Time

large group 20 minutes

Social and Emotional Development Discuss how children need to listen to each other's contributions when it is not their turn to talk. Encourage this behavior during whole group lessons.

Oral Language and Academic Vocabulary

Can children use number words to count to 30?

Talk About Number Words Display Counters. Spill out a large pile and count out thirty, emphasizing each number as you do so. Repeat, this time inviting children to count with you.

● Group the Counters in different patterns—for example, ten lines of three or five lines of six. Each time you make a different pattern, count them and stress that the overall number is always thirty.

● Ask: *How many Counters am I using? How many lines do you see? How many Counters are in each line? ¿Cuántas fichas estoy usando? ¿Cuántas filas ven? ¿Cuántas fichas hay en cada una?*

Observe and Investigate

Can children use objects appropriately to count to 30?

Counting and Building Have children re-create the building on the Math and Science Flip Chart by using Counters or Pattern Blocks to lay out the same design.

● Display the *Math and Science Flip Chart,* page 46, "Counting to 30." Call attention to the layers of building blocks used to make this structure. Count aloud from 1-30 as you point to each block.

● Then distribute 30 Counters and/or Pattern Blocks to each child. Say: *Your job is to place your markers on the floor [mat, desk] to create the same shape you see on the chart. Count and say each number name as you put each marker down.*
Coloquen sus fichas sobre el piso [tapete, escritorio] para crear la misma figura que ven en la tabla. Cuenten y digan el nombre de cada número mientras ponen cada marca en su lugar.

TIP Be sure that children sit so that they can see the chart clearly but also so that they have enough space to lay out their markers without intruding on another's space.

ELL Set up a signal system with children so that they can let you know when they are understanding the lesson well (thumbs up) and when they are becoming confused (thumbs down).

Counting to 30
Contar hasta 30

1	2	3	4	5
6	7	8	9	10
11	12	13	14	15
16	17	18	19	20
21	22	23	24	25
26	27	28	29	30

Math and Science Flip Chart, p. 46

Center Time

Center Rotation Center Time includes teacher-guided activities and independent activities. Refer to the **Learning Centers** on pages 24–25 for activities in additional centers.

  small group 30 minutes

Math and Science Center

 Center Tip

☑ **Observe children as they count to 30.**

Materials Counters, bags

It Takes Thirty Prepare sets of exactly 30 counters in small bags. Say: *Practice counting to 30.*

- Have children work in pairs. One partner should count slowly to 30 while the other partner should take one counter out of the bag for each number that is said.

- Have children switch roles and count again. This time the first partner should put one counter back in the bag each time the second partner says a number.

- If children have trouble counting to 30, encourage the partner to stack counters in groups of 10 as a visual aid.

If...children have trouble counting out exactly thirty circles, **then...**work with them to write numbers 1–30 on the circles as they gather them.

Purposeful Play

☑ **Observe children resolving problems as they make choices and play together.**

Children choose an open center for free playtime. Encourage problem-solving skills by suggesting pairs choose a game or activity together, reminding them that they should try to resolve differences of opinion before seeking your help.

Let's Say Good-Bye

  large group 15 minutes

 Read Aloud Revisit the story "Fuzzy, Wuzzy Caterpillar"/"Linda, linda oruguita" for your afternoon Read Aloud. Encourage children to listen for words that begin with the /h/ sound.

 Home Connections Refer to the Home Connections activities listed in the Resources and Materials chart on page 21. Remind children to show their families how they can count to 30. Sing the "Good-Bye Song" as children prepare to leave.

Learning Goals

Social and Emotional Development
• Child demonstrates appropriate conflict-resolution strategies, requesting help when needed.

Emergent Literacy: Writing
• Child participates in free drawing and writing activities to deliver information.

Mathematics
• Child recites number words in sequence from one to thirty.

Writing

Recap the day. Have children describe the ways in which baby animals differ from adult animals. Ask: *What did you learn about how adult animals take care of their babies? ¿Qué aprendieron acerca de cómo cuidan los animales adultos a sus crías?* Tell them to think of one important fact they've learned and list a few words that tell about this fact. Encourage them to include a drawing as well.

DAY 3

Focus Question

How do animals grow and change?
¿Cómo crecen y cambian los animales?

Vocabulary

ears	orejas	elephant	elefante
gray	gris	legs	patas
spray	rociar	trunk	trompa

Differentiated Instruction

 Extra Support
Phonological Awareness
If...children have difficulty rhyming words, **then...**use familiar nursery rhymes and draw children's attention to the words that have the same sounds at the ends.

 Enrichment
Phonological Awareness
Challenge children to hunt through the classroom to assemble pairs of objects with rhyming names.

Let's Start the Day

▶ Opening Routines and Transition Tips

For **Opening Routines** and **Transition Tips** turn to pages 178–181 and visit **DLMExpressOnline.com** for more ideas.

📖 Read **"Peanut, the Teeniest, Tiniest Pup on the Planet,"/**"Maní, el perrito más pequeñito del planeta" from the *Teacher's Treasure Book*, page 216, for your morning Read Aloud.

large group | 15 minutes

Language Time

👫👫 **Social and Emotional Development** Remind children that, if their minds start to wander, they need to bring their attention back to the activity that the group is engaged in. Praise children who stay focused on the activity.

Oral Language and Vocabulary

✓ **Can children use information they have learned to describe and to compare and contrast?**

Adults Care for Babies Talk about the care that baby animals need. Ask: *What are some things that a baby animal can not do for itself? How does the adult animal take care of its baby? ¿Cuáles son algunas de las cosas que una cría no puede hacer sola? ¿De qué manera los animales adultos cuidan a sus bebés?*

● Display *Oral Language Development Card 53*. Name the adult and the baby elephant. Then follow the suggestions on the back of the card.

Oral Language Development Card 53

Phonological Awareness

✓ **Can children produce words that rhyme?**

Produce Rhyming Words Revisit the *Rhymes and Chants Flip Chart,* page 25. Remind children that rhyming words end with the same sounds. Read the poem aloud, emphasizing the two end rhymes in each stanza. Read the poem a second time and ask children to clap when they hear the rhyming words. Ask children to listen for the words in the poem that have similar sounding endings and those that do not. Say: *The words* hat *and* cat *are in this poem. They rhyme because they both end with /at/. Can you tell me other words that rhyme with* hat *and* cat? *Las palabras hat y cat aparecen en este poema. Riman porque ambas terminan con /at/. ¿Puden decirme otras palabras que rimen con hat y cat?*

ELL To reinforce the concept of rhyming words ask children to think of Spanish words that rhyme. Have them say these words aloud to the class. Explain that all languages have sounds and words that rhyme. For additional suggestions on how to meet the needs of children at the Beginning, Intermediate, Advanced, and Advanced-High levels of English proficiency, see pages 184–187.

Rhymes and Chants Flip Chart, p. 25

Animals Grow Up
A baby kitten is very small.
He's light as a feather,
He won't chase a ball.

But after a year he'll be a cat.
He'll leap to the window
Or play with a hat.

Our dog looks big now in her bed.
She wasn't this big
At first, Dad said.

Her tiny paws were fuzzy to touch,
But now she has long hair
And barks too much!

Center Time

▶ **Center Rotation** Center Time includes teacher-guided activities and independent activities. Refer to the **Learning Centers** on pages 24–25 for activities in additional centers.

Construction Center

| | **Center Tip** |

☑ **Observe children's ability to describe and compare animal characteristics and behaviors.**

Materials books about birds that include illustrations of different bird nests; pipe cleaners; twigs; feathers; straw; coated wire pieces

Nesting Discuss with children the reasons that birds build nests. Remind them of what they've been learning about how animals care for their babies. Say: *You'll have a chance to construct a nest and to tell the class about how a bird might use it. Hoy podrán construir un nido y decirle a la clase cómo lo usaría un pájaro.*

- Have children browse through books to learn about the kinds of nests birds build.

- Ask: *What will you use to build your nest? ¿Qué usarán para construir sus nidos?* Model how choosing appropriate materials and beginning to weave a nest together. Then have children follow the same procedure. When their nests are complete, have them explain to a friend or to you how a bird would use the nest.

Center Tip

If...children have difficulty handling the materials, **then...** help them get a shape started with the wire. They can then interweave the other materials more easily.

Writer's Center

| | **Center Tip** |

☑ **Track children's ability to recognize and produce rhymes.**

Materials a variety of labeled drawings of simple, easily rhymed words like *ball* or *cat* (multiple photocopies); crayons; book binding supplies, such as yarn or tape

Rhyming Booklets Display the illustrated sheets. Point out that the top half of each page includes a word and a drawing of that word but that the bottom half is blank. Tell children that they are going to complete these pages to make an original book. Say: *Your job is to think of a word that rhymes with the object on the page. Then you'll write that word on the bottom half of the page and make a drawing of it. Su tarea es pensar en una palabra que rime con el nombre del objeto de esa página. Luego, escribirán esa palabra en la mitad inferior de la página y la ilustrarán.* Prompt children to select three different sheets and to think of rhyming word for each. When children's sheets are complete, they can use tape or yarn to bind them into a booklet.

Center Tip

If...children would prefer to staple their booklets together, **then...**have them come to you for help in using the stapler.

 Learning Goals

Emergent Literacy: Reading
- Child generates words that rhyme.
- Child describes, relates to, and uses details and information from books read aloud.

Emergent Literacy: Writing
- Child uses scribbles, shapes, pictures, symbols, and letters to represent language.

Fine Arts
- Child expresses emotions or ideas through art.

Differentiated Instruction

✋ **Extra Support**
Writer's Center
If...children have difficulty coming up with rhyming words, **then...**suggest that they say a recently learned letter sound such as /h/ or /j/. Have them drop the initial consonant sound of the word and blend in the new sound. Thus, for *ball*, they would try /h/ *all*.

 Enrichment
Construction Center
Challenge children to explore more about the way different birds build their nests and about what these varied nests look like—for example, they might research and compare eagles', orioles', and wrens' nests.

Accommodations for 3's
Construction Center
If...children have difficulty using the construction materials, **then...**suggest that they make a drawing of a nest instead.

Circle Time

Focus Question
How do animals grow and change?
¿Cómo crecen y cambian los animales?

Learning Goals

Emergent Literacy: Reading
- Child names most upper- and lowercase letters of the alphabet.
- Child identifies the letter that stands for a given sound.
- Child asks and answers questions about books read aloud (such as "Who?" "What?" "Where?").

Science
- Child identifies organisms and describes their characteristics.
- Child understands and describes the life cycles of plants and animals.

Vocabulary

attached	pegado	caterpillar	oruga
energy	energía		
extremely	extremadamente		
flapped	agitó	greedily	ávidamente

Differentiated Instruction

 Extra Support

Read Aloud

If...children have difficulty recalling the stages in sequence, **then...**go back through the story. Help children identify the names of the stages and label them: *first* (or *number one*), *second* (or *number two*), and so on.

Enrichment

Read Aloud

Challenge children to retell this same story from the point of view of a tadpole. Suggest that they call it "Little Tadpole" and have them use the same story structure but rework it to reflect what a tadpole might feel during his metamorphosis.

Literacy Time

 large group — 15 minutes

📖 Read Aloud

✓ **Can children ask and answer appropriate questions about this story?**

Build Background Tell children that you will be reading a story about a little caterpillar who goes through big changes before realizing she can now fly!

- Ask: *Would you rather be a caterpillar or a butterfly? Why?* *¿Qué preferirían: ser una oruga o un mariposa? ¿Por qué?*

Listen for Understanding Read aloud "Little Caterpillar"/"La oruga" from the *Teacher's Treasure Book*, page 222. Prompt children to pay attention to each major change that the caterpillar undergoes.

- Say: *At the end of this story, you should be able to tell me about four different stages this little caterpillar goes through.* *Al final de este cuento, deberían poder contarme acerca de las diferentes etapas por las que pasa esta pequeña oruga.*

Respond to the Story Encourage children to retell the story in sequence: egg, caterpillar, chrysalis, butterfly. Ask: *Why was the caterpillar so hungry when she came out of the egg? At the end, do you think she was surprised to discover she had wings? Why or why not?* *¿Por qué la oruga estaba tan hambrienta cuando salió del huevo? Al final, ¿creen que ella se sorprendió al ver que tenía alas? ¿Por qué?*

TIP As necessary, help children make some of the inferences in this story—for example, that the "breath of fresh air" is the caterpillar's very first breath of air and that the "blanket" is in fact the chrysalis she is spinning.

Learn About Letters and Sounds

✓ **Can children identify the /y/ sound spelled Yy?**

Learn About the Letter Yy Sing the "ABC Song" with children as you page through the *ABC Big Book*, stopping when you get to the letter *Yy*. Point to the photo of the yawn. Tell children that the word *yawn* begins with the letter *y*. The letter *y* stands for the /y/ sound. Say: *First, let's all yawn as widely as possible and then let's yell the answer to the question: "What did we do?"* *Primero, bostecemos muy fuerte y luego respondamos la pregunta: "¿Qué acabamos de hacer?"*

- Model how to write the upper case letter *Y* using the *ABC Picture Card*. Have children trace the letter *Y* with their fingers.

- While one child is tracing, the other children can be writing the letter in the air or on the floor using their finger. Have them say /y/ each time they write the letter.

- Repeat for the lower case *y*. Point out the similarities in the upper case and lower case *Yy*.

ELL Ask children questions that can be answered with a word that starts with y. For example: *What is the opposite of no? What is the color of the sun?* Help children exaggerate the beginning of each word as they say it, so that they are sure to hear the /y/ sound.

Teacher's Treasure Book, p. 222

ABC Big Book

Online Math Activity

Children can complete Dinosaur Shop 2 and Pizza Pizzazz 3 during computer time or Center Time.

Making Good Choices Flip Chart, page 25

Math Time

Observe and Investigate

✓ **Can children count up to 10 items and keep track of which objects have been counted, even in unstructured situations?**

Knock It Down

● Using safe, stackable items (coins, blocks, toy plates), build a "tower" as tall as you can to show the class.

● With children, count the items before you gently knock down the tower, and count the items again after you have knocked down the tower. Emphasize that you can pick up the items in any order as you count and the amount will still be the same. Have a volunteer choose which item to start counting.

● Encourage children to see how many items they can stack in a tower during their free time.

☥☥☥ Social and Emotional Development

Making Good Choices

✓ **Do children use independent problem-solving strategies first and turn to an adult if necessary?**

Solving Problems Display the *Making Good Choices Flip Chart,* page 25, "How can he solve his problem?" Review with children the ways the boy can try to solve his problem.

● With the Dog Puppets, role-play how the boy handles the situation. Designate Dog 1 as the adult and Dog 2 as the boy. Demonstrate, for example, how Dog 2 mops up the juice with a paper towel and how Dog 1 watches approvingly. Model as well a different scenario in which Dog 1 tries to solve the problem but winds up needing to ask for help.

● After each role play, ask: **How did Dog 1 solve his problem? Did he do it on his own or did he need help?** *¿Cómo resolvió el perrito 1 su problema? ¿Lo hizo por su cuenta o necesitó ayuda?*

ELL Help children role-play different ways of asking someone for help. Model sentences using the following sentence frame and have children repeat: **The boy said, "_____?"** (e.g. *"Please help me." "I need help, please." "Will you please help me?"*)

Learning Goals

Social and Emotional Development
● Child demonstrates appropriate conflict-resolution strategies, requesting help when needed.

Mathematics
● Child demonstrates that, when counting, the lasts number indicates how many objects were counted.

● Child understands that objects can be counted in any order.

Vocabulary

count	contar	knock	golpe
stack	pila	tower	torre

Differentiated Instruction

👋 **Extra Support**

Observe and Investigate

If...children have difficulty understanding that the scattered blocks are equal in number to the original blocks in the tower, **then...**tape a small numbered tag to each block before you knock over the tower. Afterward, have children gather up the blocks, lay them out starting with the number 1 block, and use the taped numbers to count them.

⭐ **Enrichment**

Making Good Choices

Challenge children to draw their own "How can he/she solve the problem?" poster, depicting a different problem from the one shown in the *Making Good Choices Flip Chart*. Then have partners role-play scenarios to resolve the problem.

Focus Question
How do animals grow and change?
¿Cómo crecen y cambian los animales?

Learning Goals

Social and Emotional Development
• Child shows eagerness, curiosity, and confidence while learning new concepts and trying new things.

Language and Communication
• Child uses complex sentences that include many details, tell about one topic, and communicate meaning clearly.

• Child uses appropriate nonverbal skills during conversations (making eye contact; using facial expressions).

Social Studies
• Child identifies common areas and features of home, school, and community.

Vocabulary

environment	medio	home	casa
people	personas	safe	seguro
structure	construcción	world	mundo

Differentiated Instruction

 Extra Support

Oral Language and Academic Vocabulary
If...children have difficulty recalling the town or the details of the school building, **then...**take some informal photos of town buildings or locations in the school and attach these photos to appropriate spots on the poster.

 Enrichment

Understand and Participate
Challenge children to do a 'walking tour' of a favorite place—perhaps the school library or their own room at home, to note as many details as possible, and to draw a map or grid of that place that incorporates the details they have noted.

Social Studies Time

Language and Communication During the discussion, model a good response to one of your questions. Include details and point out how you are sticking to the subject of the question.

Oral Language and Academic Vocabulary

 Can children identify common features in their immediate environment?

Talking About Where We Live Ask children what they learned about different animals' homes and environments from the *Concept Big Book, Growing and Changing/Creciendo y cambiando.* Remind them that each baby animal—the chicks, the foxes, and the elephants—lived in different environments. Each different home provided a safe living place for that animal to grow big and strong.

● Ask: *Where is your home? Describe the environment you live in.* *¿Dónde está su casa? ¿Cómo describirían el medio ambiente en el que ustedes viven?*

● Point out that, like animals, people around the world live in different kinds of homes and environments.

Understand and Participate

Can children identify and create their immediate environments?

Looking at Photos of Structures Around the World Use the "Structures" category of the Photo Library to share images of different common structures with children.

● As you display the photos, have children raise their hands and wait to be called on before speaking when they see something that looks like a structure—perhaps a bridge or a kind of home—that is familiar.

● Ask: *What makes that look like something we see in our town?* *¿En qué se parece a algo que hayan visto en nuestra ciudad?*

● Continue the discussion by challenging children to name different buildings that they see every day.

● Mount a piece of chart paper. Draw a simple grid of streets to represent a section of your town or the area near your school. Invite children to name familiar places and buildings, like the town library or post office. Write in these labels.

TIP Let children know that you will keep the poster mounted for several weeks. If they think of a building or place not yet included, you will add it.

ELL Focusing on elements that are shared and different in the two most familiar environments in children's lives—home and school. Ask: *What are three things that you have both at home and at school? What are three things that you have only at home? Only at school?* What are three things that you have both at home and at school? What are three things that you have only at home? Only at school?

Center Time

Center Rotation Center Time includes teacher-guided activities and independent activities. Refer to the **Learning Centers** on pages 24–25 for activities in additional centers.

 small group 30 minutes

Library and Listening Center

✓ **Monitor children as they browse through and learn from books about home environments.**

Materials nonfiction and fiction picture books that show a variety of homes and communities in various countries, crayons, drawing paper

Learn About Your Home by Learning About Others' Discuss that all around the world people live in homes and communities.

- With a partner, have children browse through the books, looking for what is the same and different as their homes and town.
- Have children draw a picture of their own home or street and point out the details that make it the same or different from others.

Center Tip

If...children need help focusing on the details, **then**...prompt them with questions such as, *What kinds of windows [yard, roof, fence, and so on] does your house have? Does the house in the book have?*

Purposeful Play

✓ **Observe children working together to create a dialogue.**

Children choose an open center for free playtime. Encourage children to solve problems on their own or together as they create a dialogue between an animal and a person, each of whom explains to the other what he/she loves about his/her own home.

Let's Say Good-Bye

 large group 15 minutes

 Read Aloud Revisit the story "Peanut, the Teeniest, Tiniest Pup on the Planet"/"Maní, el perrito más pequeñito del planeta" for your afternoon Read Aloud. Remind children to think about things that are alike and different as they listen.

 Home Connection Refer to the Home Connections activities listed in the Resources and Materials chart on page 21. Remind children to tell families about different kinds of homes around the world. Sing the "Good-Bye Song" as children prepare to leave.

✓ **Learning Goals**

Social and Emotional Development
- Child demonstrates appropriate conflict-resolution strategies, requesting help when needed.

Emergent Literacy: Reading
- Child describes, relates to, and uses details and information from books read aloud.

Emergent Literacy: Writing
- Child participates in free drawing and writing activities to deliver information.

Social Studies
- Child identifies common areas and features of home, school, and community.

 Writing

Recap the day. Have children name the important facts about their homes. Ask: *Why do people need homes? ¿Por qué necesita la gente un hogar?* Record children's answers on chart paper. Share the pen by having children write letters and words they know. Ask children to draw a picture to illustrate each sentence.

Focus Question
How do animals grow and change?
¿Cómo crecen y cambian los animales?

Learning Goals

Language and Communication
• Child experiments with and produces a growing number of sounds in English words. (ELL)

Emergent Literacy: Reading
• Child generates words that rhyme.
• Child describes, relates to, and uses details and information from books read aloud.

Vocabulary

brother	hermano	chase	perseguir
cute	lindo	duckling	patito
hatch	romper el cascarón	stretch	estirarse
swan	cisne	ugly	feo

Differentiated Instruction

 Extra Support
Oral Language and Vocabulary
If...children have difficulty grasping the concept of stories with lessons, **then...**read some fables with easily understood lessons (like "The Hare and the Tortoise") and take time to discuss the moral and how it relates to the story.

Enrichment
Oral Language and Vocabulary
Challenge children to create their own stories with lessons. Have them dictate the stories to you and transcribe them onto chart paper.

 Special Needs
Delayed Motor Development
Make it easier to interact with peers by providing areas for sitting or resting on the floor.

Let's Start the Day

Opening Routines and Transition Tips
For **Opening Routines** and **Transition Tips** turn to pages 178–181 and visit **DLMExpressOnline.com** for more ideas.

 Read **"Little Caterpillar"/**"La oruga" from the *Teacher's Treasure Book*, page 222, for your morning Read Aloud.

large group   15 minutes

Language Time

Social and Emotional Development Remind children that when something goes wrong—perhaps the block structure they're trying to build isn't coming out the way they hoped—they should try to figure out a way to solve the problem on their own, but if they cannot, they should turn to an adult for help.

Oral Language and Vocabulary

Can children recognize that some stories have lessons?

Stories with Lessons Talk about fables and fairy tales that teach lessons that children have previously read. Ask: *What did we learn when we read that story? At what point in the story did we learn that lesson—in the beginning, in the middle, or at the end?*
¿Qué aprendimos cuando leímos ese cuento? ¿En qué parte del cuento aprendimos esa lección: al principio, a la mitad o al final?

● Discuss how stories are different. Say: *Some stories are fun and silly and some are about serious subjects that could really happen in our lives. Others—especially fables and fairy tales—end by teaching readers a lesson.* *Algunos cuentos son divertidos y cómicos, y algunos tratan sobre temas serios que pueden pasar realmente en nuestras vidas. Otros, especialmente las fábulas y los cuentos de hadas, terminan enseñándonos una lección.*

● Prompt children to list all the fables and fairy tales they can remember and to describe the ending lesson, or moral. Use chart paper to write the titles. Next to each title, sum up in a few words the story's lesson.

Phonological Awareness

Can children produce words that rhyme?

Produce Rhyming Words Display the Dog Puppets. Tell children to pay careful attention as the first puppet says a word and the second puppet responds with another word that rhymes. If the second puppet is correct, children should clap. If he is incorrect, they'll need to correct him and provide a real rhyming word. Have Dog 2 respond at least half the time with incorrect responses and encourage children to offer real rhyming words.

ELL Support children's ability to produce rhyming words by taking a classroom walk together. Pick up or point to objects, such as a ball or a pen, that provide multiple, simple possibilities for rhymes. Prompt children to come up with a rhyming word for each.

Center Time

Center Rotation Center Time includes teacher-guided activities and independent activities. Refer to the **Learning Centers** on pages 24–25 for activities in additional centers.

 small group 60–90 minutes

Pretend and Learn Center

 Track children's ability to recognize and produce rhyming words.

Materials pack of prepared cards, each with an easy rhyming word and a simple picture illustrating that word

Act Out a Word Have children play a rhyming game with a partner. Tell them you will provide a pack of cards. Each card has one word and a picture to illustrate that word.

- Explain that one child picks up a card and acts out the word. Say: *If the card says "toe," you could point to your big toe. Si la tarjeta dice toe, señala esa parte del cuerpo.*

- The partner has two jobs: he or she has to guess the word and then say a rhyming word (for example, "no").

- Suggest that to make the game even more fun, the partner might act out his or her rhyming word rather than saying it.

Center Tip

If...children have difficulty acting out a word, **then**...model the process for them by thinking out loud as you brainstorm possibilities for how you will demonstrate the word and for how you make a final choice.

Writer's Center

 Track how well children understand stories and especially story characters' feelings.

Materials multiple sets of four cut-out paper faces—one angry, one lonely, one large smiley face, one small smiley face; crayons or pencils

Characters Have Feelings Discuss with children that characters' feelings are an important part of almost all stories. Understanding how these characters feel, and how their feelings change, is often the key to understanding a story.

- Say: *In the story we read yesterday, the characters showed many different feelings. Your job is to decide what the feelings were and who felt that way. En el cuento que leímos ayer, los personajes mostraban varios sentimientos diferentes. Su trabajo consistirá en decidir cuáles fueron esos sentimientos y quién se sintió de esa manera.*

- Display the flannel board story and the four cut-out paper faces.

- Have each child label a set of the faces with the feeling expressed and the name of the character(s) who expressed that emotion.

Center Tip

If...children have difficulty remembering the different characters, **then**...use the flannel patterns to make a list of each—the ugly duckling as a baby, the other ducklings, the Mother Duck, the grown-up ugly duckling.

Differentiated Instruction

✋ Extra Support
Writer's Center
If...children have difficulty thinking about the story as a whole, **then**...retell it in meaningful segments that reflect the characters' feelings—(1) the other ducklings' angry reactions to the ugly duckling; (2) the ugly duckling's lonely days; (3) the Mother Duck's caring for him despite his being different; (4) the grown-up ugly duckling's happy discovery.

⭐ Enrichment
Pretend and Learn Center
Challenge children to keep the game going as long as they can—coming up with and miming additional rhymes in a particular pattern.

Accommodations for 3's
Writer's Center
If...children have difficulty writing labels, **then**...have them tell you the character's name and the word for the feeling depicted.

Focus Question

How do animals grow and change? ¿Cómo crecen y cambian los animales?

Learning Goals

Emergent Literacy: Reading
• Child names most upper- and lowercase letters of the alphabet.
• Child identifies the letter that stands for a given sound.
• Child asks and answers questions about books read aloud (such as "Who?" "What?" "Where?").

Science
• Child understands and describes the life cycles of plants and animals.

Vocabulary

beautiful	hermoso	brother	hermano
duckling	patito	stronger	más fuerte
swan	cisne	ugly	feo

Differentiated Instruction

Extra Support

Learn About Letters and Sounds
If...children have difficulty differentiating lower case *j* from lower case *y*, **then**...talk about the unique details of each and help children trace a row of each letter in sand.

Enrichment

Read Aloud
Challenge children to write the next chapter in the life of the ugly duckling. Have them dictate the chapter to you or try to write it out themselves.

Literacy Time

large group · 15 minutes

📖 Read Aloud

✓ **Can children ask and answer questions about a traditional fairy tale?**

Build Background Tell children that you will be reading a fairy tale about a little bird who looks very different from his family. The other ducklings make fun of him and he wants to be like them. But in the end he learns an important lesson.

● Ask: *What are some things you can do if someone makes fun of you?* ¿Qué pueden hacer si alguien se burla de ustedes?

Listen for Enjoyment Read aloud "The Ugly Duckling"/"El patito feo" in the *Teacher's Treasure Book, page 325*. Display the flannel story patterns as you read each reference in the story to help children connect the text to its meaning.

● Ask: *When does the ugly duckling start to feel better? Why?* ¿Cuándo comienza a sentirse mejor el patito feo? ¿Qué lo hace sentirse mejor?

Respond to the Story Have children tell what the ugly duckling discovers at the end.

● Ask: *Do you think the ugly duckling will have a happy life now?* ¿Creen que el patito feo tendrá una vida feliz ahora?

● Remind children that they have been learning about how animals change as they grow up. Have children turn to a partner and ask a question about this part of the story. Then have partners switch roles.

💡 **TIP** Suggest that children use the flannel patterns to recall what happened in the story. Tell children they can use the patterns during Center Time to retell the story to a friend.

Learn About Letters and Sounds

✓ **Can children identify letters and sounds?**

Review Letters *Jj, Hh, Yy* Display *ABC Picture Cards* for these letters.

● Review each letter and sound with children. For each, have children trace the letter in the air as you trace it on the *ABC Picture Card* and say its sound aloud with you.

● Play a sorting game. Have available an assortment of easily recognizable objects in a large shopping bag. Reach in and pull out one item at a time.

● Ask: *What is this? What letter does it begin with?* ¿Qué es esto? ¿Con qué letra empieza?

● Call on a child to respond to the questions and then to come forward, place the item next to the appropriate card, and say the correct sound aloud.

● If he or she responds incorrectly, invite the class to help him or her correct the error.

Teacher's Treasure Book, p. 325

ABC Picture Cards

large group · 15 minutes

Math Time

Observe and Investigate

 Can children rote count to 30?

Count and Move in Patterns Recall the story of "Three Billy Goats Gruff." Tell children all of you, in groups of 3, will pretend to be goats bending down to eat grass. Count to 30, or more as appropriate, in patterns of 3. Once the goal number is met, have each group sit on a rug to rest after their "meal."

Mr. Mixup (Counting)

- Remind children that Mr. Mixup needs help counting and to correct him when he makes a mistake.

- Have Mr. Mixup make the following mistakes: forget to stop when producing (counting out) a certain number (show a numeral, ask Mr. Mixup to produce that amount, Mr. Mixup counts out that amount but continues); track unordered items (place up to ten counters in a random collection); double count by counting one or more items again; and skip items as they are counted. Feel free to incorporate mistakes children need to practice. Challenge them to count to 20, 30, or more while keeping track.

 large group · 15 minutes

Social and Emotional Development

Making Good Choices

 Do children use independent problem-solving strategies first and turn to an adult if necessary?

Solving Problems Display the Dog Puppets. Tell children that the puppets are running to get to the playground. Suddenly the second puppet trips and falls and starts to cry. Use the puppets to demonstrate this scenario. Model a dialogue between the puppets that shows the first puppet bending down to talk to the second puppet. He helps the second puppet to stop crying and to stand up. They talk about how to figure out if the second puppet is really hurt, but they're not sure so they look up at you and ask for help.

- Ask: **What problem did the puppets have? How did they handle their problem?**
  ¿Qué problema enfrentaron los títeres? ¿Cómo manejaron su problema?

- Remind children that they should try first to solve their problems on their own but that, if necessary, they should ask an adult for help. Play the song "Everybody Needs Help Sometimes" / *"Todos necesitan ayuda alguna vez"* from the Making Good Choices Audio CD.

Learning Goals

Social and Emotional Development
- Child demonstrates appropriate conflict-resolution strategies, requesting help when needed.

Mathematics
- Child recites number words in sequence from one to thirty.

Vocabulary

amount	cantidad	pattern	patrón
hurt	lastimado		

Differentiated Instruction

✋ Extra Support
Observe and Investigate
If...children have trouble correcting Mr. Mixup, **then...**have Mr. Mixup count slowly so that his mistakes are more obvious.

⭐ Enrichment
Observe and Investigate
For and additional challenge, have Mr. Mixup count orally without using objects, and have him say numbers twice or skip numbers.

Accommodations for 3's
Observe and Investigate
If...children struggle counting up to thirty, **then...**reduce the number to twenty (or ten) and use manipulatives such as the Farm Animals to help them count.

Learning Goals

Social and Emotional Development
• Child shows eagerness, curiosity, and confidence while learning new concepts and trying new things.

Language and Communication
• Child follows two- and three-step oral directions.

• Child names and describes actual or pictured people, places, things, actions, attributes, and events.

Mathematics
• Child recites number words in sequence from one to thirty.

Vocabulary

all number names up to and including thirty

todos los nombres de los números hasta treinta

count	contar	**shaped**	formas
total	total		

Differentiated Instruction

Extra Support

Observe and Investigate

If...children have difficulty keeping track as you count the Pattern Blocks in the different patterns, **then...**help them make the same pattern and have them tap each block as they count it along with you.

Enrichment

Observe and Investigate

Challenge children to invent new counting games and teach these to the whole class.

Math Time

Social and Emotional Development Ask children why it is important to pay attention to what is going on during group instruction rather than talking or getting up and moving. Circulate during group activities to help redirect the attention of fidgety children.

Oral Language and Academic Vocabulary

Can children use number words to count to 30?

Talk About Number Words Display Pattern Blocks. Set out a large pile and count out thirty, making sure to include different colors and shapes. Emphasize each number as you count. Repeat, this time inviting children to count with you.

● Group the Pattern Blocks to make different configurations. Each time you make a different pattern, count them and stress the total number. (30)

● Ask: *How many blocks am I using? How many red [blue, yellow, green] blocks do you see? How many differently-shaped blocks have I used? ¿Cuántos bloques estoy usando? ¿Cuántos bloques rojos [azules, amarillos, verdes] pueden ver? ¿Cuántos bloques de diferentes formas he usado?*

Observe and Investigate

Can children use actions to count to 30?

Step and Clap to 30 Invite children to play several counting games to show that they know how to count to 30.

● Tell the group that they need to listen very carefully during this game. Explain that you will clap a certain number of times and then stop. Each time you will ask: *How many times did I clap? ¿Cuántas veces aplaudí?* and children should call out the correct answer. The game will be over when you clap thirty times.

● Have children stand up and spread out. Tell them that for this next game they need to follow directions very carefully. You're going to stand in the middle of the room and call out a number. They should take that number of steps forward. Then say: *There's one trick—sometimes I'll repeat a number. The second time your hear the number, take that number of steps backward. Hay una regla especial: a veces, repetiré un número. La segunda vez que escuchen el número, den ese número de pasos hacia atrás.* When you call out "thirty," they take thirty steps and all sit.

ELL Use the Dot Cards (*Teacher's Treasure Book* pages 508–509) to reinforce number names with children. Go through the cards a few times, saying the name of each number and having the child repeat the name. Then play a game in which you hold up a card and have the child quickly call out the correct number name. For additional suggestions on how to meet the needs of children at the Beginning, Intermediate, Advanced, and Advanced-High levels of English proficiency, see pages 184–187.

Center Time

▶ **Center Rotation** Center Time includes teacher-guided activities and independent activities. Refer to the **Learning Centers** on pages 24–25 for activities in additional centers.

small group   30 minutes

Learning Goals

Language and Communication
• Child names and describes actual or pictured people, places, things, actions, attributes, and events.

Emergent Literacy: Writing
• Child participates in free drawing and writing activities to deliver information.

Mathematics
• Child recites number words in sequence from one to thirty.

• Child demonstrates that the numerical counting sequence is always the same.

Math and Science Center

Center Tip

If...children have difficulty counting to 30,

then...use a smaller target number..

✓ Observe whether children can accurately count the items in their tower.

Materials coins or other small items that can be stacked easily

Build It Up Tell children they are going to build a tower and count how many objects they used.

● Demonstrate how to stack the objects. Model counting the number of objects in the stack. Then demonstrate adding more objects and counting again.

● Challenge children to build a tower using 30 objects. Remind them to count each object once and only once.

 Writing

Recap the day. Have children describe how they should handle problems. Ask: **What should you do when you have a problem?** *¿Qué hay que hacer cuando tienen un problema?* Record children's answers on chart paper. Share the pen by having children write letters and words they know. Ask children to draw a picture to illustrate each sentence.

Purposeful Play

✓ Observe and informally assess children using language to describe and label what they see.

Children choose an open center for free playtime. Encourage partners to play an animal guessing game in which one partner acts out the behavior of a particular animal and the other partner describes the behavior and then guesses the animal.

Let's Say Good-Bye

large group   15 minutes

 Read Aloud Revisit the story **"Little Caterpillar"/"La oruga"** for your afternoon Read Aloud. Remind children to pay special attention to changes in the caterpillar's life cycle.

 Home Connection Refer to the Home Connections activities listed in the Resources and Materials chart on page 21. Remind children to tell families they can recognize and make the sounds for all three letters, *Jj*, *Hh*, and *Yy*. Sing the "Good-bye Song" as children prepare to leave.

Focus Question

How do animals grow and change?

¿Cómo crecen y cambian los animales?

✓ **Learning Goals**

Social and Emotional Development
• Child demonstrates appropriate conflict-resolution strategies, requesting help when needed.

Language and Communication
• Child recognizes the difference between similar sounding words (for example, child follows directions without confusion over the words heard; points to the appropriate picture when prompted).

Emergent Literacy: Reading
• Child generates words that rhyme.

• Child describes, relates to, and uses details and information from books read aloud.

Vocabulary

chase   perseguir   chewed   masticar

Differentiated Instruction

 Extra Support

Oral Language and Vocabulary
If...children have difficulty recalling what they've learned about animal life cycles, **then...** prompt them with the name and one fact about each animal. For example: *The caterpillar started life as an egg. What did it become at the end?*

 Enrichment

Phonological Awareness
Challenge children to come with a rhyme(s) for as many words as possible in "Animals Grow Up," including the two-syllable words such as *tiny, older,* and *scamper.*

Let's Start the Day

▶ **Opening Routines and Transition Tips**
For **Opening Routines** and **Transition Tips** turn to pages 178–181 and visit **DLMExpressOnline.com** for more ideas.

📖 Read **"The Baby Chicks"/"Los pollitos"** from the *Teacher's Treasure Book,* page 181, for your morning Read Aloud.

🕐 large group 15 minutes

Language Time

👥 **Social and Emotional Development** Encourage children to be alert to any problems that come up during today's learning activities and to remember the two ways they can handle them: first, try to solve them on their own and, if necessary, go to an adult.

Oral Language and Vocabulary

✓ **Can children share what they know about the ways animals grow and change?**

How Animals Change Talk about what children have learned this week about animals' life cycles and the changes that happen as an animal grows from a baby to an adult. Ask: **What do you know about how animals change during their lives?** *¿Qué saben sobre cómo los animales cambian a lo largo de sus vidas?*

● Display *Rhymes and Chants Flip Chart,* page 25. Read aloud the poem, "Animals Grow Up." Ask: **What does the kitten look like? What will he do when he grows up? What does the dog look like now? Where does she sleep?** *¿Cómo es el gatito? ¿Qué hará cuando crezca? ¿Cómo luce la perrita ahora? ¿Dónde duerme?*

ELL Choose some animal photos, such as a cow, lion, sheep, from the Photo Library. Ask children what each animal is called. Then teach the name of each baby animal, *calf, cub, lamb.* Play a game. You say, "The mother is a _____." Children respond by saying, "The baby is a _____." For additional suggestions on how to meet the needs of children at the Beginning, Intermediate, Advanced, and Advanced-High levels of English proficiency, see pages 184–187.

Phonological Awareness

✓ **Can children produce words that rhyme?**

Produce Rhyming Words Using *Rhymes and Chants Flip Chart,* page 25, read aloud "Animals Grow Up" once more with children. Remind children that rhyming words end with the same sounds. Point to the kitten in the picture. Ask: **What do kittens grow up to be? What are some words that rhyme with cat?** *¿Cuáles son algunas palabras que riman con cat?*

Animals Grow Up

A baby kitten is very small.
He's light as a feather,
He won't chase a ball.

But after a year he'll be a cat.
He'll leap to the window
Or play with a hat.

Our dog looks big now in her bed.
She wasn't this big
At first, Dad said.

Her tiny paws were fuzzy to touch,
But now she has long hair
And barks too much!

Rhymes and Chants Flip Chart, p. 25

Center Time

Center Rotation Center Time includes teacher-guided activities and independent activities. Refer to the **Learning Centers** on pages 24–25 for activities in additional centers.

 small group 60–90 minutes

ABC Center

Center Tip

 Monitor children's ability to recognize letter names and sounds.

Materials big bucket; "fishing poles" with magnet attached to the end of fishing line; magnetic letters representing the letters children have learned thus far (or fewer, to make the game easier)

Fishing for Letters Explain to children that they have by now learned so many letters that they're ready to play the Fishing for Letters game.

- Have partners take turns fishing out a letter from the bucket. Say: *When you fish out a letter, you need to say the name of the letter, make the sound for that letter, and think of a word or a friend's name that begins with that letter-sound.* *Cuando pesquen una letra, deben decir el nombre de la letra, hacer el sonido de esa letra, y pensar en una palabra, o en el nombre de un amigo, que comience con esa letra.*

- If children are able to complete a turn successfully, they keep the letter. If not, they toss it back into the bucket. The game is over when the bucket is empty.

If...children have difficulty deciding if answers are correct, **then**...make sure they call you over to make the decision. This is an opportunity to remind children of the good choices behavior they have been learning this week: if they can't solve a problem on their own, they need to ask for help.

Creativity Center

Center Tip

 Observe children's ability to expand and express their knowledge in creative ways.

Materials Photo Library pictures from the Animals, Home, Structures, and Clothing categories

What If? Remind children of what they've learned about where different animals live and/or how they bring up their babies. Tell them today they will have a chance to imagine "What If?"

- Display the Photo Library pictures. Explain that first children should choose an Animal picture, either a Home or a Structures picture, and a Clothing picture. Say: *Imagine a story about your animal. What would happen if he/she lived in that building and wore those clothes? What kinds of things would he/she do every day? Tell me or a partner your story.* *Imaginen un cuento sobre su animal. ¿Qué pasaría si viviera en ese edificio y usara esa ropa? ¿Qué tipo de cosas haría todos los días? Cuéntenme a mí o a un compañero sus cuentos.*

If...children have difficulty making choices about how and what to combine, **then**...present a few specific options to them and hone in on a few possible scenarios to help them get started.

Learning Goals

Language and Communication
- Child uses complex sentences that include many details, tell about one topic, and communicate meaning clearly.

Emergent Literacy: Reading
- Child names most upper- and lowercase letters of the alphabet.
- Child identifies the letter that stands for a given sound.

Science
- Child understands and describes life cycles of plants and animals.
- Child observes, understands, and discusses the relationship of plants and animals to their environments.

Differentiated Instruction

✋ Extra Support

ABC Center
If...children have difficulty achieving all three tasks (letter name, letter sound, new word), **then**...narrow the scope of the game to focus on only one at a time.

⭐ Enrichment

Creativity Center
Challenge children to incorporate pictures from additional Photo Library categories—for example, from the Toys or Occupations categories. Encourage them to use these additional pictures to further embellish their imaginary scenarios.

Learning Goals

Emergent Literacy: Reading
- Child names most upper- and lowercase letters of the alphabet.
- Child identifies the letter that stands for a given sound.
- Child describes, relates to, and uses details and information from books read aloud.

Science
- Child understands and describes life cycles of plants and animals.

Vocabulary

adult	adulto
baby	cría
egg	huevo
elephant	elefante
hatches	romper el cascarón
nest	nido
safe	seguro

Differentiated Instruction

 Extra Support

Learn About Letters and Sounds

If...children struggle to recognize the initial letter in the word you hold up, **then...**say the word aloud at the same time that you hold up the card.

 Enrichment

Learn About Letters and Sounds

Play a more complicated version of the game with children by including all three letters at once. Children need to decide if the word card you hold up starts with one of the three letters (or the word you say starts with one of the three sounds).

Literacy Time

 large group 15 minutes

📖 Read Aloud

✅ **Can children use information learned from books to compare and contrast?**

Build Background Tell children that you will be rereading the *Concept Big Book* selection about how animals change and grow from babies to adults.

- Ask: *What did we learn about how adult animals take care of their babies?* *¿Qué aprendimos sobre los animales adultos cuidan a sus crías?*

Listen for Understanding Display *Concept Big Book 3: Growing and Changing/ Creciendo y cambiando*, page 17, and read the title.

- Reread pages 18–21. Stop and have children compare and contrast.

- Ask: *What are the differences in how a baby chick looks compared to an adult chicken? What does a baby animal need that an adult does not need? What do both adults and babies need?* *¿Cuáles son las diferencias entre el aspecto de un pollito y el de un pollo adulto? ¿Qué necesita una cría que no necesite un animal adulto? ¿Qué necesitan los adultos y sus crías?*

Respond and Connect Have children connect their new learning to their daily lives. Ask: *Do you have a baby brother or sister, or a puppy or kitten? Or do you know someone who does? What happens as those babies grow up?* *¿Tienen un hermano o hermana bebé, o un cachorro o un gatito? De lo contrario, ¿conocen a alguien que sí tenga? ¿Qué sucede a medida que crecen esos bebés y esas crías?*

TIP Be sure to include children who do not have younger siblings or pets by encouraging them to think about their extended family and neighbors.

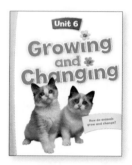

Growing and Changing
Creciendo y cambiando

Learn About Letters and Sounds

✅ **Can children identify letters and sounds?**

Review Letters *Jj, Hh, Yy* Display the *ABC Picture Cards* for these letters.

- Review each letter and sound with children. For each, have children trace the letter in the air as you trace it on the *ABC Picture Card* and say its sound aloud with you.

- Play a version of Simon Says. Display the *ABC Picture Card* for *Jj*. Say: *I'm going to hold up another card with a word. If it also starts with the letter J, do what I say. If it does not start with J, just stand still.* *Voy a sostener otra tarjeta con una palabra. Si también comienza con la letra J, hagan lo que digo. Si no comienza con J, quédense quietos.*

- For each turn, give directions such as "Jump up and down" or "Clap." Play the same game for the letters *Hh* and *Yy*. Vary the game by saying works aloud, rather than showing letter cards.

ELL Preview game rules and direction words with children. Tell them beforehand exactly which words—*clap, jump, skip, tap,* and so on—you'll be using. Check comprehension by having children act out the meaning of each.

ABC Picture Cards

Building Blocks

Online Math Activity

Children can complete Dinosaur Shop 2 and Pizza Pizzazz 3 during computer time or Center Time.

Math Time

Observe and Investigate

☑ **Can children count up to 10 items and keep track of which objects have been counted, even in unstructured situations?**

Dinosaur Shop (Fill Orders)

- Provide dinosaur counters, toy dinosaurs, and play money for children to fill orders at the Dinosaur Shop. To add realism, you may also provide a toy register, bags and boxes to pack dinosaurs, and so on.

- Children take turns being customers and salespeople. For example, a customer orders ten dinosaurs, the salesperson counts out ten dinosaurs, and then the customer counts out ten dollars to pay.

- Observe whether or not children can produce amounts to 10 or more, and if they can count unordered sets.

✗✗✗ Social and Emotional Development

Making Good Choices

☑ **Do children use independent problem-solving strategies first and turn to an adult if necessary?**

Solving Problems Display *Making Good Choices Flip Chart* page 25, "How can he solve his problem?"

- Point to the flip chart illustration. Ask: **What did you learn about how to solve a problem?** *¿Qué aprendieron sobre cómo resolver un problema?*

- Tell children about a problem you faced recently and how you managed to solve it. You might discuss two different scenarios—one in which you solved the problem on your own and one in which you needed help to resolve it.

- Invite children to tell about a problem they had this week and how they fixed it. Encourage discussion about the ways we can address problems.

ELL Work on vocabulary with children by presenting and discussing common English/Spanish cognates. Examples relevant to this lesson include: *problem—problema; solve—resolver; adult—adulto; dollar—dolar; customer/client—cliente; count (v.)—contar; count (n.)—cuenta.*

Making Good Choices Flip Chart, p. 25

☑ Learning Goals

Social and Emotional Development
- Child demonstrates appropriate conflict-resolution strategies, requesting help when needed.

Mathematics
- Child understands that objects, or parts thereof, can be counted.
- Child counts 1–10 concrete objects correctly.
- Child demonstrates that, when counting, the last number indicates how many objects were counted.

Social Studies
- Child understands basic concepts of buying, selling, and trading.

Vocabulary

customer	cliente
register	caja registradora
salesperson	vendedor

orders	órdenes

Differentiated Instruction

✋ **Extra Support**

Observe and Investigate

If...children have difficulty counting out the correct number of dinosaurs for dollars, **then...** have them lay out one dinosaur next to each dollar as they receive it and do their full count by tapping, one by one, each dinosaur they are about to sell.

⭐ **Enrichment**

Making Good Choices

Encourage children to role-play problem-solving scenarios with a partner. One is the child, the other the adult. Challenge them to come up with multiple solutions to one problem and to discuss afterward which solution was best and why.

💙 **Special Needs**

Cognitive Challenges

When doing any kind of counting activity, hold up the number of fingers to help the child see you are counting.

Focus Question
How do animals grow and change?
¿Cómo crecen y cambian los animales?

Learning Goals

Social and Emotional Development
• Child shows eagerness, curiosity, and confidence while learning new concepts and trying new things.

Science
• Child identifies organisms and describes their characteristics.
• Child understands and describes life cycles of plants and animals.
• Child follows basic health and safety rules.

Art
• Child uses and experiments with a variety of art materials and tools in various art activities.

Vocabulary

animal	animal	detail	detalle
feel	sentir	nature	naturaleza
shape	figura	stage	etapa

Differentiated Instruction

 **Extra Support**
Explore and Express
If…children have difficulty making the two decisions (which photo to choose and how to interpret it), **then…**work through the decision process with them for one of the two factors and help them use that choice to make the second decision.

Enrichment
Explore and Express
Challenge children to add a sentence (at the bottom of the painting or on the back) to explain what the painting represents or how they were feeling as they painted it.

Art Time

large group 20 minutes

Personal Safety Skills With a volunteer helper, model how art tools and supplies should be handled, cleaned, and stored.

Oral Language and Academic Vocabulary

☑ **Can children describe the changes that happen as different animals grow up?**

Animals Change as They Grow Remind children that they learned how some animals go through very different life cycle changes. They also learned that most animals start out as helpless babies who need care. Have students use the *Sequence Cards* "Metamorphosis" to sequence the life cycle of a butterfly.

● Ask: *Which animals go through different stages, changing how they look and their shape as they grow up? What are these stages? What is the most important difference between baby animals and adult animals? ¿Qué animales pasan por diferentes etapas y cambian de apariencia a medida que crecen? ¿Cuáles son esas etapas? ¿Cuál es la diferencia más importante entre las crías y los animales adultos?*

Explore and Express

☑ **Can children paint a picture that represents their reaction to a detail from nature?**

Paint What You See or Feel Tell children that they will have a chance to paint their reactions to a photograph of an animal detail.

● Display about a half dozen photos (from the Photo Library, nature magazines, or the Internet) that depict detailed images such as the silk fibers of a caterpillar's chrysalis, the markings on a butterfly's wing, or the webbed feet of a frog. Say: *Your first job is to examine the photos closely and choose your favorite. Su primera tarea es examinar las fotos de cerca y escoger su favorita.*

● Distribute art supplies. Invite children to paint either a realistic version of what they see *or* a design/image that reflects how they feel when they look at the nature picture. When completed, say: *Why did you choose to do your painting this way? What do you think about your painting? ¿Por qué elegiste hacer tu cuadro de esta manera? ¿Qué piensas de tu pintura?*

TIP Display children's paintings next to the corresponding photo. Encourage children to look at each other's artwork and to ask the painter to explain why he/she reacted to the detail from nature in that particular way.

ELL Use cause/effect sentence frames to help children work through the decision process. For example,

I like this photo best because_____.

I want to [paint what I see/paint what I feel] because _____.

I'm going to use _____ colors because _____.

Center Time

▶ **Center Rotation** Center Time includes teacher-guided activities and independent activities. Refer to the **Learning Centers** on pages 24–25 for activities in additional centers.

 small group — 30 minutes

Construction Center

✓ **Observe children as they create sculptures to depict stages in an animal's life cycle.**

Materials clay, coated wire, sticks, cotton balls, construction paper, other standard art supplies, animal books and photos

Construct a Life Cycle Stage Tell children that they will use clay and other art materials to create a stage from an animal's life cycle. They can choose any animal, such as a frog, caterpillar, or kitten.

- Prompt children to make their choice: *Which animal are you really interested in? Which stage in its life would you like to build? What happens to the animal during this stage? ¿Qué animal les interesa? ¿Qué etapa de su vida les gustaría construir? ¿Qué sucede con el animal durante esa etapa?*

- Have all children who built a stage from the same animal's life gather their pieces. Lay them out in order on a table and examine the way they go together to tell a story.

Center Tip

If...children need help deciding which material to use, **then...**discuss the characteristics of the stage they've selected and what kind of materials would best match up.

Purposeful Play

✓ **Observe children problem solving as they work together.**

Children choose an open center for free playtime. Encourage problem-solving skills by having children work in pairs to decide the best way to solve a given problem—anything from completing a block puzzle to solving a 'mystery scenario.'

Let's Say Good-Bye

 large group — 15 minutes

 Read Aloud Revisit the story, **"The Baby Chicks"**/ "Los pollitos" for your afternoon Read Aloud. Remind children to listen for words that tell how animals change and grow.

 Home Connection Refer to the Home Connections activities listed in the Resources and Materials chart on page 21. Remind children to tell families what they learned about how animals change as they grow up. Sing the "Good-Bye Song" as cildren prepare to leave.

✓ Learning Goals

Social and Emotional Development
• Child demonstrates appropriate conflict-resolution strategies, requesting help when needed.

Emergent Literacy: Writing
• Child participates in free drawing and writing activities to deliver information.

Science
• Child identifies organisms and describes their characteristics.

• Child understands and describes life cycles of plants and animals.

Fine Arts
• Child uses and experiments with a variety of art materials and tools in various art activities.

✏ Writing

Recap the day and week. Say: *Tell me one thing you learned this week about how animals grow and change. Díganme una cosa que hayan aprendido esta semana sobre cómo crecen y cambian los animales.* Encourage them to think of one important fact they've learned and list a few words that tell about this fact. Encourage them to include a drawing as well.

Week 2

Focus Question

How do plants grow and change?

¿Cómo crecen y cambian las plantas?

This week children will learn about the needs and life cycles of plants. They will plant beans, record plant observations, retell the sequence of a plant's life cycle, label plant parts, measure plants, and read about gardens.

Social and Emotional Development	DAY 1	2	3	4	5
Child demonstrates initiative in independent activities; makes independent choices.	✓	✓	✓	✓	✓
Child uses classroom materials carefully.	✓				✓

Language and Communication	1	2	3	4	5
Child demonstrates an understanding of oral language by responding appropriately.				✓	✓
Child follows basic rules for conversations (taking turns, staying on topic, listening actively).				✓	
Child recognizes the difference between similar sounding words (for example, child follows directions without confusion over the words heard; points to the appropriate picture when prompted).	✓	✓		✓	
Child names and describes actual or pictured people, places, things, actions, attributes, and events.	✓		✓		✓
Child exhibits an understanding of instructional terms used in the classroom.		✓		✓	
Child uses newly learned vocabulary daily in multiple contexts.	✓	✓	✓	✓	✓
Child builds English listening and speaking vocabulary for common objects and phrases. (ELL)					✓
Child understands and uses sentences having two or more phrases or concepts.		✓			
Child uses individual words and short phrases to communicate. (ELL)				✓	

Emergent Literacy: Reading	1	2	3	4	5
Child enjoys and chooses reading-related activities.				✓	
Child generates words that rhyme.	✓	✓	✓	✓	✓
Child independently engages in pre-reading behaviors and activities (such as, pretending to read, turning one page at a time).			✓		
Child names most upper- and lowercase letters of the alphabet.	✓	✓		✓	✓
Child identifies the letter that stands for a given sound.	✓	✓	✓	✓	✓
Child retells or reenacts poems and stories in sequence.	✓	✓			✓

Emergent Literacy: Writing	1	2	3	4	5
Child uses scribbles, shapes, pictures, symbols, and letters to represent language.	✓		✓		✓
Child writes own name or a reasonable approximation of it.	✓	✓			

Mathematics	DAY 1	2	3	4	5
Child counts 1–10 concrete objects correctly.					✓
Child measures the length and height of people or objects using standard or non-standard tools.	✓	✓	✓	✓	
Child measures passage of time using standard or non-standard tools.		✓			

Science	1	2	3	4	5
Child uses basic measuring tools to learn about objects.	✓	✓		✓	
Child identifies organisms and describes their characteristics.	✓	✓	✓	✓	✓
Child understands and describes life cycles of plants and animals.	✓	✓	✓	✓	✓
Child observes, understands, and discusses the relationship of plants and animals to their environments.	✓	✓	✓		✓
Child follows basic health and safety rules.	✓				

Social Studies	1	2	3	4	5
Child understands basic concepts of buying, selling, and trading.			✓		

Fine Arts	1	2	3	4	5
Child expresses emotions or ideas through art.			✓		
Child participates in a variety of music activities (such as listening, singing, finger plays, musical games, performances).					✓

Materials and Resources

DAY 1	DAY 2	DAY 3	DAY 4	DAY 5

Program Materials

• Book: *I Am a Peach* • Connecting Cubes • Oral Language Development Cards 54 and 55 • Dog Puppets • Alphabet Wall Cards: *Hh* and *Jj* • Home Connections Resource Guide • Jumbo Hand Lenses • Making Good Choices Flip Chart • Math and Science Flip Chart • Rhymes and Chants Flip Chart • Sequence Cards: Seed to Flower • Teacher's Treasure Book • Building Blocks Online Math Activities	• Book: *I Am a Peach* • Connecting Cubes • Dog Puppets • ABC Wall Cards: *Hh* and *Jj* • Making Good Choices Flip Chart • Math and Science Flip Chart • Teacher's Treasure Book • Building Blocks Online Math Activities	• Concept Big Book 3: Growing and Changing • Home Connections Resource Guide • Oral Language Development Card 56 • Making Good Choices Flip Chart • Rhymes and Chants Flip Chart • Teacher's Treasure Book • ABC Wall Cards: *Hh* and *Jj* • Dog Puppets • Book: *I Am a Peach* • Photo Library Cards: Trees (summer, spring, winter, fall) • Building Blocks Online Math Activities	• Teacher's Treasure Book • Math and Science Flip Chart • Home Connections Resource Guide • Dog Puppets • Alphabet Wall Card: *Jj* Jump Rope • Connecting Cubes • Building Blocks Online Math Activities	• Teacher's Treasure Book • Rhymes and Chants Flip Chart • Making Good Choices Flip Chart • Home Connections Resource Guide • Alphabet/Letter Tiles: *Hh* and *Jj* • ABC Picture Cards: *Hh* and *Jjj* • Book: I Am a Peach • Photo Library Cards: Flash Cards • ABC Wall Cards: *Hh* and *Jj* • Counting Cards • Sequence Cards: Seed to Flower • Building Blocks Online Math Activities

Other Materials

• flower books • long paper • crayons • flowering plants • blank books for plant journal	• house-shape cut-outs from file folders • magazines • crayons • construction paper • craft sticks • scissors, glue, yarn • flat buttons • plants • wooden blocks • cut string pieces	• cut fruit • plant journals • poster paper • glue, tissue and/or crepe paper • yarn, markers, crayons • construction paper • blocks • boxes • clay, craft sticks • paper cups, paper bags • small stones	• books about flowers, fruits, vegetables, trees • seed catalogs, garden supply store ads • plant journals • Nursery rhyme: Mary, Mary, Quite Contrary, How Does Your Garden Grow? • garden tools • artificial flowers and vegetables • sun hats, gardening gloves • scissors • cups, potting soil, lima beans	• poster board labels • markers, tape • a jump rope • heavy paper • glue • beans • musical instruments • rulers, rubber bands, buttons

Home Connection

Encourage children to tell their families what they learned about plants and flowers. Send home the following materials: Weekly Family Letter, Home Connections Resource Guide, pp. 55-56.	Encourage children to tell their families about how plants grow and change. Remind children to tell their families how they learned to measure different objects in the classroom.	Encourage children to tell their families what they learned about the parts of a plant. Remind children to tell their families about problems in different situations and how they helped solve the problems.	Encourage children to tell their families what happened to Jack in the story *Jack and the Beanstalk*. Send home Storybook 16, Home Connections Resource Guide, pp. 141-142 (English), and pp. 143-144 (Spanish).	Encourage children to tell their families what they learned this week about plants and how they grow. Remind children to tell their families about the sounds that different musical instruments make.

Assessment

As you observe children throughout the week, you may fill out an Anecdotal Observational Record Form to document an individual's progress toward a goal or signs indicating the need for developmental or medical evaluation. You may also choose to select work for each child's portfolio. The Anecdotal Observational Record Form and Weekly Assessment rubrics are available in the assessment section of DLMExpressOnline.com.

More Literature Suggestions

- **Tom's Tree** by Gillian Shields
- **Carrot Soup** by John Segal
- **Pumpkin Circle** by George Levenson
- **From Seed to Plant** by Gail Gibbons
- **Inch By Inch** by Leo Lionni
- **La semilla de zanahoria** por Ruth Krauss

- **Árboles por todas partes** por Rosanela Álvarez
- **El jardín de Bessey, la desordenada** por Pat McKissack y Fredrick McKissack
- **El árbol de Rita** por Rosa Flores
- **Un día feliz** por Ruth Krauss

Daily Planner

		DAY 1	DAY 2
Let's Start the Day Language Time	large group	**Opening Routines** p. 64 **Morning Read Aloud** p. 64 **Oral Language and Vocabulary** p. 64 Plants Grow **Phonological Awareness** p. 64 Produce Rhyming Words	**Opening Routines** p. 70 **Morning Read Aloud** p. 70 **Oral Language and Vocabulary** p. 70 I Am a Peach **Phonological Awareness** p. 70 Produce Rhyming Words
Center Time	small group	**Focus On:** **Library and Listening Center** p. 65 **Pretend and Learn Center** p. 65	**Focus On:** **ABC Center** p. 71 **Creativity Center** p. 71
Circle Time Literacy Time	large group	**Read Aloud** I Am a Peach/Yo Soy el Durazno p. 66 **Learn About Letters and Sounds:** /j/ and /h/ p. 66	**Read Aloud** I Am a Peach/Yo Soy el Durazno p. 72 **Learn About Letters and Sounds:** j and h p. 72
Math Time	large group	**Measure Length** p. 67	**Length Riddles** p. 73
Social and Emotional Development	large group	**Solving Problems** p. 67	**Solving Problems** p. 73
Content Connection	large group	**Science:** **Oral Language and Academic Vocabulary** p. 68 Talking About Flowers **Observe and Investigate** p. 68 Looking at Flowers	**Math:** **Oral Language and Academic Vocabulary** p. 74 Talk About Measuring **Observe and Investigate** p. 74 Mr. Mixup's Measuring Mess
Center Time	small group	**Focus On:** **Math and Science Center** p. 69 **Purposeful Play** p. 69	**Focus On:** **Math and Science Center** p. 75 **Purposeful Play** p. 75
Let's Say Good-Bye	large group	**Read Aloud** p. 69 **Writing** p. 69 **Home Connection** p. 69	**Read Aloud** p. 75 **Writing** p. 75 **Home Connection** p. 75

DAY 3

Opening Routines p. 76
Morning Read Aloud p. 76
Oral Language and Vocabulary
p. 76 How Gardens Grow
Phonological Awareness
p. 76 Recognize Rhyming Words

Focus On:
Writer's Center p. 77
Creativity Center p. 77

Read Aloud
*Growing and Changing/Creciendo
y cambiando* p. 78
Learn About Letters and Sounds:
Jj and Hh p. 78

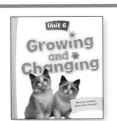

Road Blocks p. 79

Solving Problems p. 79

Social Studies:
Oral Language and Academic Vocabulary
p. 80 Talking About Time Passing
Understand and Participate
p. 80 Looking at Changes

Focus On:
Construction Center p. 81
Purposeful Play p. 81

Read Aloud p. 81
Writing p. 81
Home Connection p. 81

DAY 4

Opening Routines p. 82
Morning Read Aloud p. 82
Oral Language and Vocabulary
p. 82 Real and Make-Believe
Phonological Awareness
p. 82 Produce Rhyming Words

Focus On:
Library and Listening Center p. 83
Pretend and Learn Center p. 83

Read Aloud
*Jack and the Beanstalk/Jaime
y los frijoles magicos* p. 84
Learn About Letters and Sounds:
/j/ and /h/ p. 84

Length Riddles p. 85

Solving Problems p. 85

Math:
Oral Language and Academic Vocabulary
p. 86 Talk About Measuring Length
Observe and Investigate
p. 86 I'm Thinking of a Number (Length)

Focus On:
Math and Science Center p. 87
Purposeful Play p. 87

Read Aloud p. 87
Writing p. 87
Home Connection p. 87

DAY 5

Opening Routines p. 88
Morning Read Aloud p. 88
Oral Language and Vocabulary
p. 88 Plants Grow and Change
Phonological Awareness
p. 88 Produce Rhyming Words

Focus On:
Writer's Center p. 89
ABC Center p. 89

Read Aloud
I Am a Peach/Yo Soy el Durazno p. 90
Learn About Letters and Sounds:
Jj and Hh p. 90

X-Ray Vision p. 91

Solving Problems p. 91

Music and Movement Time:
Oral Language and Academic Vocabulary
p. 92 Talking About Sounds
Explore and Express
p. 92 Wake Up Sleepy Seeds

Focus On:
Construction Center p. 93
Purposeful Play p. 93

Read Aloud p. 93
Writing p. 93
Home Connection p. 93

Learning Centers

Math and Science Center

My Plant Journal
Children keep a plant journal for the week. Each day, they draw and write what they learn about plants. See p. 69.

Measuring Match
Children use string in different lengths to measure objects that are the same length as the string. See p. 75.

Growing Beans
Children plant lima beans and describe what they see over time as the beans sprout and grow. They record their observations in their Plant Journals. See p. 87.

Fruit Grab Bag
Children reach in a sack filled with different kinds of fruit. Without looking, they touch a piece of fruit and guess what it is.

ABC Center

Letter House
Children draw a large door and windows on the front of a folder house shape. Inside the folder, they draw pictures whose names begin with /h/. See p. 71.

Matching Letters
Children use Letter Tiles to match upper case and lower case *Jj* and *Hh*. They write *Jj* and *Hh* on heavy paper, trace the letters with glue, and press beans over the glue. See p. 89.

A Hat for *Hh*
Children draw a large hat on a sheet of construction paper. On the hat, they write the letters *Hh* and draw pictures of objects whose names begin with /h/, such as *hen, heart,* and *hammer*.

Creativity Center

Peach Puppets
Children draw a picture of a peach and cut it out. They add a face and glue the peach to a craft stick. See p. 71.

Poster Plants
Children use a variety of art supplies to create a flower garden on poster paper. They take turns giving "tours" of their garden. See p. 77.

Apple Tree
Children paint a big apple tree on a sheet of butcher paper. Each child cuts and pastes a round, red circle on the apple tree.

Flower Puzzles
Children glue a picture of a flower on a piece of poster board and cut the picture into three or four pieces. Partners exchange puzzles and put them together.

Library and Listening Center

Browsing Flower Books
Children browse through books about flowers, choose a favorite flower, and make a large drawing of it. They fold and unfold the drawing to make the flower grow. See p. 65.

Growing Library
Partners browse through books about flowers, fruits, vegetables, and trees. They talk about how a plant begins and grows over time. See p. 83.

Plant Power
Partners look through books about plants and flowers with the goal of identifying five different fruits, four different flowers, and two different trees.

Construction Center

Build a Garden Store
Children use blocks, boxes, and clay to build a garden store. They role-play clerks and customers during the grand opening of their store. See p. 81.

Build a Musical Instrument
Children use blocks, boxes, and other materials to make a musical instrument. They play the instrument to wake up the tiny seed. See p. 93.

Fruit Collage
Children cut out pictures of fruits from magazines and glue them to a large sheet of butcher paper to form a collage. Children point to each fruit and name it.

Writer's Center

Write About Seeds
Children examine pieces of fruit that have seeds. They draw and label pictures in their plant journals to show what they notice about seeds. See p. 77.

Planting Labels
Children write labels for planting tools and plants in the Math and Science Center. They also label their bean plants with names, descriptions, and markings that show how the plants are growing. See p. 89.

Berry Good
Children talk about the different kinds of berries they like to eat, such as strawberries, blueberries, and raspberries, and share any experiences they have had with berry picking. Children draw and label a picture of their favorite kind of berry.

Pretend and Learn Center

Growing Seeds
Children pretend to be tiny seeds and use their bodies to show what happens as seeds grow and change. See p. 65.

Plant a Garden
Children use gardening props, such as small shovels and rakes, gardening gloves, and a watering can to pretend to plant a garden. See p. 83.

Fruit and Vegetable Stand
Children use boxes, crates, and pictures of fruits and vegetables to set up a fruit stand. They use a cash register and play money to act out purchases.

Food Rhymes
Children make up simple rhymes about fruits they like, for example: "An orange is juicy and sweet. For me, it's the best treat!"

Focus Question
How do plants grow and change?
¿Cómo crecen y cambian las plantas?

Learning Goals

Language and Communication
• Child recognizes the difference between similar sounding words (for example, child follows directions without confusion over the words heard; points to the appropriate picture when prompted).
• Child uses newly learned vocabulary daily in multiple contexts

Emergent Literacy: Reading
• Child generates words that rhyme.

Vocabulary

flower	flor	leaves	hojas
plant	planta	pot	maceta
soil	tierra	window	ventana

Differentiated Instruction

 Extra Support
Phonological Awareness
If...children have difficulty producing words that rhyme, **then...**read aloud each couplet on the *Rhymes and Chants Flip Chart* and have children echo. Then read the couplet again, pausing to have children produce the second word in each rhyming pair.

 Enrichment
Phonological Awareness
Challenge children to produce a rhyming couplet with the first phrase on the *Rhymes and Chants Flip Chart*. For example: *I'm a little seed. What do I need?*

Let's Start the Day

▶ **Opening Routines and Transition Tips**
For **Opening Routines** and **Transition Tips** turn to pages 178–181 and visit DLMExpressOnline.com for more ideas.

📖 Read **"Shade Trees"**/*"Arbol frondoso"* from the *Teacher's Treasure Book,* page 110, through twice for your morning Read Aloud.

large group | 15 minutes

Language Time

👥 **Social and Emotional Development** Encourage children to offer solutions during class discussions.

Oral Language and Vocabulary

✓ **Can children use descriptive words to describe a plant?**

Plants Grow Talk about *plants* and how they grow. Ask: **What plants have you seen? How do you know when it's growing?** *¿Qué plantas han visto? ¿Cómo saben que una planta está creciendo?*

● Display *Oral Language Development Card 54.* Name parts of the *plant.* (*flower, leaves*) Point out two things that plants need to grow (*soil,* light from the *window*), noting that plants also need water. Ask: **Where is the best place for a plant to grow in our classroom? Why?** *¿Cuál es el mejor lugar para que una planta crezca en nuestro salón? ¿Por qué?* Then follow the suggestions on the back of the card.

Phonological Awareness

✓ **Can children produce words that rhyme with *grow*?**

Produce Rhyming Words Display *Rhymes and Chants Flip Chart,* page 26. Read "A Plant Grows". Tell children that rhyming words end with the same sound. Call attention to the rhyming words *below* and *grow.* Then have children produce real and nonsense words that rhyme with *grow.* Have them squat and then grow like the flower in the rhyme each time a rhyming word is suggested.

 Use the *Rhymes and Chants Flip Chart* and focus on the word *grows.* Pronounce and act out the word. Then have children say the word and pantomime with you. Continue with *mow.* Say: **grows, mows, toes. These words end with the same sound, /ō/. These words rhyme.** Have children repeat the words with you.

Oral Language Development Card 54

Rhymes and Chants Flip Chart, p. 26

Center Time

> **Center Rotation** Center Time includes teacher-guided activities and independent activities. Refer to the **Learning Centers** on pages 62–63 for activities in additional centers.

 small group · 60–90 minutes

Library and Listening Center

 Track the use of rhyming words as children unfold favorite flower drawings.

Materials flower books, long paper, crayons

Browsing Flower Books Have children browse through books that show pictures of flowers and choose a favorite flower. Help them describe the flower.

- Have children make a large drawing of their favorite flower vertically on a long sheet of paper. Help them fold the drawing four times.

- To make the flower grow, have a child unfold one section of the drawing at a time, say a real or nonsense word that rhymes with *seed*, and then pass the picture to another child who names another rhyming word.

Center Tip

If...children have difficulty describing their favorite flower, **then**...use sentence frames. *The color is _____. The leaves are _____.*

Pretend and Learn Center

 As children problem solve, point out creative solutions.

Growing Seeds Have children pretend to be tiny seeds. Have them figure out how to use their bodies to show what happens as seeds grow and change. Provide *Sequence Cards* "Seed to Flower" for children to practice sequencing the life cycle of plants.

- Say: *Show how you grow and change, tiny seeds. Semillitas, muéstrenme cómo crecen y cambian.*

- Say: *Tiny seeds, you are done growing! What do you look like now? Semillitas, ¡ya han crecido! ¿Cómo se ven ahora?*

Center Tip

If...children do not persist in figuring out a way to show how seeds grow and change, **then**... offer prompts and encouragement, for example: *A seed is tiny. You can make yourself tiny.*

Learning Goals

Social and Emotional Development
- Child demonstrates initiative in independent activities; makes independent choices.

Language and Communication
- Child uses newly learned vocabulary daily in multiple contexts.

Emergent Literacy: Reading
- Child generates words that rhyme.

Differentiated Instruction

Extra Support
Library and Listening Center
If...children have difficulty producing rhyming words for *seed*, **then**...say a rhyming word pair and have them repeat.

Enrichment
Library and Listening Center
Challenge children to produce silly rhyming names for flowers in the books.

Accommodations for 3's
Pretend and Learn Center
If...children have difficulty pretending to grow, **then**...have them follow your actions.

Focus Question

How do plants grow and change?

¿Cómo crecen y cambian las plantas?

Learning Goals

Emergent Literacy: Reading
- Child names most upper- and lowercase letters of the alphabet.
- Child identifies the letter that stands for a given sound.
- Child retells or reenacts poems and stories in sequence.

Science
- Child identifies organisms and describes their characteristics.
- Child understands and describes life cycles of plants and animals.
- Child observes, understands, and discusses the relationship of plants and animals to their environments.

Vocabulary

branch	rama	market	mercado
matured	maduro	peach	durazno
trunk	tronco		

Differentiated Instruction

 Extra Support

Read Aloud

If...children have difficulty identifying the sequence of events, **then...**point out specific parts of the story illustrations: the flower, the green peach, the ripe peach.

Enrichment

Read Aloud

Challenge children to sequence events without using the illustrations.

 Special Needs

Behavioral Social/Emotional

Praise the child often, especially when he or she accomplishes something new or stays on task for a given amount of time.

Literacy Time

large group — 15 minutes

📖 Read Aloud

✓ **Can children identify a sequence of events?**

Build Background Tell children that you will be reading a book about how a plant grows and changes.

- Ask: **How do plants change over time?** *¿Cómo cambian las plantas con el paso del tiempo?*

- **Listen for Enjoyment** Display the book *I Am a Peach, Yo soy el durazno,* and read the title. Explain that a peach is a fuzzy fruit. Then conduct a picture walk. *¿Cómo se ve el durazno ahora? ¿Cómo se veía antes? picture walk.*

- Browse through the pages focusing on how the peach grows and changes. Ask: **What does the peach look like now? What did the peach look like before?** *¿Cómo es el durazno ahora?Cómo era antes?*

- Tell children that the peach is telling the story. Then read *I Am a Peach* aloud. Pause to explain that the peach's heart is the seed.

Respond to the Story Have children use the illustrations to retell the beginning of the story. Say: **First, the peach is a flower. What happens next? What happens last?** *Primero, el durazno es una flor. ¿Qué pasa después? ¿Qué pasa al final?*

TIP To reinforce sequence, have children draw the three events in order that show the peach growing and changing from a blossom, to a green fruit, to a ripe fruit.

ELL Have children point to pictures in the book *I Am a Peach* as you sequence these events: **First, the peach is a flower. Next, the peach is a green fruit. Last, the peach is a ripe fruit.**

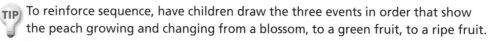

I Am a Peach
Yo soy el durazno

Learn About Letters and Sounds

✓ **Can children identify the /j/ sound spelled *Jj* and the /h/ sound spelled *Hh?***

Learn About *J* and *H* Review how to write upper case *J* and *H* using the Alphabet Cards. Have children practice writing each letter in the air and on a Alphabet Card.

- Use the Dog Puppet to say: **I am thinking of a letter. It is upper case J.** *Estoy pensando en una letra. Es la J mayúscula.* Have children look closely at the two Letter Cards and compare their shapes to find the letter. Have them hold up the Alphabet Card. Repeat the process several times.

- Review sounds /j/ and /h/. Have children match the beginning sound of a word with one of the Alphabet Cards, J or H. Have the Dog Puppet say: **jacks, hug, jelly, heart, horse, jacket.**

Math Time

Observe and Investigate

✅ **Can children measure lengths of common objects?**

Measure Length Explain that measuring is finding a number that tells how long or how much. Tell children that a length in units tells how many units can fit along something from one end to the other. For example, a book may be the length of one standard ruler or twelve inches long. Use Connecting Cubes to measure classroom objects.

- Ask children whether they do any measuring outside of school. Using their examples or your own, measure something together as a model, such as measuring a rug to discover it is about three feet long.

- Discuss how you can use measuring to tell how much a plant has grown. Then tell children there will be much measuring done in class this week.

- Have children measure a volunteer and an adult to compare the heights of each.

Building Blocks

Online Math Activity

Introduce Reptile Ruler (online activity) in which children learn about linear measurements by using an on-screen ruler to determine the length of various reptiles.

👫👫 Social and Emotional Development

Making Good Choices

✅ **Do children attempt to solve problems?**

Solving Problems Discuss a classroom problem and how it was solved. Display the *Making Good Choices Flip Chart*. Point to the children in the scene.

- Ask: **What problems do these children have? How can they solve their problems?**
  ¿Qué problemas enfrentan estos niños? ¿Cómo pueden solucionarlos?

- Then discuss the children's problems and possible solutions. As children offer solutions, point out that there are often different ways to solve the same problem. Play the song "Excuse Me"/"Permiso" from the Making Good Choices Audio CD. Ask children what they think the song is telling them about selfishness.

ELL Point to the illustrations on the *Making Good Choices Flip Chart* and describe the problems for children. Say: **The boy and the girl both want the pot. The girl spills the soil and makes a mess.** For additional suggestions on how to meet the needs of children at the Beginning, Intermediate, Advanced, and Advanced-High levels of English proficiency, see pages 184–187.

Making Good Choices Flip Chart, p. 26

✅ Learning Goals

Social and Emotional Development
- Child demonstrates initiative in independent activities; makes independent choices.

Mathematics
- Child measures the length and height of people or objects using standard or non-standard tools.

Science
- Child uses basic measuring tools to learn about objects.

Vocabulary

length	longitud	measure	medida
problem	problema	ruler	regla
olution	solución	solve	resolver

Differentiated Instruction

✋ Extra Support

Observe and Investigate
If...children have difficulty measuring length, **then...**have them place small objects at one end of a ruler and ask them to count "how many" (objects).

⭐ Enrichment

Observe and Investigate
Have children measure objects in the classroom, record lengths, and then compare results.

Accommodations for 3's

Observe and Investigate
If...children lack focus when you are measuring together, **then...**guide a hand to move the ruler.

Focus Question

How do plants grow and change?
¿Cómo crecen y cambian las plantas?

Learning Goals

Social and Emotional Development
• Child uses classroom materials carefully.

Language and Communication
• Child names and describes actual or pictured people, places, things, actions, attributes, and events.

Science
• Child identifies organisms and describes their characteristics.

• Child understands and describes life cycles of plants and animals.

• Child follows basic health and safety rules.

Vocabulary

apple tree	manzano	blossoms	pimpollos
branches	ramas	spring	primavera
sunlight	luz solar	trunk	tronco

Differentiated Instruction

 Extra Support

Oral Language and Academic Vocabulary
If...children have difficulty describing a flower, **then**...ask questions: *Is this flower white? Is this flower tall or small? Is this flower shaped like a circle or a square?*

⭐ **Enrichment**

Observe and Investigate
Challenge children to draw and label their observations.

Accommodations for 3's

Observe and Investigate
Model how to gently touch and smell a flower. Provide practice with an artificial plant.

Science Time

large group — 20 minutes

Health Skills Model good cleanliness routines by washing your hands before and after handling plants.

Oral Language and Academic Vocabulary

✓ **Can children use words to describe plants and how they grow and change?**

Talking About Flowers Point to the seeds on the *Math and Science Flip Chart*, page 47. Say: **Here are some seeds. The seeds grew and grew.** *Aquí hay algunas semillas. Estas semillas crecieron y crecieron.*

• Ask: **How did the seeds change?** *¿Cómo cambiaron las semillas?* Help children recognize that over time the seeds grew into small plants and then grew and changed into plants with flowers. Introduce *Sequence Cards*, "Seed to Flower" to show how a plant grows and changes.

• Discuss the flowers. Ask: **What color are the flowers in the pots? Look at this flower shape. What does it remind you of?** *¿De qué color son las flores de la maceta? Observen la forma de esta flor. ¿Qué les recuerda?*

• Display *Oral Language Development Card 55*. Tell children that this tree is an apple tree in the spring. Say: **Sunlight helped this tree grow. Look at the strong branches. The flowers on an apple tree are called blossoms. What do you notice about the apple blossoms?** *La luz solar ayudó a este árbol a crecer. Miren sus ramas robustas. Las flores, antes de abrirse, son pimpollos. ¿Qué observan en los pimpollos del manzano?*

Math and Science Flip Chart, p. 47

Observe and Investigate

✓ **Can children use words to describe the characteristics of flowers?**

Looking at Flowers Display flowering plants in pots on a table. Have children observe and compare the plants.

• Have children talk about the color and shape of the flowers. Say: **Compare two flowers. Tell how the flowers are the same. Tell how the flowers are different.** *Comparen dos flores. Díganme en qué se parecen las flores. Díganme en qué se diferencian.*

• Let children take turns using a hand lens to observe the flowers more closely.

• Encourage children to smell the flowers and gently touch the leaves and petals. Ask: **Are the leaves smooth or rough? Are the petals soft or stiff?** *¿Las hojas son suaves o ásperas? ¿Los pétalos son blandos o duros?*

💡 **TIP** Check health records for allergies before allowing children to touch or smell the flowers.

Oral Language Development Card 55

Center Time

▶ **Center Rotation** Center Time includes teacher-guided activities and independent activities. Refer to the **Learning Centers** on pages 62–63 for activities in additional centers.

small group · 30 minutes

Math and Science Center

Center Tip

If...children need support in understanding the function of written language, **then...** encourage children to connect meaning to their drawing by asking what they wrote.

☑ **Encourage children to draw and write about plants in a journal.**

Materials *Oral Language Development Cards* 54, 55; *Math and Science Flip Chart*, Looking at Flowers; real flowering plants; blank books

My Plant Journal Display the *Oral Language Development Cards*, the *Math and Science Flip Chart*, and real plants. Distribute blank books. Say: *This is a plant journal. Éste es un diario de plantas.*

- Have children write their names at the bottom of the cover. Have children talk about plants and how they grow. Have them recall their experiences with real plants.

- Have children draw and write about what they learned about plants today in their plant journals. Have them keep the plant journal to use throughout the week.

Purposeful Play

☑ **Observe children appropriately handling classroom materials.**

Children choose an open center for free playtime. Encourage cooperation skills by suggesting they work together to create a skit about a tiny seed that wanted to grow.

Let's Say Good-Bye

large group · 15 minutes

 Read Aloud Revisit the poem, "Shade Trees"/"Arbol frondoso" for your afternoon Read Aloud. Read it twice. Remind children to listen for words with the /j/ or /h/ sound.

 Home Connection Refer to the Home Connections activities listed in the Resources and Materials chart on page 59. Remind children to tell families about plants and flowers. Sing the "Good-Bye Song"/"Hora de ir casa" as as children prepare to leave.

✓ Learning Goals

Social and Emotional Development
- Child demonstrates initiative in independent activities; makes independent choices.

Language and Communication
- Child names and describes actual or pictured people, places, things, actions, attributes, and events.

Emergent Literacy: Writing
- Child uses scribbles, shapes, pictures, symbols, and letters to represent language.
- Child writes own name or a reasonable approximation of it.

Science
- Child identifies organisms and describes their characteristics.
- Child understands and describes life cycles of plants and animals.
- Child observes, understands, and discusses the relationship of plants and animals to their environments.

Writing

Recap the day by having children share what they wrote in their plant journals. Say: *The title of a book tells what the book is about. El título de un libro dice de qué se trata.* Then have children write a title for their journal on the first page.

Focus Question
How do plants grow and change?
¿Cómo crecen y cambian las plantas?

✓ Learning Goals

Language and Communication
- Child recognizes the difference between similar sounding words (for example, child follows directions without confusion over the words heard; points to the appropriate picture when prompted).
- Child uses newly learned vocabulary daily in multiple contexts.
- Child understands and uses sentences having two or more phrases or concepts.

Emergent Literacy: Reading
- Child generates words that rhyme.

Vocabulary

oranges	naranjas	story	cuento
themselves	ellos mismos		

Differentiated Instruction

Extra Support
Oral Language and Vocabulary
If...children have difficulty describing the orange, **then...**have them hold a real orange and talk about it.

Enrichment
Oral Language and Vocabulary
Ask: **What if other fruits could talk? Whose story would you like to tell?** Have children name other fruits. Encourage them to tell the fruit's story.

Special Needs
Cognitive Challenges
Present new concepts in short segments and use as many of the child's senses as possible.

Let's Start the Day

▶ **Opening Routines and Transition Tips**
For **Opening Routines** and **Transition Tips** turn to pages 178–181 and visit DLMExpressOnline.com for more ideas.

📖 Read **"My Father Picks Oranges"/**"Mi papá cosecha naranjas" from the *Teacher's Treasure Book,* page 186, for your morning Read Aloud.

large group 🕐 *15 minutes*

Language Time

👧👧👧 **Social and Emotional Development** Encourage children to actively participate and contribute to the discussion about how fruit grows and changes.

Oral Language and Vocabulary

✓ **Can children describe fruit and how fruit grows and changes?**

I Am a Peach Talk about the unique point of view of the book *I Am a Peach/ Yo soy el durazno,.* Ask: **Did you like hearing a story that was told by a peach? Tell why or why not.** *¿Les gustó oír un cuento contado por un durazno? ¿Por qué?*

- Ask: **Suppose the oranges we read about today could talk. What might they say about themselves?** *Supongan que las naranjas sobre las que leímos hoy pudieran hablar. ¿Qué podrían decir sobre ellas mismas?* Encourage children to use sentences with phrases to describe an orange. Model first: **I am round and orange, and I have rough skin. When you bite into me, juice comes out.** *Soy redonda y de color naranja, y tengo la piel áspera. Cuando me das una mordida, me sale jugo.*

- Compare how an orange grows with how the peach grew: seed, small plant, tree. Encourage children to tell the orange's growing story. Ask: **How does the orange begin? How does the orange grow and change over time? What happens first, next, and last?** *¿Qué ocurre al principio? ¿Cómo va creciendo y cambiando la naranja? ¿Qué sucede primero, después y al final?*

ELL To demonstrate how the fruit is talking about itself, use facial expressions and gestures. Say: **I am an orange.** Point to yourself. **I am round.** Move your hands in a circle. **My skin is rough.** Rub your skin.

Phonological Awareness

✓ **Can children produce words that rhyme?**

Produce Rhyming Words Display the Dog Puppets. Tell children that one puppet will say a word and they will help the other puppet say a word that rhymes with it. Remind children that words rhyme when they have the same ending sounds, like *grow* and *row*. Model first, using one puppet. Say: *pot.* Have the other puppet reply: *dot.*

- Have the puppet say these words: *cat, pit, ten, lake, bun.* Pause after each word and call on a child to use the second puppet to respond with a rhyming word. For each set, repeat the rhyming words children name and have them echo. For example: *cat, hat, bat, sat, mat, fat, pat.*

Center Time

▶ **Center Rotation** Center Time includes teacher-guided activities and independent activities. Refer to the **Learning Centers** on pages 62–63 for activities in additional centers.

small group 60–90 minutes

Learning Goals

Social and Emotional Development
• Child demonstrates initiative in independent activities; makes independent choices.

Emergent Literacy: Reading
• Child names most upper- and lowercase letters of the alphabet.
• Child identifies the letter that stands for a given sound.

Science
• Child understands and describes life cycles of plants and animals.

ABC Center

✓ Keep track of the letter-sounds children are beginning to master.

Materials *Alphabet Wall Cards* Jj, Hh; cut-out house shapes from file folders; magazines; crayons

Letter House Display the *Alphabet Wall Card* Hh. Remind children that the letter Hh stands for /h/ as in /h/ /h/ house.

• Provide folder house shapes. Have children draw a large door and windows on the front.

• Say: ***The letter*** h ***is in the house today. Write*** Hh ***on the door.*** *La letra h hoy está en casa. Escriban Hh en la puerta.* Inside the folder, have children draw or cut out of magazines pictures whose names begin with /h/. Repeat with a new house folder and the letter Jj.

Center Tip

If...children have difficulty remembering the sound for Hh, **then...**give them a clue by telling them to listen for the first sound in /h/ /h/ house.

Differentiated Instruction

✋ Extra Support

ABC Center

If...children have difficulty matching a sound with a picture, **then...**provide them with picture cards to sort and place inside the house.

⭐ Enrichment

ABC Center

Challenge children to write words that begin with Hh in the house. Repeat for the letter Jj.

Accommodations for 3's

ABC Center

If...children have difficulty matching a sound with a picture, **then...**suggest a simple drawing. For example: hat. Then have children repeat /h/ /h/ /h/ hat as they draw.

Creativity Center

✓ Notice if children are eager to try out new materials.

Materials construction paper, craft sticks, crayons, scissors, glue, yarn, flat buttons

Peach Puppets Tell children that they will make peach puppets.

• Have children draw a picture of a peach and then cut it out. Have them use art materials to add a face. Have them glue the fruit to a craft stick to make a puppet.

• Encourage children to have the peach puppets tell how they grow.

Center Tip

If...children are reluctant to use yarn or buttons, **then...**model how to glue them to paper. Encourage children to persist if they don't succeed on the first attempt.

Focus Question

How do plants grow and change?
¿Cómo crecen y cambian las plantas?

Emergent Literacy: Reading
• Child names most upper- and lowercase letters of the alphabet.
• Child identifies the letter that stands for a given sound.
• Child retells or reenacts poems and stories in sequence.

Science
• Child identifies organisms and describes their characteristics.
• Child understands and describes life cycles of plants and animals.
• Child observes, understands, and discusses the relationship of plants and animals to their environments.

Vocabulary

sentence	oración	tree	árbol
word	palabra		

Differentiated Instruction

✋ Extra Support

Read Aloud
If...children have difficulty retelling the story, **then**...repeat the main events and have children act them out.

⭐ Enrichment

Read Aloud
Help children recognize the story pattern. Display the last page of the book. Have children draw and label a picture to show what will happen next to the peach.

Literacy Time

large group · 15 minutes

📖 Read Aloud

🕐 **Can children retell story events in order?**

Build Background Tell children that you will read *I Am a Peach* again. Ask: *How does the peach start out at the beginning of the story?* *¿Qué era el durazno cuando nació?*

Listen for Understanding Have children listen to find out how the peach grows and changes over time. Read aloud *I Am a Peach/Yo soy el durazno,* pausing to have children retell main story events in their own words. Ask: *Where is the peach in this picture? What is happening to the peach now?* *¿Dónde está el durazno en esta imagen? ¿Qué le está ocurriendo ahora al durazno?*

Respond to the Story Have children retell the story. Write their responses on sentence strips and display them in a pocket chart in story order. Point to one sentence. Say: *This is a sentence. Let's count the words together.* *Ésta es una oración. Vamos a contar juntos las palabras.*

Learn About Letters and Sounds

🕐 **Can children identify the /j/ sound spelled *j* and the /h/ sound spelled *h*.**

Learn About *j* and *h* Review how to write lower case *j* and *h* using the *Alphabet Wall Cards*. Have children practice writing the letters in the air and on the cards.

● Use the Dog Puppet to say: *I am thinking of a letter. It is lower case j.* *Estoy pensando en una letra. Es la j minúscula.* Have children look closely at the two *Alphabet Wall Cards* and compare their shapes to find the letter. Have them hold up the *Alphabet Wall Card*. Repeat the process several times.

● Review sounds /j/ and /h/.

● Have children match the beginning sound of a word with one of the *Letter Cards, j* or *h*. Have the Dog Puppet, say: *jet, hat, jump, happy, jeep, hide.*

I Am a Peach
Yo soy el durazno

large group
15 minutes

Building Blocks

Online Math Activity

Introduce Number Compare 1: Dots and Numerals (online activity) in which children compare two cards to see the one that is greater.

Math Time

Observe and Investigate

☑ **Can children estimate the length of common objects?**

Length Riddles Provide group members with riddle items: real plants, pencils, crayons, books, wooden blocks of the same shape, and scissors. Have at least two of every item, one of which is the cube length in the riddle. Give children enough Connecting Cubes with which to measure items. Pairs of children should guess each item, measuring with cubes as needed. Use or adapt the following riddles:

● *I am 14 cubes long. I have leaves. What am I?* (plant) *Mido 14 cubos. Tengo hojas. ¿Qué soy? (una planta)*

● *I am 10 cubes long. You use me to write and erase. What am I?* (pencil) *Mido 10 cubos. Me usan para escribir y borrar. ¿Qué soy? (un lápiz)*

● *I am 5 cubes long. You use me to color. What am I?* (crayon) *Mido 5 cubos. Me usan para colorear. ¿Qué soy? (un crayón)*

● *I am 9 cubes long. I have words and a hard cover. What am I?* (book) *Mido 9 cubos. Tengo palabras y mi cubierta es dura ¿Qué soy? (un libro)*

● *I am 8 cubes long. I am a (insert shape) made of wood. What am I?* (block) *Mido 8 cubos. Soy un [insertar figura] hecho de madera ¿Qué soy? (un bloque)*

● *I am 7 cubes long. You use me to cut paper and string. What am I?* (scissors) *Mido 7 cubos. Me usan para cortar papeles y cintas. ¿Qué soy? (unas tijeras)*

♔♔♔ Social and Emotional Development

15 minutes
15 minutes

Making Good Choices

☑ **Do children attempt to solve problems?**

Solving Problems Revisit the *Making Good Choices Flip Chart* page 26, "What Should I Do?"

● Display the Dog Puppet. Say: *Tell the puppet about the children's problems. Tell him what they can do to solve their problems.* *Cuéntenle al títere sobre los problemas de los niños. Díganle qué pueden hacer los niños para resolver sus problemas.*

● Provide each child a turn to tell the puppet about the children's problems and how to solve them. Ask children to tell you what they should do if they find that something is hard for them to do.

ELL Talk about and act out solutions to the problems. Then have children repeat and pantomime actions. For example: Act out using a scoop to get soil from the bag to fill the pot. Say: *I get a cup. I take soil from the bag. I put it in the pot. The soil does not spill.*

Making Good Choices Flip Chart, p. 26

✓ Learning Goals

Social and Emotional Development

● Child demonstrates initiative in independent activities; makes independent choices.

Mathematics

● Child measures the length and height of people or objects using standard or non-standard tools.

Science

● Child uses basic measuring tools to learn about objects.

Vocabulary

color	color	cubes	cubos
erase	borrar	long	largo
riddle	adivinanza		

Differentiated Instruction

 Extra Support

Observe and Investigate

If...children need help with Length Riddles, **then...**use shorter items and make clues more obvious.

 Enrichment

Observe and Investigate

Use longer items and make clues more difficult in the Length Riddles.

Focus Question
How do plants grow and change?
¿Cómo crecen y cambian las plantas?

Math Time

 large group · 20 minutes

Oral Language and Academic Vocabulary

✓ Can children use measurement words to compare and describe length?

Talk About Measuring Display *Math and Science Flip Chart*, page 48: "How long are the vines?"

● Ask: *How long are the vines? What can we do to find out?* (measure) *We can use a ruler to measure. We can use Connecting Cubes or paper clips. We can even use our fingers! What else can we use to measure the vines?* *¿De qué largo son las parras? ¿Qué haremos para saberlo?* (medir) *Podemos usar una regla para medir. Podemos usar cubos conectables o clips. ¡Hasta podemos usar los dedos! ¿Qué más podemos usar para medir las parras?*

● Use several of the items children name as well as a ruler and Counting Cubes to measure the vines. Model first and then call on children to measure on the chart. As children measure, encourage them to explain what they are doing. Ask: *How many [crayons] long is this vine? ¿Cuántos [crayones] de largo mide esta parra?*

Observe and Investigate

✓ Can children observe and correct mistakes made in measuring?

Mr. Mixup's Measuring Mess Model proper measurement of several objects. Then introduce Mr. Mixup.

● Show children a length of string eight Connecting Cubes long. Explain that Mr. Mixup has measured the string incorrectly, and show the cubes he will use to measure.

● While measuring the string with Connecting Cubes, alternate having Mr. Mixup make these mistakes: gaps between cubes, string end misaligned with cubes, and string or cubes not in a straight line. Pause after each mistake for children to correct Mr. Mixup.

TIP Practice polite ways to tell people they are doing things incorrectly. For example, say: *I noticed you left a space between cubes. I do that sometimes, too. It's an easy mistake to make. Noté que has dejado un espacio entre los cubos. A veces, yo también lo hago. Es muy común cometer este error.*

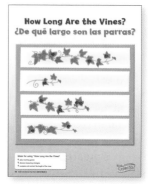

Math and Science Flip Chart, p. 48

Center Time

▶ **Center Rotation** Center Time includes teacher-guided activities and independent activities. Refer to the **Learning Centers** on pages 62–63 for activities in additional centers.

small group 🕐 30 minutes

Math and Science Center

	Center Tip

☑ **Observe children as they use string to measure objects.**

Materials string cut into pieces of different lengths that are the same as the length of objects in the center

Measuring Match Show pieces of string to the group and have each child choose a piece. Say: *Use your string to measure things in the center. Find something that is the same length as your string.* *Usen su cuerda para medir cosas del centro. Encuentren algo que tenga la misma longitud que su cuerda.*

- Have children hold their piece of string along different objects until they find a match. Encourage children to measure each other.

- Record their measurements on a chart. Have each child tape the piece of string to the chart, write his or her name, and draw a picture of the object that is the same length.

Center Tip

If...children are frustrated when they don't find a match quickly,
then...offer words that will encourage them to keep trying.

Learning Goals

Social and Emotional Development
• Child demonstrates initiative in independent activities; makes independent choices.

Language and Communication
• Child exhibits an understanding of instructional terms used in the classroom.

Mathematics
• Child measures the length and height of people or objects using standard or non-standard tools.

Writing

Recap the day. Then have children draw three pictures to show how a peach seed grows and changes. Have them label the pictures with the words, *first*, *next*, and *last*. *primero, luego y por último.*

Purposeful Play

☑ **Observe children sharing classroom materials and working cooperatively.**

Children choose an open center for free playtime. Encourage cooperation skills by suggesting they work together to put on a puppet show with their peach puppets.

Let's Say Good-Bye

large group 🕐 15 minutes

📖 **Read Aloud** Revisit the story, "My Father Picks Oranges"/"Mi papá cosecha naranjas" for your afternoon Read Aloud. Remind children to listen for words that begin with /j/ or /h/.

Home Connection Refer to the Home Connections activities listed in the Resources and Materials chart on page 59. Remind children to tell families about how plants grow and change. Sing the "Good-Bye Song" as children prepare to leave.

Let's Start the Day

Focus Question
How do plants grow and change?
¿Cómo crecen y cambian las plantas?

 Learning Goals

Social and Emotional Development
• Child demonstrates initiative in independent activities; makes independent choices.

Language and Communication
• Child uses newly learned vocabulary daily in multiple contexts.

Emergent Literacy: Reading
• Child generates words that rhyme.

Vocabulary

garden	huerta	plant (verb)	plantar
rows	surcos	vegetables	verduras
water (verb)	regar		

Differentiated Instruction

 Extra Support
Phonological Awareness
If...children have difficulty producing words that rhyme, **then...**give them two ABC Picture Cards that rhyme with words you say. Have them select the rhyming word. For example, give children ABC Cards *fish* and *pie*. Say: **dish** and have children hold up the rhyming card.

Enrichment
Phonological Awareness
Have children draw a big sunflower on paper. Then have children draw and label a picture of something whose name rhymes with *big* in the center.

 Opening Routines and Transition Tips
For **Opening Routines** and **Transition Tips** turn to pages 178–181 and visit **DLMExpressOnline.com** for more ideas.

📖 Read **"Once I Ate an Orange"/**"Mi naranjo" from the *Teacher's Treasure Book*, page 115, for your morning Read Aloud.

Language Time

large group / 15 minutes

👪 **Social and Emotional Development** Encourage children to persist when they have a challenging task such as producing a rhyming word.

Oral Language and Vocabulary

✓ **Can children use descriptive words to tell about a garden?**

How Gardens Grow Talk about gardens. Ask: **What is fun about growing a garden? What is hard?** *¿Qué tiene de divertido plantar una huerta? ¿Qué tiene de difícil?*

● Display *Oral Language Development Card 56*. Talk about the vegetables and what they need to grow. Ask: **How is the person helping?** *¿De qué manera ayuda esta persona?* Then follow the suggestions on the back of the card.

Phonological Awareness

✓ **Can children produce words that rhyme?**

Recognize Rhyming Words Revisit *Rhymes and Chants Flip Chart*, page 26. Remind children that rhyming words end with the same sounds.

Reread the first rhyming couplet. Have children identify the rhyming words: *underground/sound*. Then have them produce words that rhyme with *ground* and *sound*. Repeat for *sun/none* and *below/grow*.

ELL Use the *Rhymes and Chants Flip Chart* to revisit the word *up*. Use actions and gestures to teach the meaning of the word, such as crouching down and standing up or pointing up. Then name words that rhyme with *up* and have children repeat: *pup, cup*.

Oral Language Development Card 56

Rhymes and Chants Flip Chart, p. 26

Center Time

▶ **Center Rotation** Center Time includes teacher-guided activities and independent activities. Refer to the **Learning Centers** on pages 62–63 for activities in additional centers.

small group — 60–90 minutes

Writer's Center

✓ **Track children's ability to write words to describe seeds.**

Materials various fruits cut so that the seeds are visible, such as apples and peaches; plant journals

Write About Seeds Have children examine pieces of fruit that have seeds.

- Guide children to observe the different seeds in each fruit. Have them describe the seeds. Ask: *What color is the seed? How is it shaped? Is it a big or little seed? How does it feel? ¿De qué color es la semilla? ¿Qué forma tiene? ¿Es una semilla grande o pequeña? ¿Cómo se siente?*

- Have children draw and label pictures to show what they notice about seeds in their plant journals. Encourage them to share pictures and read the words they wrote to a partner.

Center Tip

If...children have difficulty writing words to describe seeds, **then...**have them dictate words for you to write.

Creativity Center

✓ **Track children's ability to incorporate plant details in their artwork.**

Materials poster paper, glue, assorted art supplies (yarn, construction paper, tissue paper, bendable sticks, markers, crayons)

Poster Plants Tell children that they will make a flower garden.

- Give each child a piece of poster paper. Ask: *What flowers would you grow in a flower garden? Why? ¿Qué flores plantarían en un jardín? ¿Por qué?*

- Prompt children to use a variety of art supplies, such as chenille stems for the stems, construction paper leaves, and tissue paper petals.

- Display children's posters in an area labeled "Our Flower Garden." Children can take turns giving tours of the garden.

Center Tip

If...children are not eager to try new materials, such as chenille stems or tissue paper **then...** demonstrate how the materials can be used to form flowers. Notice if children move on to independent work.

✓ Learning Goals

Social and Emotional Development
- Child demonstrates initiative in independent activities; makes independent choices.

Emergent Literacy: Writing
- Child uses scribbles, shapes, pictures, symbols, and letters to represent language.

Fine Arts
- Child expresses emotions or ideas through art.

Differentiated Instruction

 Extra Support

Creativity Center

If...children have difficulty deciding which flower to create, **then...**display photos and illustrations of flowers and real flowering plants for children to use as models.

 Enrichment

Writer's Center

Children can compare and contrast seeds in their plant journals. Ask: *Which seed is the largest? the smallest? Does the peach seed feel rougher than the apple seed?*

Accommodations for 3's

Writer's Center

If...children label seed pictures with scribbles or mock letters, **then...**ask them what they wrote.

Focus Question

How do plants grow and change?
¿Cómo crecen y cambian las plantas?

Emergent Literacy: Reading

• Child independently engages in pre-reading behaviors and activities (such as, pretending to read, turning one page at a time).

• Child names most upper- and lowercase letters of the alphabet.

• Child identifies the letter that stands for a given sound.

Science

• Child identifies organisms and describes their characteristics.

• Child understands and describes life cycles of plants and animals.

• Child observes, understands, and discusses the relationship of plants and animals to their environments.

Vocabulary

food	comida	root	planta
stem	tallo	strong	fuerte
water (noun)	agua		

Differentiated Instruction

 Extra Support

Read Aloud

If...children have difficulty making a prediction about what the seed will become, **then**...remind them how the peach seed grew and changed in *I Am the Peach*.

 Enrichment

Learn About Letters and Sounds

Challenge children to produce /j/ and /h/ words for the dog puppet to say.

 Special Needs

Speech and Language Delays

Use simple sentences and ask the child to tell you what you just said.

Literacy Time

📖 Read Aloud

✓ **Can children identify a sequence of events?**

Build Background Tell children that you will read how plants grow and change.

● Ask: *What do you know about how a plant grows? ¿Qué saben acerca de cómo crece una planta?*

Listen for Understanding Display Concept Big Book 3: *Growing and Changing*, page 22 and read it aloud.

● Ask children to predict what the seed will become. Ask: *What do you think the seed will look like next? ¿Cómo creen que la semilla se verá después?* Have children use the photo on page 23 to make a prediction and then read page 23 aloud.

● Have children revise or confirm their predictions. Ask: *Was your answer right? If not, how do you have to change it? ¿Tu respuesta era correcta? ¿Si no lo era, cómo tienes que cambiarla?*

● Point to the labels in the photographs and read them aloud. Then say: *Name a part of a plant.* Point to the photo as children name a plant part.

Respond to the Story Have children talk about how the seed changes and grows. Say: *The seed grows roots. What happens next? What happens then? A la semilla le crecen raíces. ¿Qué pasa después? ¿Y después?* Write children's responses on sentence strips and label them 1, 2, 3.

💡 **TIP** If children need to change their prediction, point to photos on page 23 and ay: **1. The seed grows roots. 2. There is a stem with leaves. 3. There is a plant.** *1.A la semilla le crecen raíces. 2. Hay un tallo con hojas. 3. Hay una planta.*

Learn About Letters and Sounds

✓ **Can children identify the /j/ sound spelled *Jj* and the /h/ sound spelled *Hh*?**

Learn About *Jj* and *Hh* Review how to write upper case and lower case *Jj* and *Hh* using the *Alphabet Wall Cards*. Have children practice writing the letters in the air and on a *Alphabet Wall Card*.

● Use the Dog Puppet to say: *I am thinking of a letter. It is lower case j. Estoy pensando en una letra. Es la j minúscula.* Have children look closely at the four *Alphabet Wall Cards* and compare their shapes to find the letter. Have them hold up the *Alphabet Wall Card*. Repeat the process several times.

● Review sounds /j/ and /h/. Have children match the beginning sound of a word with one of the *Alphabet Wall Cards*, *j* or *h*. Have the Dog Puppet say: **hook, juice, jam, hay, heel, jug.** Repeat with *J* or *H* and **Jen, Hank, June, Harry.**

ELL In Spanish, the /h/ sound is spelled *j*. Provide extra practice for those who need support with words with /j/ spelled *j* and /h/ spelled *h*.

Plants also need water to grow and nutrients, too. A plant begins as a tiny **seed**. What will this seed become?
22

Concept Big Book, p. 22

Alphabet Wall Cards

large group 15 minutes

Math Time

Building Blocks

Online Math Activity

Children can complete Reptile Ruler during computer time or Center Time.

Observe and Investigate

Can children understand the concept of length?

Road Blocks Provide children with blocks. Have them count ten blocks.

- Have children make several different roads using only ten blocks. Be sure to observe their work. Ask: ***If the roads are different shapes, how are their lengths the same?*** *Si los caminos tienen diferente forma, ¿por qué su longitud es la misma?* Guide children to conclude that it is because all the roads are made with ten blocks.

large group 15 minutes

Social and Emotional Development

Making Good Choices Flip Chart, p. 26

Making Good Choices

Do children attempt to solve problems?

Solving Problems Display *Making Good Choices Flip Chart* page 26, "What Should I Do?" Review with children the ways the children solved their problems. Ask: ***What did the children decide to do when they both wanted to use the pretty flower pot? How did the girl fill the pot with soil without making a mess?*** *¿Qué decidieron hacer los niños cuando ambos querían usar esa maceta tan hermosa? ¿Cómo llenó la niña la maceta sin ensuciarla?*

- With the Dog Puppet, role-play other situations to model children solving problems. For example, explain that the puppet wants to water his plant, but he can't find the watering can. Model what you would say and do to help the puppet solve his problem.
- After each role-play, have the children tell you how you helped solve the Dog Puppet's problem. Ask: ***What did I do and say?*** *¿Qué hice y qué dije?*
- Play the song "Excuse Me"/"Permiso" from the Making Good Choices Audio CD. Ask children what they think the song is telling them about being selfish.

ELL Act out the dog's actions, such as looking around the sink or using a cup to water his plant. Say simple phrases: ***I will look by the sink. I will use a cup.*** For additional suggestions on how to meet the needs of children at the Beginning, Intermediate, Advanced, and Advanced-High levels of English proficiency, see pages 184–187.

Learning Goals

Social and Emotional Development

• Child demonstrates initiative in independent activities; makes independent choices.

Mathematics

• Child measures the length and height of people or objects using standard or non-standard tools.

Vocabulary

add	sumar	caring	cuidado
count	contar	helpful	útil
how many	cuántas		

Differentiated Instruction

Extra Support

Making Good Choices

If...children struggle finding a solution to the problem, **then...**ask questions: ***Where do you fill the watering can? Who else uses the watering can? What else can you use to water a plant?***

Enrichment

Making Good Choices

Challenge children to tell what the puppet might be thinking when he can't find the watering can.

Accommodations for 3's

Making Good Choices

If...children struggle with the review of the problems/solutions from the chart, **then...**have them act out the scenarios on the chart using props. Have them use the same props to act out solutions you present.

Focus Question
How do plants grow and change?
¿Cómo crecen y cambian las plantas?

Learning Goals

Language and Communication
• Child names and describes actual or pictured people, places, things, actions, attributes, and events.

Mathematics
• Child measures passage of time using standard or non-standard tools.

Vocabulary

passes	pasa	time	tiempo
today	hoy	tomorrow	mañana
yesterday	ayer		

Differentiated Instruction

👋 Extra Support

Oral Language and Academic Vocabulary
If...children have difficulty describing what they did yesterday, **then...**mention one thing they did at school today and one thing they did yesterday and have them choose.

⭐ Enrichment

Understand and Participate
Challenge children to draw pictures to show how a plant or tree they see outdoors changes over time.

Social Studies Time

large group — 20 minutes

Oral Language and Academic Vocabulary

☑️ **Can children use words to describe time intervals?**

Talking About Time Passing Tell children that yesterday they read about a peach seed. Ask: *What kind of seed did we read about today? ¿Sobre qué tipo de semilla leímos ayer?*

● Write these sentence frames on a chart. Read them aloud, and have children complete them orally.

> Yesterday I _____. Ayer, yo _____.
> Today I _____. Hoy, yo _____.
> Tomorrow I will _____. Mañana, yo _____.

Understand and Participate

☑️ **Can children recognize changes in the environment over time?**

Looking at Changes Display *I Am a Peach/Yo Soy el Durazno* and use the illustrations to point out the changes in the environment over time.

● Turn to page 5. Say: *Look at the peach tree. What do you notice? Miren el árbol de durazno. ¿Qué observan?*

● Turn to page 7. Say: *Time passes. What do the peaches look like now? How do you know the days are hot? El tiempo pasa. ¿Cómo se ven ahora los duraznos? ¿Cómo saben que los días son calurosos?*

● From the Photo Library, display photos of trees in summer, spring, winter, and fall. Place them in seasonal order. Have children discuss how the trees change over time.

● After pointing to each photo, say: *Time passes. The tree changes. El tiempo pasa. Los árboles cambian.* Then ask: *What does the tree look like now? How does the tree change when time passes? ¿Cómo se ve ahora el árbol? ¿Cómo cambia el árbol cuando el tiempo pasa?*

💡 **TIP** Help children stay focused by not mentioning seasons. Guide them to concentrate on changes in the environment over time.

ELL Use the Photo Library pictures to teach children phrases that describe changes in the environment. *The tree has green leaves. The tree has red leaves. The tree does not have leaves. There is snow. The tree has flowers.*

CD-ROM

Center Time

▶ **Center Rotation** Center Time includes teacher-guided activities and independent activities. Refer to the **Learning Centers** on pages 62–63 for activities in additional centers.

  small group 30 minutes

Construction Center

	Center Tip
✓ **Monitor children as they build and describe a garden store.** **Materials** blocks, boxes, modeling clay, paper cups, construction paper, paper bags, small stones, craft sticks, markers, tape, glue **Build a Garden Store** Ask: *What did we make yesterday?* Say: *Today, we will make a garden store.* ¿Qué hicimos ayer? Diga: Hoy, vamos a hacer una tienda de jardinería. ● Have children talk about times when they went to the garden section of a store. Ask: *What did you buy? What did you see?* ¿Qué compraron? ¿Qué vieron? ● Encourage children to use problem-solving skills as they construct the store. Stress that they should share their ideas with the group. ● When the garden store is finished, encourage children to have a grand opening. Have them role play clerks and customers.	**If...**children use your suggestions to solve problems but not their own, **then...**remind them that problems can have more than one solution and yours is not the only good one.

 Learning Goals

Social and Emotional Development
• Child demonstrates initiative in independent activities; makes independent choices.

Language and Communication
• Child names and describes actual or pictured people, places, things, actions, attributes, and events.

Social Studies
• Child understands basic concepts of buying, selling, and trading.

Writing

Recap the day. Draw a large sunflower on chart paper, including the seed and roots. Have children name what they learned about parts of plants. Share the pen by having children write letters and words they know as they label the parts of the sunflower: seed, root, stem, leaf, flower.

Purposeful Play

✓ **Observe children as they work in small groups.**

Children choose an open center for free playtime. Encourage cooperation by suggesting they take turns sitting in an author's chair to share what they wrote about seeds in their plant journal. Remind speakers to talk clearly and listeners to listen politely.

Let's Say Good-Bye

  large group 15 minutes

 Read Aloud Revisit the story, "Once I Ate an Orange"/"Mi naranjo" for your afternoon Read Aloud. Remind children to listen for the names of things that grow and change.

 Home Connection Refer to the Home Connections activities listed in the Resources and Materials chart on page 59. Remind children to tell families about the parts of a plant. Sing the "Good-Bye Song" as children prepare to leave.

DAY 4

Let's Start the Day

Focus Question

How do plants grow and change?

¿Cómo crecen y cambian las plantas?

 Learning Goals

Language and Communication

• Child follows basic rules for conversations (taking turns, staying on topic, listening actively).

• Child recognizes the difference between similar sounding words (for example, child follows directions without confusion over the words heard; points to the appropriate picture when prompted).

Emergent Literacy: Reading

• Child generates words that rhyme.

Vocabulary

characters	personajes
make-believe	fantástico
real	real

Differentiated Instruction

 Extra Support

Oral Language and Vocabulary

If...children have difficulty distinguishing real from make-believe, **then...**show pictures of characters performing magical feats. Ask: *Is this person acting like a person you have seen in the real world? Are real people able to do this? Tell why or why not.*

 Enrichment

Oral Language and Vocabulary

Challenge children to talk about the next thing a make-believe character will do. Remind them that it must be something that a real person could never do.

Opening Routines and Transition Tips

For **Opening Routines** and **Transition Tips** turn to pages 178–181 and visit DLMExpressOnline.com for more ideas.

Read **"The Fall of the Last Leaf"/**"La caída de la última hoja" from the *Teacher's Treasure Book*, page 198, for your morning Read Aloud.

Language Time

Oral Language and Vocabulary

☑ **Can children distinguish real from make-believe?**

Real and Make-Believe Tell children that the people and animals in stories are called characters. Say: *Some stories are make-believe. The characters in make-believe stories do things that real people could never do. Algunos cuentos son de fantasía. Los personajes en los cuentos de fantasía hacen cosas que las personas reales jamás harían.*

- Help children to remember any make-believe stories previously read that have characters that do things that real people can't do.

- Ask: *What did the character do? How do you know that a real person could never do this? ¿Qué hace el personaje? ¿Cómo saben que una persona real jamás haría eso?*

- Have children act out scenes from familiar tales, such as Goldilocks going into the bears' home or Little Red Riding Hood talking to the wolf.

- Afterwards have children discuss whether or not a real person would do this. Ask: *Would you be able to do this? Why not? ¿Podrían hacer eso? ¿Por qué no?*

ELL Display books with cover illustrations that clearly show a make-believe or real-world scene. Model first, and then have children point to a book cover and say, *real* or *make-believe*.

Phonological Awareness

☑ **Can children produce words that rhyme?**

Produce Rhyming Words Display the Dog Puppet. Have children sit in a circle. Use the Dog Puppet to say: *I'm going on a trip to a make-believe place. I will take a wig. Me voy de viaje a un lugar imaginario. Llevo un wig..* Give the Dog Puppet to a child in the circle. Model how to continue by having the Dog Puppet produce another rhyming word: *I will take a wig and a pig. Yo llevo un wig y un pig..* Proceed around the circle and then begin again with another word.

Center Time

▶ **Center Rotation** Center Time includes teacher-guided activities and independent activities. Refer to the **Learning Centers** on pages 62–63 for activities in additional centers.

 small group 60–90 minutes

Library and Listening Center

Center Tip

✓ Track children's use of plant part names and words that describe plant growth.

Materials fiction and nonfiction books about growing flowers, fruits, vegetables, and trees; seed catalogs; garden supply store ads; children's plant journals; chart with familiar nursery rhyme, "Mary, Mary, Quite Contrary, How Does Your Garden Grow?"

Growing Library Place books in the center. Tell children it is their Growing Library. Have children browse through the books with a partner and talk about the illustrations.

- Say: *Look carefully at the illustrations. What does the plant look like now? How did the plant begin? What happened between when it was planted and now? Observen cuidadosamente las imágenes. ¿Cómo se ve la planta en este momento? ¿Cómo se forma una planta? ¿Qué le sucedió entre que la plantaron y este momento?*

- Display the chart with the nursery rhyme "Mary, Mary, Quite Contrary" in the center. Recite it several times with children. Then have them produce words that rhyme with *grow* and *row*.

If...children are reluctant to select a variety of books to discuss,
then...pick up a book and talk about what you notice on the cover: *Wow! These flowers are growing in a box on a windowsill. I wonder who planted the seeds.*

Pretend and Learn Center

Center Tip

✓ Track how well children can act out planting a garden.

Materials garden tools, safe with no sharp edges (trowel, small shovels and rakes, watering can); artificial flowers and vegetables; sun hats; gardening gloves

Plant a Garden Share an experience you have had with gardening. Have children talk about what people do when they garden.

- Pass the props around for children to examine and discuss how they are used.

- Have children pretend to plant a garden. To get them started, ask: *How will you plant the seeds? What will the rows look like? How will you dig the holes? ¿Cómo plantarían las semillas? ¿Cómo serán los surcos? ¿Cómo cavarán los hoyos?*

If...children have difficulty sharing props,
then...encourage them to find ways to solve the problem on their own.

 Learning Goals

Social and Emotional Development
- Child demonstrates initiative in independent activities; makes independent choices.

Language and Communication
- Child uses newly learned vocabulary daily in multiple contexts.

Emergent Literacy: Reading
- Child enjoys and chooses reading-related activities.
- Child generates words that rhyme.

Differentiated Instruction

 Extra Support
Pretend and Learn Center
If...children have difficulty using new vocabulary while they pretend, **then...**prompt with questions and comments: *I think the ground is dry around your plant. What can you do to help your plants grow?*

⭐ **Enrichment**
Pretend and Learn Center
Challenge children to pretend to set up a Farmer's Market for their harvested flowers, fruits, and vegetables. Children can role-play farmers and customers.

Accommodations for 3's
Pretend and Learn Center
If...children have difficulty with interactive play, **then...**provide additional gardening tools so children can each choose a few.

Focus Question

Focus Question

How do plants grow and change?
¿Cómo crecen y cambian las plantas?

Learning Goals

Language and Communication
• Child demonstrates an understanding of oral language by responding appropriately.

Emergent Literacy: Reading
• Child names most upper- and lowercase letters of the alphabet.
• Child identifies the letter that stands for a given sound.

Vocabulary

bargain	regatear	curious	curioso
exchange	intercambiar	magic	magia
shocked	asombrado	value	valor

Differentiated Instruction

 Extra Support

Read Aloud

If...children have difficulty retelling the story, **then...**reread each event that takes place in the giant's castle and have children draw a picture to show what happened. Encourage children to talk about their story picture.

Enrichment

Read Aloud

Read aloud different versions of *Jack and the Beanstalk*. Have children compare and contrast the characters, settings, and plots.

Literacy Time

 large group · 15 minutes

📖 Read Aloud

✓ **Can children answer questions about a story read aloud?**

Build Background Tell children that you will be reading a make-believe story about a boy named Jack. Explain that Jack was surprised when a plant grew and grew. Have children talk about tall plants they have seen.

● Ask: *Where was the plant growing? What did the plant look like? Could you reach the top? ¿Dónde estaba creciendo esa planta? ¿Cómo era esa planta? ¿Pudieron llegar hasta arriba?*

Listen for Enjoyment Read aloud "Jack and the Beanstalk"/*"Jaime y los frijoles mágicos"* from the *Teacher's Treasure Book,* page 230.

● Tell children to listen carefully to find out what Jack does that a real boy could never do.

● Ask: *What is Jack's problem? What does he do to solve it? Could a real boy climb up a tall beanstalk into the clouds? ¿Qué problema enfrenta Jaime? ¿Qué hace para resolverlo? ¿Un niño real podría trepar por una enorme planta de frijoles hasta meterse entre las nubes?*

Respond to the Story Have children retell how Jack took the big bag of gold coins and the magic goose from the giant's castle. Ask: *Why did Jack, his mother, and the goose live happily ever after? ¿Por qué vivieron felices para siempre Jaime, su madre y la gallina?*

ELL Explain these sentences to children: *"Never mind, Mother," said Jack. "Done!" cried Jack. Jack started down the beanstalk lickity-split.* For additional suggestions on how to meet the needs of children at the Beginning, Intermediate, Advanced, and Advanced-High levels of English proficiency, see pages 184–187.

Learn About Letters and Sounds

✓ **Can children identify the /j/ sound spelled *j* and the /h/ sound spelled *h*?**

Learn About the /j/ and /h/ Sounds.

● Display *ABC Picture Card* Jump Rope. Remind children that *jump* begins with the /j/ sound. Then ask children to say /j/ when they see a picture whose name begins with /j/. Show several picture cards, including those whose names begin with /j/: *jar, jet, jeep, jug,* and *jacks*. Allow time for children to respond.

● Repeat with the *ABC Picture Card* Horse and assorted picture cards, including *horn, hive, hat, hook,* and *hose*.

Teachers's Treasure Book, p. 230

Math Time

Building Blocks

Online Math Activity

Children can complete Number Compare 1 and Reptile Ruler during computer time or Center Time.

Observe and Investigate

 Can children estimate the length of objects?

Length Riddles

● Provide group members with riddle items (have at least two of every item, one of which is the cube length in the riddle) and enough Connecting Cubes with which to measure items. Pairs of children should guess each item, measuring with cubes as needed. Use the following riddles or adapt them to match items of your choice and their cube lengths.

> *I am 12 cubes long. I have a soft cover with printed words and pictures. What am I?* (magazine) *Mido 12 cubos. Mi cubierta es blanda y tengo palabras impresas y dibujos. ¿Qué soy? (una revista)*
>
> *I am 7 cubes long. You use me to write and erase. What am I?* (pencil) *Mido 7 cubos. Me pueden usar para escribir y borrar. ¿Qué soy? (un lápiz)*
>
> *I am 5 cubes long. I have four tires, and you can put me in a race. What am I?* (toy car) *Mido 5 cubos. Tengo cuatro ruedas y me pueden poner en una carrera. ¿Qué soy? (un auto de juguete)*
>
> *I am 9 cubes long. I have words and a hard cover. What am I?* (book) *Mido 9 cubos. Mi cubierta es dura y tengo palabras. ¿Qué soy? (un libro)*
>
> *I am 4 cubes long. I can lock and unlock things. What am I?* (a key) *Mido 4 cubos. Puedo abrir y cerrar cosas. ¿Qué soy? (una llave)*
>
> *I am 8 cubes long. You use me to cut paper. What am I?* (scissors) *Mido 8 cubos. Pueden usarme para cortar papel. ¿Qué soy? (unas tijeras)*

ELL Before you begin Length Riddles, point to and name each item. Have children repeat. Then name items and have children locate the item.

☼☼☼ Social and Emotional Development

Making Good Choices

 Do children attempt to solve problems?

Solving Problems Display the Dog Puppets and a flower drawing with water spilled on it. Tell children that one dog has spilled water on the other dog's drawing. Now the dog doesn't know what to do. Model a dialogue between the puppets that ends with the dog apologizing for spilling the water and then both dogs drawing a new flower picture together. Ask: ***What problem did the puppets have? How did they solve their problem?*** *¿Qué problema enfrentaron los títeres? ¿Cómo resolvieron su problema?* Ask: ***What should you do if your first try does not work?*** *¿Qué harían si no logran algo en el primer intento?*

Learning Goals

Social and Emotional Development
• Child demonstrates initiative in independent activities; makes independent choices.

Mathematics
• Child measures the length and height of people or objects using standard or non-standard tools.

Science
• Child uses basic measuring tools to learn about objects.

Vocabulary

cover	cubierta	cubes	cubos
tires	ruedas	unlock	abrir

Differentiated Instruction

✋ **Extra Support**

Observe and Investigate

If...children need help with Length Riddles, **then...**help them use cubes to measure.

⭐ **Enrichment**

Observe and Investigate

Challenge children by giving them several of each item in various lengths with only one to match the specified length.

Accommodations for 3's

Observe and Investigate

If...children struggle solving the riddles, **then...** instead of giving a numeric measurement, show a cube train of the same length as the mystery object.

Focus Question
How do plants grow
and change?
¿Cómo crecen y cambian las
plantas?

Learning Goals

Language and Communication
• Child exhibits an understanding of instructional terms used in the classroom.
• Child uses individual words and short phrases to communicate. (ELL)

Mathematics
• Child measures the length and height of people or objects using standard or non-standard tools.

Vocabulary

length	largo	longer	más largo
measure	medir	same	igual
shorter	corto		

Differentiated Instruction

 Extra Support
Observe and Investigate
If...children struggle during I'm Thinking of a Number (Length), **then...**point to steps as you provide clues. For example, say: **The secret step is more than 3** while gesturing to all steps greater than 3, or do the activity with fewer steps.

 Enrichment
Observe and Investigate
Challenge children to build more steps or have children explain why their guess is a good guess.

Math Time

large group · 20 minutes

Oral Language and Academic Vocabulary

✓ **Can children use words to make length comparisons?**

Talk About Measuring Length Give children construction paper and scissors.

• Have children remove their shoes and trace around one of their feet. Have them cut out the tracing. Ask: **How can you use your foot to measure? How many feet long is your chair?** *¿Cómo pueden usar su pie para medir? ¿Cuántos pies de largo mide su silla?*

• Have partners measure various objects in the classroom using their feet. As children measure, encourage them to discuss the measurements. Ask: **What things are longer than your foot? What things are shorter? Did you find anything that was the same size?** *¿Qué cosas son más largas que su pie? ¿Cuáles son más cortas? ¿Encontraron algo que sea del mismo tamaño?*

Observe and Investigate

✓ **Can children figure out the missing number length?**

I'm Thinking of a Number (Length) Make a Connecting Cube step between 1 and 10, and hide it.

• Show children the set of Connecting Cubes 1–10 you prepared beforehand, and count each step with them. Tell children a secret step is hidden that is the same length as one of the steps on display, and ask them to guess its number.

• When a child guesses correctly, excitedly reveal the secret step. Count the cubes of the secret step with children, and show how it matches the corresponding step in the complete set. For other guesses, say: **The secret step is more (or less) than your guess.** *El escalón secreto es más largo (o más corto) que el que señalaron.* Repeat the activity several times.

• As children become familiar with the activity, ask them to tell why they made their guess. Encourage answers like "Three was too little and nine was too much so I guessed a number in between."

• Children can complete Number Compare 1 during computer time or Center Time.

TIP Suggest children use their feet to measure plants in the classroom.

ELL Help children compare the length of objects. Focus on the concepts "shorter" and "longer". Place two Mini Motors Counters next to each other. The counters should not be the same length. For example, set out a boat and a train. Point to a boat. Say: **This boat is shorter than the train.** Then point to the train. Say: **This train is longer than the boat.** Have children point to a counter and say *shorter* or *longer*. Continue with other pairs of counters.

Center Time

Center Rotation Center Time includes teacher-guided activities and independent activities. Refer to the **Learning Centers** on pages 62–63 for activities in additional centers.

small group   30 minutes

Math and Science Center

 Track children's ability to describe and measure plant growth.

Materials cups, potting soil, lima beans (soaked overnight in water)

Growing Beans Tell children that they will plant bean seeds.

- Give children cups, soil, and lima beans. Have them plant the seeds and then observe what happens. Remind them that it will take time for the bean plants to grow. Ask: **What do your plants need to grow?** *¿Qué necesitan sus plantas para crecer?*

- Over time, encourage children to describe what they see as the beans sprout and grow. Have children draw pictures in their plant journal at regular intervals to record their observations.

- Have children record the growth of their bean plant by measuring it with string. Have them tape the string to the corresponding picture in their plant journal.

Center Tip

If...children forget to water their plants, **then...**allow them to problem-solve independently.

Purposeful Play

 Observe how children incorporate what they know about make-believe stories in their play.

Children choose an open center for free playtime. Encourage cooperation skills by suggesting they work together to tell a make-believe story about what happens when one of their bean plants grows as tall as Jack's beanstalk.

Let's Say Good-Bye

large group   15 minutes

 Read Aloud Revisit the story, "The Fall of the Last Leaf"/"La caída de la última hoja" for your afternoon Read Aloud. Remind children to listen for words with /j/ and /h/.

 Home Connection Refer to the Home Connections activities listed in the Resources and Materials chart on page 59. Remind children to tell families what happened to Jack. Sing the "Good-Bye Song" as children prepare to leave.

 Learning Goals

Social and Emotional Development
- Child demonstrates initiative in independent activities; makes independent choices.

Mathematics
- Child measures the length and height of people or objects using standard or non-standard tools.

Science
- Child identifies organisms and describes their characteristics.
- Child understands and describes life cycles of plants and animals.

Writing

Recap the day. Have children tell about a make-believe boy they have read about. Ask: **What did this make-believe boy do that a real boy cannot do?** *¿Qué hace este niño de mentira que no podría hacer un niño de verdad?* Record their answers in a list. Read them back as you track the print, and emphasize the correspondence between speech and print.

Let's Start the Day

Focus Question
How do plants grow and change?
¿Cómo crecen y cambian las plantas?

 Learning Goals

Language and Communication
• Child uses newly learned vocabulary daily in multiple contexts.
• Child builds English listening and speaking vocabulary for common objects and phrases. (ELL)

Emergent Literacy: Reading
• Child generates words that rhyme.

Vocabulary

curled	rizado	farmer	granjero
raindrops	riego	stout	fuerte
stretch	estirar	underground	suelo

Differentiated Instruction

 Extra Support
Oral Language and Vocabulary
If...children have difficulty describing how a plant grows, **then...**in order, point to pictures on the chart: seed, sprout, flower. Have children tell what happens first, next, last.

 Enrichment
Oral Language and Vocabulary
Challenge children to describe characteristics of other plants, using the Photo Library.

▶ Opening Routines and Transition Tips
For **Opening Routines** and **Transition Tips** turn to pages 178–181 and visit DLMExpressOnline.com for more ideas.

📖 Read **"My Grandmother's Garden"/**"El jardín de mi abuela" from the *Teacher's Treasure Book,* page 266, for your morning Read Aloud.

large group — 15 minutes

Language Time

Social and Emotional Development Encourage children to find more than one way to solve a problem.

Oral Language and Vocabulary

✓ **Can children share what they know about how plants grow and change?**

Plants Grow and Change Talk about what children have learned this week about plant growth. Ask: *What do you know about how plants grow and change?* *¿Qué saben sobre la manera en que crecen y cambian las plantas?*

● Display *Rhymes and Chants Flip Chart*, page 26. Read "A Plant Grows" with children. Say: *First, the plant is a seed.* *Primero, la planta es una semilla.* Ask: *Where does it grow? What happens next? What happens last? What happens to the tiny roots as they grow? ¿Dónde crece? ¿Qué pasa después? ¿Qué pasa por último? ¿Qué les sucede a las pequeñas raíces a medida que crecen?*

● Say: *Suppose you have a sunflower seed. What would you do to help it grow? What if your sunflower seed doesn't grow? How will you solve the problem?* *Imaginen que tienen una semilla de girasol. ¿Qué harían para ayudarla a crecer? ¿Qué harían si su semilla de girasol no creciera? ¿Cómo resolverían el problema?*

Phonological Awareness

✓ **Can children produce words that rhyme?**

Produce Rhyming Words Using *Rhymes and Chants Flip Chart*, page 26, read "A Plant Grows" once more with children. Remind children that rhyming words end with the same sounds. Point to the *seed* in the picture. Say: *Name words that rhyme with* seed. *Nombren palabras que rimen con seed.* Continue with the picture of a *sprout* and the picture of the *sunflower*.

ELL Call on children to point to specific pictures on the chart as you say: *First, you plant a seed. Next, the seed is a little plant. Last, the plant is a big flower.* Have children repeat the phrases.

Rhymes and Chants Flip Chart, p. 26

Center Time

▶ **Center Rotation** Center Time includes teacher-guided activities and independent activities. Refer to the **Learning Centers** on pages 62–63 for activities in additional centers.

small group   60–90 minutes

Writer's Center

Center Tip

✓ Track the words children use to label planting materials and plants.

Materials poster board labels, markers, tape

Planting Labels Have children write labels for planting materials and plants in the Math and Science Center.

- Discuss materials in the Center. Have children organize the materials. For example, pots, tools, and soil can be placed on shelves. Have children label items. When the labels are in place, ask: **How do the labels help us?** *¿Cómo nos ayudan los rótulos o las etiquetas?*

- Have children label their own bean plants or other growing plants with names, descriptions, or markings that show how the plants are growing.

If...children offer more than one idea for organizing and labeling, **then...**comment positively on their contribution.

ABC Center

Center Tip

✓ Track children's ability to match upper and lower case letters.

Materials Alphabet Letter Tiles, a jump rope, heavy paper, glue, uncooked beans

Matching Letters Explain to children that they will use Alphabet *Letter Tiles* to match the upper and lower case forms of *Jj* and *Hh*. Reinforce each letter's sound as children work.

- Form an upper case *J* on the floor with a jump rope. Have children devise ways to make it a lower case *j*. (Add a lid, ball, circle-shape block and so on.)

- Have children write a big *J* and *j* on heavy paper and then trace each with glue. Have them press beans over the glue. When the glue dries, have children trace the *J* or *j* with a finger as they say /j/ /j/ /j/. Children can draw pictures of things whose names begin with /j/ around the letters.

- Have children form *H* and *h* with yarn on the floor and then repeat the procedure.

If...children have difficulty finding a way to change upper case *J* to lower case *j*, **then...**have them look closely at the *Letter Tiles*. Ask: **What is at the top of lower case j? What shape is a dot? What does it remind you of?** *¿Qué hay arriba de la j minúscula? ¿Qué forma tiene el punto? ¿A qué les recuerda?.*

Learning Goals

Language and Communication
- Child names and describes actual or pictured people, places, things, actions, attributes, and events.

Emergent Literacy: Reading
- Child names most upper- and lowercase letters of the alphabet.
- Child identifies the letter that stands for a given sound.

Emergent Literacy: Writing
- Child uses scribbles, shapes, pictures, symbols, and letters to represent language.

Differentiated Instruction

 Extra Support

Writer's Center

If...children have difficulty labeling plants, **then...**ask them questions, such as: **What color is your bean plant? How many leaves does it have?** *¿De qué color es su planta de frijol? ¿Cuántas hojas tiene?*

⭐ **Enrichment**

Writer's Center

Challenge children to label pictures they draw with words.

Accommodations for 3's

ABC Center

If...children have difficulty tracing a large letter they write with glue, **then...**guide their hand.

Focus Question
How do plants grow and change?
¿Cómo crecen y cambian las plantas?

Circle Time

Literacy Time

 large group   15 minutes

Read Aloud

 Can children identify a sequence of events?

Build Background Tell children that you will be rereading *I Am a Peach*/*Yo soy el durazno*. Ask children to tell you how the peach in the story grows and changes.

- Ask: **What did we learn about how plants grow and change?** *¿Qué aprendimos sobre cómo creecen y cambian las plantas?*

Listen for Understanding Display the Big Book, *I Am a Peach*/*Yo soy el durazno*, and read the title.

- Reread the beginning of the story. Have children identify the sequence of events by retelling this part of the story. (The peach is a flower. The peach is a green fruit. The peach is a ripe fruit.) Continue reading the middle and end of the story.

- Have children identify sequence at the end of the story by retelling what happened to the peach after the boy ate it. (The peach is a seed. The peach is a small plant. The peach is a tree with flowers.)

- Use *Sequence Cards* "Seed to Flower" to reinforce the concept of the growth cycle of a plant.

Respond and Connect To help children connect the text to the world, ask: **What will happen to the peach next?** *¿Qué le pasará al durazno más tarde?*

I Am a Peach
Yo soy el durazno

Learning Goals

Emergent Literacy: Reading
- Child names most upper- and lowercase letters of the alphabet.
- Child identifies the letter that stands for a given sound.
- Child retells or reenacts poems and stories in sequence.

Science
- Child identifies organisms and describes their characteristics.
- Child understands and describes life cycles of plants and animals.
- Child observes, understands, and discusses the relationship of plants and animals to their environments.

Vocabulary

city	ciudad	countryside	campo
delicious	delicioso	happily	felizmente

Learn About Letters and Sounds

 Can children identify letters and sounds?

Review Letters *Jj* and *Hh* Review letters and sounds /j/ and /h/.

- Give partners pie tins that contain a thin layer of tiny seeds. Have them write with their fingers in the seeds the letter you name. Have one child write the letter you name (upper case) and then have the other child write the partner letter (lower case). Show children how to gently shake the tin to make each letter disappear. Repeat several times for each letter.

- Display picture flashcards from the Photo Library: ham, jeans, hands, jacket, hose, jelly.

- Give children Alphabet Wall Cards *Jj* and *Hh*. Say a riddle. Have children answer with a picture name that has the beginning sound. For example: **I am a kind of meat. I start with /h/. What am I?** (ham) *Conmigo se hacen emparedados. Mi nombre comienza con /h/. ¿Qué soy?* (ham) Then have children hold up the matching *Alphabet Wall Cards*. (Hh)

ELL Provide more examples for children using *ABC Picture Cards*: jar, jellybeans, horse, hammer.

Differentiated Instruction

✋ Extra Support

Read Aloud

If...children have difficulty retelling events in order, **then**...ask: **What does the peach look like when it is in the ground? What does the peach look like when it is small? What does the peach look like when it grows big?** *¿Cómo es el durazno cuando está en el suelo? ¿Cómo es el durazno cuando es aún pequeño? ¿Cómo es el durazno cuando termina de crecer?*

⭐ Enrichment

Read Aloud

Challenge children to draw a conclusion. Ask: **Why does the peach call its seed "my heart?"** *¿Por qué el durazno llama a su semilla "mi corazón"?*

Math Time

Observe and Investigate

☑ **Can children focus on identifying numbers just before or after a given number?**

X-Ray Vision 2 Show Counting Cards 1–10 in numerical order. Count them with children. Then place the cards facing down still in order. Tell children that they are going to play X-Ray Vision in a new way. To encourage counting forward and back, tell children they will keep their cards facing up after they guess.

- Point to any card. Ask children to use their X-Ray vision to figure out which card it is. Flip the card to check their answer. If the answer is correct, keep the card face up.

- Point to the card that is located right after the card facing up. Ask children to use their X-ray vision to figure out which card it is. Have children tell how they figured it out.

- Now with both cards facing up, repeat with another card that does not come right before a face up card. Continue the game, sometimes choosing a card that is two away from the nearest card facing up.

👬👬 Social and Emotional Development

Making Good Choices

☑ **Do children show a desire to be helpful and caring?**

Solving Problems Display the *Making Good Choices Flip Chart* page 26, "What Should I Do?"

- Point to the flip chart illustration. Ask: ***What did we learn about solving problems?*** *¿Qué aprendimos sobre la solución de problemas?*

- Point to a trash can that is filled with paper. Say: ***We are wasting paper. That's not good for our Earth. How can we solve this problem? One way is to write or draw on both sides of a sheet of paper. What else should we do?*** *Estamos desperdiciando papel. Esto no es bueno para nuestro planeta. ¿Cómo podemos resolver este problema? Una manera es escribir o dibujar en los dos lados de la hoja de papel. ¿Qué más debemos hacer?* Allow time for children to think about and share solutions. Graph solutions on an interactive whiteboard. Say: ***We'll see if these ideas help, and we'll keep trying to find ways to save paper.*** *Veremos si estas ideas son útiles, y seguiremos intentado encontrar otras maneras de ahorrar papel.*

 Encourage children at all proficiency levels to join in the discussion. Say: ***Where is the problem? Point to it. Do we waste paper?***

Making Good Choices Flip Chart, p. 26

Building Blocks

Online Math Activity

Children can complete Reptile Ruler and Number Compare 1 during computer time or Center Time.

✓ Learning Goals

Social and Emotional Development
- Child demonstrates initiative in independent activities; makes independent choices.

Mathematics
- Child counts 1–10 concrete objects correctly.

Vocabulary

backward	atrás	count	contar
facing up	vuelta	forward	adelante

Differentiated Instruction

 Extra Support

Observe and Investigate

If...children have difficulty explaining their reasoning for determining which card is located right after the card facing up, **then...**discuss how you can count forward from the card facing up.

⭐ **Enrichment**

Observe and Investigate

Challenge children to play with cards 1–20.

Accommodations for 3's

Observe and Investigate

If...children struggle with the game, **then...**play with fewer cards or guide children to point to a card as they count.

💜 **Special Needs**

Behavioral Social/Emotional

Praise the child when s/he sits quietly without outbursts. If it is necessary for the child to leave the circle for a few minutes to go to the "calm-down" area, acknowledge when they rejoin the group by looking at them and smiling.

Learning Goals

Social and Emotional Development
• Child uses classroom materials carefully.

Language and Communication
• Child demonstrates an understanding of oral language by responding appropriately.

Fine Arts
• Child participates in a variety of music activities (such as listening, singing, finger plays, musical games, performances).

Vocabulary

beat	ritmo	fast	rápido
loud	fuerte	music	música
slow	lento	soft	suave

Differentiated Instruction

 Extra Support

Explore and Express
If...children have difficulty choosing an instrument, **then...**limit their choices.

⭐ **Enrichment**

Explore and Express
Have children compose a chant and use an instrument to sound out the beat.

Accommodations for 3's

Explore and Express
If...children have difficulty playing to the beat of the chant, **then...**tap it out in manageable parts and have them follow you.

Music and Movement Time

 large group 20 minutes

Personal Safety Skills Model how to properly use and store musical instruments.

Oral Language and Academic Vocabulary

✓ **Can children use words to describe the beat and sounds of music?**

Talking About Sounds Revisit the *Rhymes and Chants Flip Chart*, page 26. Read the first two lines of "A Plant Grows."

● Say: ***The tiny seed is deep underground. We can pretend the seed is sleeping. Let's play some music to wake up the sleepy seed.*** *La semillita está muy hondo bajo tierra. Imaginemos que está durmiendo. Vamos a pasar algo de música para despertar a la semilla dormilona.*

● Play a variety of very short selections of music that reflect a variety of tempos and styles. Encourage children to listen to what the music sounds like. After children listen to each selection, ask: ***What was the speed (or tempo) of the music? Was the music loud or soft?*** *¿La música fue rápida o lenta? ¿La música sonó fuerte o suave?*

● Say: ***Suppose you are sleeping. You need to wake up for school. What kind of music do you want to hear?*** *Supongan que están durmiendo. Necesitan despertarse para ir a la escuela. ¿Qué tipo de música prefieren oír?* Have children describe musical selections they would like to hear.

Explore and Express

✓ **Can children invent their own music and movements?**

Wake Up Sleepy Seeds Tell children that they will make musical sounds to wake up the tiny seed.

● Distribute classroom musical instruments, such as bells, blocks, sticks, triangles, and drums.

● Have children choose an instrument and use it to make sounds. Encourage children to add their own movements and sounds to wake up the tiny seed. Then begin to chant:

It's time to wake up. It's time we know.
It's time to change— and grow, grow, grow!

● Model clapping a steady beat and have children follow with their instruments. Then slow down the beat and use a softer chant.

● To conclude the activity, say: ***Listen! The tiny seed is waking up.*** *¡Escuchen! La semillita se está despertando.* Ask: ***What will happen next?*** *¿Qué pasará ahora?* Tell children they will wake up the tiny seed again with instruments they build in the Construction Center.

TIP Have plenty of open space available. If sound must be controlled, have children take turns making sounds to wake up the tiny seed while the others form a circle, move their bodies, and clap.

Center Time

▶ **Center Rotation** Center Time includes teacher-guided activities and independent activities. Refer to the **Learning Centers** on pages 62–63 for activities in additional centers.

 small group   30 minutes

Learning Goals

Social and Emotional Development
• Child demonstrates initiative in independent activities; makes independent choices.

Fine Arts
• Child participates in a variety of music activities (such as listening, singing, finger plays, musical games, performances).

Construction Center

	Center Tip
✓ **Monitor children as they construct musical instruments.** **Materials** blocks, boxes, paper plates, oatmeal boxes, rulers, rubber bands, buttons, dried beans, tape **Build a Musical Instrument** Tell children that they will use blocks and other materials to make a musical instrument. • Have children decide which materials to work with. Ask: **What instrument will you make? What materials will you use?** *¿Qué instrumentos van a hacer? ¿Qué materiales van a usar?* • Have children tell how they made the instrument. Encourage them to play it to wake up the tiny seed.	**If**...children make independent decisions about which materials to use, **then**...use them as role models for children who ask you to select the materials for them.

Writing

Recap the day and week. Have children write one thing that they want to tell a family member about plants. Say: **What do you want to tell your family about plants? Write about it on the last page of your plant journal. Draw a picture to go with your writing.** *¿Qué le dirán a sus familiares acerca de las plantas? Escríbanlo en la última página de su diario. Hagan un dibujo para ilustrar lo que escribieron.* Suggest that children take their bean plant and their plant journal home to share with their family members.

Purposeful Play

✓ **Observe and informally assess children sharing classroom materials and working cooperatively.**

Children choose an open center for free playtime. Encourage cooperation skills by suggesting they work together to form a band and play music with classroom instruments and those they made.

Let's Say Good-Bye

 large group   15 minutes

 Read Aloud Revisit the story, **"My Grandmother's Garden"**/"El jardín de mi abuela" for your afternoon Read Aloud. Remind children to listen for words about plants and how they grow.

Home Connection Refer to the Home Connections activities listed in the Resources and Materials chart on page 59. Remind children to tell families what they learned this week about plants and how they grow. Sing the "Good-Bye Song" as children prepare to leave.

Week 3

Focus Question

How do people grow and change?

¿Cómo crece y cambia la gente?

This week children will learn about the human life cycle. They will identify what people need to grow, draw and label bodies, match family members with growth stages, compare and contrast babies and adults, and describe growth changes.

Unit 6 Growing and Changing

Week 3

 Learning Goals

Social and Emotional Development	1	2	3	4	5
Child identifies self by categories (such as gender, age, family member, cultural group).	✓	✓	✓	✓	✓
Child describes personal interests and competencies positively (such as, "I can hop.").	✓	✓	✓	✓	✓
Child shows eagerness, curiosity, and confidence while learning new concepts and trying new things.				✓	

Language and Communication	1	2	3	4	5
Child demonstrates an understanding of oral language by responding appropriately.				✓	
Child uses oral language for a variety of purposes.				✓	
Child begins and ends conversations appropriately.		✓			
Child follows basic rules for conversations (taking turns, staying on topic, listening actively).		✓			
Child names and describes actual or pictured people, places, things, actions, attributes, and events.	✓		✓		✓
Child exhibits an understanding of instructional terms used in the classroom.	✓	✓			
Child uses newly learned vocabulary daily in multiple contexts.			✓		✓
Child builds English listening and speaking vocabulary for common objects and phrases. (ELL)	✓	✓			
Child speaks in complete sentences of four or more words including a subject, verb, and object.	✓		✓	✓	✓
Child understands and uses sentences having two or more phrases or concepts.		✓			

Emergent Literacy: Reading	1	2	3	4	5
Child enjoys and chooses reading-related activities.				✓	
Child names most upper- and lowercase letters of the alphabet.	✓	✓		✓	✓
Child identifies the letter that stands for a given sound.	✓	✓	✓	✓	✓
Child describes, relates to, and uses details and information from books read aloud.	✓	✓	✓	✓	✓

Emergent Literacy: Writing	1	2	3	4	5
Child uses scribbles, shapes, pictures, symbols, and letters to represent language.		✓	✓		
Child writes own name or a reasonable approximation of it.					✓
Child writes some letters or reasonable approximations of letters upon request.					✓
Child experiments with and uses some writing conventions when writing or dictating.	✓			✓	✓

Mathematics	1	2	3	4	5
Child demonstrates that the numerical counting sequence is always the same.				✓	
Child recognizes, names, describes, matches, compares, sorts common two-dimensional shapes (such as circle, square, rectangle, triangle, rhombus).		✓		✓	
Child creates two-dimensional shapes; recreates two-dimensional shapes from memory.	✓	✓			✓
Child compares the length, height, weight, volume (capacity), area of people or objects..	✓				✓
Child manipulates (flips, rotates) and combines shapes.		✓		✓	
Child sorts objects and explains how the sorting was done.			✓		
Child identifies, duplicates, and creates simple patterns.					✓

Science	1	2	3	4	5
Child identifies organisms and describes their characteristics.	✓	✓	✓	✓	✓
Child understands and describes life cycles of plants and animals.	✓	✓	✓	✓	✓
Child recognizes and selects healthy foods.	✓		✓		✓

Social Studies	1	2	3	4	5
Child understands basic human needs for food, clothing, shelter.			✓		
Child understands basic concepts of buying, selling, and trading.			✓		
Child participates in voting for group decision-making.			✓		

Fine Arts	1	2	3	4	5
Child expresses emotions or ideas through art.	✓				
Child expresses ideas, emotions, and moods through individual and collaborative dramatic play.					✓

Materials and Resources

	DAY 1	DAY 2	DAY 3	DAY 4	DAY 5
Program Materials	• Teacher's Treasure Book • Oral Language Development Card 57 • Rhymes and Chants Flip Chart • Making Good Choices Flip Chart • Math and Science Flip Chart • Home Connections Resource Guide • ABC Picture Cards *Hh* and *Yy* • Book: *I'm Growing!* • Pattern Blocks • Sequence Cards: The Life Span • Building Blocks Online Math Activities	• Teacher's Treasure Book • Making Good Choices Flip Chart • Dog Puppets • Book: *I'm Growing!* • ABC Picture Cards: *Hh* and *Yy* • Math and Science Flip Chart • Pattern Blocks • Building Blocks Online Math Activities	• Teacher's Treasure Book • Oral Language Development Card 58 • Rhymes and Chants Flip Chart • ABC Picture Cards: *Hh* and *Yy* • Making Good Choices Flip Chart • Concept Big Book: 3 *Growing and Changing* • ABC Big Book • Pattern Blocks • Dog Puppets • Building Blocks Online Math Activities	• Teacher's Treasure Book • Math and Science Flip Chart • Home Connections Resource Guide • Dog Puppets • ABC Picture Cards: *Hh* and *Yy* • Counting Cards 1–5 • Pattern Blocks • Book: *I'm Growing!* • Building Blocks Online Math Activities	• Teacher's Treasure Book • Rhymes and Chants Flip Chart • Making Good Choices Flip Chart • Book: *I'm Growing!* • ABC Picture Cards: *Hh* and *Yy* • Pattern Blocks • Building Blocks Online Math Activities
Other Materials	• paper plates • food pictures from old magazines • crayons, markers, glue • pasta shapes • dried beans • paper	• butcher paper • pencils, crayons, markers • bowl of plastic fruit, artificial flowers • small box • drawing paper	• butcher paper • pictures from magazines of people, animals, and plants • scissors, glue, crayons • toy register • play money or counters • construction paper	• folktale and fairy tale books • paper, crayons, markers • scissors	• poster board • crayons, markers • scissors, glue, tape
Home Connection	Encourage children to tell their families what they learned today about growing and changing. Send home the following materials: Weekly Family Letter, Home Connections Resource Guide, pp. 57-58.	Encourage children to tell their families about the book, *I'm Growing!*. Remind children to tell their families how they learned to make puzzles.	Encourage children to tell their families what they learned today about the way all living things change and grow. Remind children to tell their families how they learned to sort Pattern Block shapes into groups.	Encourage children to retell the story "The Boy Who Cried Wolf" to their families. Send home Storybook 17, Home Connections Resource Guide, pp. 145-146 (English), and 147-148 (Spanish).	Encourage children to tell their families what they learned this week about how people change and grow. Remind children to tell their families about how they learned to try new things.

Assessment

As you observe children throughout the week, you may fill out an Anecdotal Observational Record Form to document an individual's progress toward a goal or signs indicating the need for developmental or medical evaluation. You may also choose to select work for each child's portfolio. The Anecdotal Observational Record Form and Weekly Assessment rubrics are available in the assessment section of DLMExpressOnline.com.

More Literature Suggestions

- **The Growing-up Tree** by Vera Rosenberry
- **Growing Like Me** by Anne Rockwell
- **How Kids Grow** by Jean Marzollo and Nancy Sheehan
- **Me and My Amazing Body** by Joan Sweeney
- **Harold and the Purple Crayon** by Crockett Johnson
- **Zapatos nuevos para Silvia** por Johanna Huwitz
- **Soy importante** por Elvia Vargas Trujillo
- **La fiesta de cumpleaños** por Ana María Pecanins
- **La leyenda del pincel indio** por Tomie dePaola
- **Sílbale a Willie** por Ezra Jack Keats

	DAY 1	DAY 2
Let's Start the Day **Language Time** large group	**Opening Routines** p. 102 **Morning Read Aloud** p. 102 **Oral Language and Vocabulary** p. 102 Family Time **Phonological Awareness** p. 102 Recognize Final Sounds	**Opening Routines** p. 108 **Morning Read Aloud** p. 108 **Oral Language and Vocabulary** p. 108 I'm Growing!/¡Estoy creciendo! **Phonological Awareness** p. 108 Recognize Final Sounds
Center Time small group	**Focus On:** **Construction Center** p. 103 **ABC Center** p. 103	**Focus On:** **Math and Science Center** p. 109 **Pretend and Learn Center** p. 109
Circle Time **Literacy Time** large group	**Read Aloud** *I'm Growing!/¡Estoy creciendo!* p. 104 **Learn About Letters and Sounds:** /h/ and /y/ p. 104	**Read Aloud** *I'm Growing!/¡Estoy creciendo!* p. 110 **Learn About Letters and Sounds:** /h/ and /y/ p. 110
Math Time large group	**Puzzles** p. 105	**I Spy** p. 111
Social and Emotional Development large group	**Trying New Things** p. 105	**Trying New Things** p. 111
Content Connection large group	**Science:** **Oral Language and Academic Vocabulary** p. 106 Talk About the Human Life Cycle **Observe and Investigate** p. 106 How We Grow	**Math:** **Oral Language and Academic Vocabulary** p. 112 Talk About Puzzles **Observe and Investigate** p. 112 Pattern Block Puzzle
Center Time small group	**Focus On:** **Creativity Center** p. 107 **Purposeful Play** p. 107	**Focus On:** **Library and Listening Center** p. 113 **Purposeful Play** p. 113
Let's Say Good-Bye large group	**Read Aloud** p. 107 **Writing** p. 107 **Home Connection** p. 107	**Read Aloud** p. 113 **Writing** p. 113 **Home Connection** p. 113

DAY 3

Opening Routines p. 114
Morning Read Aloud p. 114
Oral Language and Vocabulary
p. 114 Learn from Family Members
Phonological Awareness
p. 114 Recognize Final Sounds

Focus On:
ABC Center p. 115
Creativity Center p. 115

Read Aloud
Growing and Changing/Creciendo y cambiando p. 116
Learn About Letters and Sounds:
/h/ and/ y/ p. 116

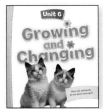

Guess My Rule p. 117

Trying New Things p. 117

Social Studies:
Oral Language and Academic Vocabulary
p. 118 Take a Vote
Understand and Participate
p. 118 Shop for New Clothes

Focus On:
Construction Center p. 119
Purposeful Play p. 119

Read Aloud p. 119
Writing p. 119
Home Connection p. 119

DAY 4

Opening Routines p. 120
Morning Read Aloud p. 120
Oral Language and Vocabulary
p. 120 Good Choices
Phonological Awareness
p. 120 Recognize End Sounds

Focus On:
Library and Listening Center p. 121
Writer's Center p. 121

Read Aloud
The Boy Who Cried Wolf/El niño y el lobo p. 122
Learn About Letters and Sounds:
/h/ and /y/ p. 122

What's the Missing Card? p. 123

Trying New Things p. 123

Math:
Oral Language and Academic Vocabulary
p. 124 Talk About Symmetry
Observe and Investigate
p. 124 Use Pattern Blocks

Focus On:
Math and Science Center p. 125
Purposeful Play p. 125

Read Aloud p. 125
Writing p. 125
Home Connection p. 125

DAY 5

Opening Routines p. 126
Morning Read Aloud p. 126
Oral Language and Vocabulary
p. 126 Same and Different
Phonological Awareness
p. 126 Recognize Final Sounds

Focus On:
Creativity Center p. 127
Pretend and Learn Center p. 127

Read Aloud
I'm Growing!/¡Estoy creciendo! p. 128
Learn About Letters and Sounds:
/h/ and /y/ p. 128

Pattern Block Puzzles p. 129

Trying New Things p. 129

Dramatic Play Time:
Oral Language and Academic Vocabulary
p. 130 Name Family Members
Explore and Express
p. 130 A Family Birthday

Focus On:
Writer's Center p. 131
Purposeful Play p. 131

Read Aloud p. 131
Writing p. 131
Home Connection p. 131

Week 3

People Change

Learning Centers

Math and Science Center

What's Inside?
Children stretch out on a sheet of butcher paper and allow a partner to trace the outline of their body. They use page 11 of the Big Book, *I'm Growing!* to draw and label their own body parts. See p. 109.

Line Symmetry
Children fold a sheet of paper in half and draw half of a body along the fold. They unfold the paper to see a whole body shape that is symmetrical, and then draw facial features. See p. 125.

Make a Timeline
Children create a timeline with three markers, as well as drawings of themselves at 3 months, 2 years, and their current age. They describe how they have changed over the years.

ABC Center

Pasta and Bean Letters
Children use glue to draw the capital letters *H* and *Y* on paper, and place bean and pasta shapes on the glue to form special letters. See p. 103.

Letter Teams
Children form teams and hunt for the letters *Hh*, which are hidden around the classroom. Each team counts the number of *Hh* cards they find, and the team with more cards wins. Children repeat to find *Yy* cards. See p. 115.

Yy is for Yellow
Children write the letters *Yy* on a large sheet of yellow construction paper, and draw pictures of things whose names begin with /y/, such as *yarn*, *yawn*, *yak*, and *yo-yo*.

Creativity Center

When We Grow Up
Children draw a picture of what they think they will look like as an adult and show what kind of job they might have. See p. 107.

"How It Grows" Collage
Children make a collage that shows animals, plants, or people. They cut out pictures of their subject from magazines and glue them on butcher paper, including pictures that show stages of growth and what those living things need to grow. See p. 115.

Try a New Game
Children create a new classroom game that everyone can play. They make up rules for the game and draw pictures that show how the game is played. See p. 127.

"Me" Puzzles
Children draw a self-portrait on poster board and cut the picture into four pieces. Partners trade and put together each other's puzzles.

Library and Listening Center

How Are We the Same?
Children listen to the story CD for *I'm Growing!* as they follow along in the Big Book. They draw pictures to show one way they are like the boy and one thing his family does that their family does. See p. 113.

Talk About Story Characters
Partners look through fairy tale and folk tale books and tell each other stories that include wolves, such as "Little Red Riding Hood" and "The Three Little Pigs." They discuss how animals in stories often act like people. See p. 121.

What Can You Do?
Partners look through storybooks about children who are about their age, talk about what the characters do, and tell whether they can do the same things.

Construction Center

A Family Dinner
Children cut out pictures of food from magazines and glue them on a paper plate to display a healthful dinner. Then they describe the different foods they selected. See p. 103.

Caterpillars and Butterflies
Children trace and cut out circles from green construction paper, overlap the circles, and glue them to make a caterpillar. They make a butterfly by coloring a sheet of paper, folding it accordion style, and wrapping a chenille stick around the middle. See p. 119.

Grow and Learn
Children think of a new skill they learned this year and create a poster that shows what they are able to do. They write or dictate a label for their poster and place it on a bulletin board titled, "We Grow and Learn."

Writer's Center

Write a Tale
Children write a fairy tale about a child and an animal that are friends. They draw pictures to show what happens in the beginning, in the middle, and at the end of the story. See p. 121.

Thank-You Notes
Children fold a sheet of drawing paper in half to make a card. They draw a picture that shows a party scene on the front of the card and complete a sentence frame inside the card. See p. 131.

Healthy Habits for Us
Children illustrate and write about healthy behaviors that help them grow. For example: *I eat healthful food. I exercise every day. I get plenty of sleep.*

Pretend and Learn Center

A Visit from a Friend
Children act out the scene from the Big Book, *I'm Growing!* in which the boy's family has a friend visit them. They use polite and friendly words as they act out the scene. See p. 109.

New Clothes
Children draw a figure of a child on poster board. They draw their own face and hair on the figure, but no other details. Then they draw and cut out paper clothes for the figure and tell how they feel about having new clothes. See p. 127.

Do "The Hokey Pokey"
Children practice naming parts of their body by doing "The Hokey Pokey."

Happy Feelings
Children sing "If You're Happy and You Know It" and take turns leading the group in new actions, such as: tap your knees, jump around, and laugh out loud.

Let's Start the Day

Focus Question
How do people grow and change?
¿Cómo crece y cambia la gente?

▶ Opening Routines and Transition Tips
For **Opening Routines** and **Transition Tips** turn to pages 178–181 and visit **DLMExpressOnline.com** for more ideas.

Read **"When I Was One"/**"Cuando yo tenía un año" from the *Teacher's Treasure Book*, page 128, for your morning Read Aloud.

✓ Learning Goals

Social and Emotional Development
• Child identifies self by categories (such as gender, age, family member, cultural group).
• Child describes personal interests and competencies positively (such as, "I can hop.").

Language and Communication
• Child names and describes actual or pictured people, places, things, actions, attributes, and events.
• Child speaks in complete sentences of four or more words including a subject, verb, and object.

Vocabulary

children	niños	family	familia
meal	comida	parents	padres
table	mesa	young	jóvenes

Differentiated Instruction

 Extra Support
Oral Language and Vocabulary
If...children have difficulty identifying final sounds, **then...**segment the phonemes in each word: /k/ /i/ /d/, *kid*. Ask children to say the last sound they hear.

 Enrichment
Phonological Awareness
Challenge children to name other words that end with the same sound as *way, walk,* and *glad*.

Language Time

large group   15 minutes

👥 **Social and Emotional Development** Identify and praise children's competence in oral language, and provide help when requested.

Oral Language and Vocabulary

✓ **Can children use a wide variety of words to tell about families?**

Family Time Ask children to recall what they learned from lessons presented earlier in the year. Talk about what makes a family. Explain that family members can be many different ages. **Who is in a family?** *¿Quiénes forman una familia?*

● Display *Oral Language Development Card 57.* Ask: **Who are the parents in this family? Point to them. Who are the children?** *¿Quienes son los padres en esta familia? Señálenlos. ¿Quiénes son los niños?* Then follow the suggestions on the back of the card.

Oral Language Development Card 57

Phonological Awareness

✓ **Can children identify final sounds?**

Recognize Final Sounds Display *Rhymes and Chants Flip Chart,* page 27. Use hand movements and pantomime as you chant "A Baby Grows." Repeat, having children join you in the movements. Then say: **Listen to these words from the chant. Tell me the last sound in each word.** *Escuchen estas palabras de la canción. Díganme cuál es el último sonido de cada palabra.* Say *day, way, walk, talk, tricycle,* and *bicycle* slowly. Pause to allow children to name each sound.

ELL Explain to children that a bicycle has two wheels. A tricycle is a bicycle with three wheels. Then demonstrate the word *tricycle.* Pretend to ride a tricycle. Say: **I rode a tricycle when I was a little child.**

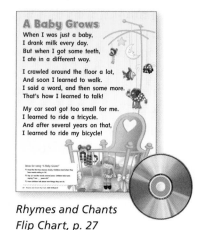
Rhymes and Chants Flip Chart, p. 27

Center Time

Center Rotation Center Time includes teacher-guided activities and independent activities. Refer to the **Learning Centers** on pages 100–101 for activities in additional centers.

small group   60–90 minutes

Refer to the **Learning Centers** on pages 100–101 for activities in additional centers.

Construction Center

Center Tip

If...children need more drawing space, **then...**suggest that they use more than one plate and draw only one or two foods on each plate.

✓ **Track children's ability to identify nutritious foods.**

Materials *Oral Language Development Card 57,* uncoated white paper plates, food pictures from old magazines and catalogs, crayons or washable markers

A Family Dinner Display *Oral Development Language Card 57,* "What's for Dinner?" Have children tell each other what they like to eat at family dinners.

● Give children white paper plates. Have them cut out foods for a family dinner and glue them onto a plate. Children may also draw foods if they wish. Encourage them to include healthy foods in the meal.

● Have children use their plates to set up a dinner on a table. Have them tell about their food. Help them identify foods that are healthy.

ABC Center

Center Tip

If...children have difficulty forming letters with glue, **then...**have them practice writing *H* and *Y* on paper and then try to draw the letters with glue again.

✓ **Track children's ability to form letters *H* and *Y*.**

Materials *ABC Picture Cards Hh* and *Yy,* paper, glue, small pasta shapes and dried beans

Pasta and Bean Letters Display *ABC Picture Cards Hh* and *Yy* in the center. Have children take turns going to the cards and tracing the capital letters with a finger as they say /h/ and /y/.

● Have children use glue to draw the capital letters *H* and *Y* on paper.

● Give children a variety of beans and small pasta shapes to place onto the glue to form bean and pasta letters.

Learning Goals

Emergent Literacy: Reading
● Child names most upper- and lowercase letters of the alphabet.
● Child identifies the letter that stands for a given sound.

Science
● Child recognizes and selects healthy foods.

Differentiated Instruction

✋ Extra Support

Construction Center

If...children have difficulty choosing healthy foods for their plate, **then...**review a healthy dinner menu with them that includes protein, milk, fruits, and vegetables.

⭐ Enrichment

ABC Center

Challenge children to also make lower case letters *h* and *y.*

Accommodations for 3's

ABC Center

If...three-year-olds have trouble creating pasta and bean letters, **then...**use glue to draw *H* and *Y* on paper for children and have them cover the letters with glitter or colored sand.

Focus Question

How do people grow and change?

¿Cómo crece y cambia la gente?

large group 15 minutes

Literacy Time

 **Read Aloud**

 Can children describe ways that people grow?

Build Background Tell children that they will read a book about growing.

- Ask: **Have you grown since you were a baby? What are some ways that you have grown?** ¿Siguieron creciendo desde que eran bebés? ¿De qué manera crecieron?

Listen for Enjoyment Display *I'm Growing!/¡Estoy creciendo!* and read the title. Ask: **Who is bigger in this picture?** Explain that the child in the yellow shirt is bigger, but both children are growing. Then conduct a picture walk.

- Browse through the pages. Point out the main character in the pictures. Ask: **How do you think this boy has grown since he was a baby?** ¿En qué creen que cambió este niño desde que era bebé?

- Read the book aloud, pointing to details in the pictures that support the text.

Respond to the Story Discuss the story. Ask: **How does the boy change as he grows? What helps him grow bigger and stronger?** ¿Cómo cambia el niño a medida que crece? ¿Qué cosas lo ayudan a crecer sano y fuerte?

TIP Revisit the illustrations in the book as needed to help children describe how the boy changes as he grows.

ELL As you read aloud, encourage children to point to corresponding parts of their body as they learn how the boy grows, for example, their face, arms, and teeth. Model for children by pointing to your own body parts.

I'm Growing!
¡Estoy creciendo!

Learning Goals

Emergent Literacy: Reading

- Child names most upper- and lowercase letters of the alphabet.
- Child identifies the letter that stands for a given sound.
- Child describes, relates to, and uses details and information from books read aloud.

Science

- Child identifies organisms and describes their characteristics.
- Child understands and describes life cycles of plants and animals.

Vocabulary

baby	bebé	growing	creciendo
heavier	más pesado	teens	adolescentes
taller	más alto	grown-up	adulto
older	mayor de edad		

Differentiated Instruction

 Extra Support

Learn About Letters and Sound

If...children difficulty making sound-spelling associations for /h/*h* and /y/*y*, **then...**have them trace over the letters on the *ABC Picture Cards* as you say sounds of the letters with them.

 Enrichment

Read Aloud

After reading aloud the book once, invite children to page through the book and take turns describing how the boy grows.

 Special Needs

Cognitive Challenges

Use simple sentences when explaining something new.

Learn About Letters and Sounds

 Can children identify sounds and letters /h/ and /y/?

Review Letters and Sounds /h/, /y/ Display *ABC Picture Cards* for *Hh* and *Yy*. Remind children that they made capital *H* and *Y* letters earlier.

- Then point to each letter as you name it and say the sound: *The letter is* h. *The sound is* /h/. **What is the letter? What is the sound?** ¿Qué letra es? ¿Qué sonido tiene?

- Have children lightly tap the top of their head as they chant, "Head, head, head. Head begins with /h/." Then have them nod their head as they chant, "Yes, yes, yes. Yes begins with /y/."

- Trace each letter on the letter cards as children write the letters in the air.

ABC Picture Cards

large group · 15 minutes

Math Time

Observe and Investigate

☑ **Can children compose shapes to make puzzle designs?**

Puzzles This serves as an introduction to puzzles, helping children put this week's activities in perspective. Show a wooden puzzle, and explain that doing puzzles often involves combining shapes to make new shapes and pictures. Tell children they will do many puzzles this week—even on the computer!

- Display *Math and Science Flip Chart, page 50.* Point out Pattern Block Puzzle 1 (*Teacher's Treasure Book,* page 512), and ask for volunteers to solve it with actual Pattern Blocks. You can put tape on the blocks to hold them, or place the flip chart on the floor.

- Generally, if children need more help with puzzles, move from easy off-computer wooden puzzles to simple off-computer outline puzzles, gradually increasing complexity. For a challenge, ask children to solve the same puzzle once it is completed but with different shapes.

ELL Identify each shape in Pattern Block Puzzle 1 by name as you point to it. Have children trace over each shape on the puzzle as they say the name with you. Then have them use Pattern Blocks to solve the puzzle.

ᜄᜄᜄ Social and Emotional Development

Making Good Choices

☑ **Do children recognize the benefits of trying new things?**

Trying New Things Discuss how children can have fun and feel good about themselves by trying new things. Display the *Making Good Choices Flip Chart, page 27.* Point to the children playing the jumping game.

- Say: ***The children are trying a new game. Do you think they are having fun? What might they say about being good jumpers?*** *Los niños están intentando un juego nuevo. ¿Creen que están divirtiéndose? ¿Qué dirían ellos sobre sí mismos al ver que saltan tan bien?*

- Point out the children who can't jump as high as the others. Say: ***Do you think these children are still having fun? It's important to know how much you can do and be proud of it!*** *¿Creen que estos niños también se divierten? Es importante saber hasta dónde pueden llegar, ¡y sentirse orgullosos de eso!*

Pattern Block Puzzles
Rompecabezas de bloques con patrones

Math and Science Flip Chart, p. 50

Building Blocks

Online Math Activity

Children can complete Piece Puzzler 1 during computer time or Center Time.

Trying New Things
Aprendamos cosas nuevas

Making Good Choices Flip Chart, p. 27

☑ Learning Goals

Social and Emotional Development
- Child identifies self by categories (such as gender, age, family member, cultural group).
- Child describes personal interests and competencies positively (such as, "I can hop.").

Mathematics
- Child creates two-dimensional shapes; recreates two-dimensional shapes from memory.

Vocabulary

pattern	patrón	proud	orgulloso
puzzle	rompecabezas	shapes	figuras
solve	resolver		

Differentiated Instruction

✋ **Extra Support**

Math Time

If...children have difficulty solving Pattern Block Puzzle 1, **then...**draw simple puzzles with three or four shapes for them to solve with Pattern Blocks.

⭐ **Enrichment**

Math Time

Have children build Pattern Block Puzzle 1 in as many ways as they can, using Pattern Blocks in different colors or rotating the design.

Focus Question

How do people grow and change?
¿Cómo crece y cambia la gente?

Learning Goals

Language and Communication
• Child exhibits an understanding of instructional terms used in the classroom.

• Child builds English listening and speaking vocabulary for common objects and phrases. (ELL)

Mathematics
• Child compares the length, height, weight, volume (capacity), area of people or objects.

Science
• Child identifies organisms and describes their characteristics.

• Child understands and describes life cycles of plants and animals.

• Child recognizes and selects healthy foods.

Vocabulary

baby	bebé	child	niño
grown-up	adulto	older	mayor
teen	adolescente	younger	más joven

Differentiated Instruction

 Extra Support

Oral Language and Academic Vocabulary
If...children have difficulty identifying how abilities change as we grow, **then...**point to the chart as you give specifics: *Babies can crawl and reach. Children can jump, run, and throw. Teens can play games like baseball. Grown-ups can work on a job.*

 Enrichment

Oral Language and Academic Vocabulary
Challenge children to look through the illustrations in the Big Book *I'm Growing!* and find examples of babies, children, and grown-ups.

Science Time

large group   20 minutes

Personal Safety and Health Skills Remind children that in order to grow to be strong and healthy, they must eat nutritious food, or good food with proteins, vitamins, and minerals.

Oral Language and Academic Vocabulary

✓ **Can children identify stages in the life cycle of humans?**

Talk About the Human Life Cycle Display *Math and Science Flip Chart*, page 49. Say: *This chart shows how we grow. It starts from when we are very young, and shows how we grow up.* *Esta tabla muestra la manera en que crecemos. Comienza desde que éramos muy pequeños y muestra cómo vamos creciendo.*

● Point to and read aloud the labels below the people on the chart. Ask: *Who is younger, the child or the baby? Who is older, the teen or the grown-up?* *¿Quién es más joven, el niño o el bebé? ¿Quién es mayor el adolescente o el adulto?*

● Have children compare the weights of the people in each picture. Ask: *Who do you think weighs the most? Who do you think weighs the least?* *¿Quién creen que es más pesado? ¿Quién es más ligero?*

● Use *Sequence Cards,* "The Life Span" to sequence the life cycle of a person.

Observe and Investigate

✓ **Can children describe how they grow?**

How We Grow Have children bring in baby pictures or draw a picture of what they looked like as a baby.

● Say: *Look at the chart. How do our bodies change as we grow?* *Observen la tabla. ¿Cómo nos cambia el cuerpo a medida que crecemos?*

● Ask: *What can we do when we get older that we can't do when we are young?* *¿Qué cosas podemos hacer cuando somos mayores que no podemos hacer cuando somos más pequeños?*

● Have children show their baby pictures and talk about how they changed as they grew. *Did you get taller? Did your legs and arms get longer? What can you do now that you couldn't do when you were a baby?* *¿Son ahora más altos? ¿Sus piernas y sus brazos son más largos? ¿Qué pueden hacer ahora que no podían hacer cuando eran bebés?*

TIP Remind children that they saw details about how a person grows in the book *I'm Growing!*

ELL Support language on the chart with additional examples. Point to children and then to yourself. *You are a child. I am a grown-up.* Act out rocking a baby. *A baby is very young.* Write numerals 13–19 on the board. *A teen can be this old. How old are you?* Have children repeat each phrase and answer the question in English.

Math and Science Flip Chart, p. 49

Center Time

Center Rotation Center Time includes teacher-guided activities and independent activities. Refer to the **Learning Centers** on pages 100–101 for activities in additional centers.

  small group 30 minutes

Creativity Center | Center Tip

✓ Track children's knowledge of adult characteristics and abilities.

Materials paper, crayons or washable markers

When We Grow Up Provide children with drawing materials and invite them to draw themselves as grown-ups.

- Encourage children to discuss how children change as they grow to be adults. Then have them draw what they think they will look like as a grown-up.

- As children draw, encourage them to also show what they might do as a grown-up, such as working at a job or enjoying time with friends or family.

Center Tip

If...children have difficulty identifying specific ways that people change as they grow into adults, **then...**display Big Book *I'm Growing!* again and have them look through the illustrations.

Purposeful Play

✓ **Observe children engaging in conversations about themselves.**

Children choose an open center for free playtime. Help build children's awareness of their potential abilities by suggesting that they act out what they will be when they grow up.

Let's Say Good-Bye

 large group 15 minutes

 Read Aloud Revisit the story, "When I Was One"/"Cuando yo tenía un año" for your afternoon Read Aloud. Remind children to listen for ways that people change as they grow.

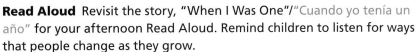 **Home Connection** Refer to the Home Connections activities listed in the Resources and Materials chart on page 97. Remind children to tell families what they learned today about growing and changing. Sing the "Good-Bye Song"/"Hora de ir casa" as children prepare to leave.

✓ Learning Goals

Social and Emotional Development
- Child identifies self by categories (such as gender, age, family member, cultural group).
- Child describes personal interests and competencies positively (such as, "I can hop.").

Emergent Literacy: Writing
- Child experiments with and uses some writing conventions when writing or dictating.

Science
- Child identifies organisms and describes their characteristics.
- Child understands and describes life cycles of plants and animals.

Fine Arts
- Child expresses emotions or ideas through art.

Writing

Recap the day. Say: **Let's quickly retell how people grow.** *Volvamos a contar rápidamente cómo crece la gente.* Write and ask: What are we first? Have children dictate other sentences for you to write. As you write their responses, point out the way you write from left to right and leave spaces between words.

DAY 2

Let's Start the Day

Focus Question

How do people grow and change?

¿Cómo crece y cambia la gente?

 **Learning Goals**

Social and Emotional Development
• Child identifies self by categories (such as gender, age, family member, cultural group).
• Child describes personal interests and competencies positively (such as, "I can hop.").

Language and Communication
• Child uses newly learned vocabulary daily in multiple contexts.
• Child builds English listening and speaking vocabulary for common objects and phrases. (ELL)
• Child understands and uses sentences having two or more phrases or concepts.

Vocabulary

arms	brazos	brain	cabeza
legs	piernas	muscles	músculos
nose	nariz	skin	piel
teeth	dientes		

Differentiated Instruction

 Extra Support

Oral Language and Vocabulary
If...children have difficulty remembering details about how their bodies change as they grow, **then...**display the Big Book *I'm Growing!* and point out specifics in the illustrations.

 Enrichment

Phonological Awareness
Give partners the dog puppets and have them name words that end with the same sound.

▶ **Opening Routines and Transition Tips**
For **Opening Routines** and **Transition Tips** turn to pages 178–181 and visit DLMExpressOnline.com for more ideas.

Read **"Growing Up Dream"/"El sueño de crecer"** from the *Teacher's Treasure Book,* page 116, for your morning Read Aloud.

Language Time

 large group   15 minutes

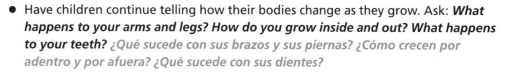 **Social and Emotional Development** Encourage children to continue to try new things, and remind them that as they grow they will be able to do new things that they could not do before.

Oral Language and Vocabulary

✓ **Can children identify ways their bodies change as they grow?**

I'm Growing! Remind children that they read about how people grow and change in the book *I'm Growing!/¡Estoy creciendo!* Review that one way that children change as they grow is that their bodies get bigger. Point to your nose: **Children's noses get bigger as they grow. How else do you change as you grow?** *La nariz de los niños se hace más grande a medida que crecen. ¿Qué otras cosas cambian a medida que crecen?*

I'm Growing!
¡Estoy creciendo!

● Have children continue telling how their bodies change as they grow. Ask: **What happens to your arms and legs? How do you grow inside and out? What happens to your teeth?** *¿Qué sucede con sus brazos y sus piernas? ¿Cómo crecen por adentro y por afuera? ¿Qué sucede con sus dientes?*

● Encourage children to point to body parts such as arms and legs, muscles (arm muscle), brain (head), skin, teeth as they talk about how they grow.

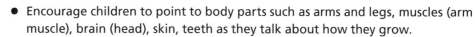 Display pictures of body parts in the Photo Library, such as arm, head, leg, nose, teeth. Have children listen to the names in English and state the name in their own language. Then encourage them to talk about how their bodies change as they grow.

Phonological Awareness

 **Can children identify final sounds?**

Recognize Final Sounds Display the Dog Puppets. Explain that each puppet will say a word. Tell children to listen closely for the end sound in each word. If both words end with the same sound, children should clap their hands. If the words don't end with the same sound, they should shake their head no. Have the puppets say these and other word pairs slowly, emphasizing the final sounds: *bib/crib, arm/leg, walk/duck, lid/Dad, foot/brain, small/tall, big/day, nose/rose.*

Center Time

▶ **Center Rotation** Center Time includes teacher-guided activities and independent activities. Refer to the **Learning Centers** on pages 100–101 for independent activity ideas.

 small group 60–90 minutes

Math and Science Center

☑ **Track children's knowledge of body parts.**

Materials butcher paper, pencils, crayons or washable markers, Big Book *I'm Growing*

What's Inside? Display page 11 in the Big Book *I'm Growing!* and read aloud the labels on the diagram that shows what the boy looks like inside. Invite children to draw and label their own body in the same way.

● Have children stretch out on a sheet of butcher paper and allow a partner to trace their body on the paper.

● Have children use the illustration in the Big Book to draw and label their own body parts: heart, lungs, stomach, intestines.

● Have children write their name on their drawing and display it in the center.

Center Tip

If...children prefer not to have their body traced, **then...**have them draw a body on chart paper and label body parts on it.

Pretend and Learn Center

☑ **Track children's ability to participate in social conversations.**

Materials bowl of plastic fruit, artificial flowers, small box, Big Book *I'm Growing!*

A Visit from a Friend Display page 17 in the Big Book *I'm Growing!* Invite children to act out the scene in which the boy's family has a visit from a friend.

● Have four children at a time stand up and act out the scene using props for items shown on the page.

● Encourage children to use polite and friendly words as they act out the scene. The boy and his family should welcome the visitor to their home, and the visitor should express his appreciation for the invitation.

● Make sure all children have the opportunity to act out one or more of the characters.

Center Tip

If...children have difficulty knowing what to say, **then...**model the beginning of a polite social conversation: *Hello. Welcome to our home. It's nice to see you....I'm glad to be here. Thank you for inviting me.* *Hola. Bienvenido a nuestra casa. ¡Qué bonita visita! Gracias invitarme.*

✓ Learning Goals

Language and Communication
• Child begins and ends conversations appropriately.
• Child follows basic rules for conversations (taking turns, staying on topic, listening actively).

Science
• Child identifies organisms and describes their characteristics.

Differentiated Instruction

 Extra Support

Math and Science Center

If...children have difficulty writing labels for their body tracing, **then...**have them point to body parts on the tracing as they name the parts with you.

 Enrichment

Pretend and Learn Center

Challenge children to extend the role-play and act out what happens when the boy and his parents go to the visitor's home.

Accommodations for 3's

Math and Science Center

If...children cannot add details or labels to their body tracing, **then...**have them trace their body and name external body parts, for example: *"This is my head. Here are my legs."* *"Ésta es mi cabeza. Aquí están mis piernas."*

Focus Question

How do people grow and change?

¿Cómo crece y cambia la gente?

Learning Goals

Emergent Literacy: Reading

• Child names most upper- and lowercase letters of the alphabet.

• Child identifies the letter that stands for a given sound.

• Child describes, relates to, and uses details and information from books read aloud.

Science

• Child identifies organisms and describes their characteristics.

• Child understands and describes life cycles of plants and animals.

Vocabulary

bottom	abajo	children	niños
grown-ups	adultos	left	izquierda
right	derecha	top	arriba

Differentiated Instruction

 Extra Support

Learn About Letters and Sounds

If...children have difficulty pronouncing /h/ or /y/, **then...**model the mouth position for each sound and have children repeat these words after you: *he, has, hair, hand; you, year, yarn, yard.*

 Enrichment

Learn About Letters and Sounds

Challenge partners to find the letters *Hh* and *Yy* in the text of the Big Book *I'm Growing!*

Circle Time

Literacy Time

 large group / 15 minutes

📖 Read Aloud

✓ **Can children use information in the book to describe the growth cycle?**

Build Background Display the Big Book *I'm Growing!/¡Estoy creciendo!* and read the title.

● Ask: *What do you remember about the way children grow? ¿Qué recuerdan sobre la manera en que los niños crecen?*

● Display the first two pages of the book. Say: *When we read, we go from left to right and from top to bottom. What do we do when we finish a page? Cuando leemos, vamos de izquierda a derecha y de arriba hacia abajo. ¿Qué hacemos cuando terminamos de leer una página?* Read the first two pages and track the text to demonstrate moving from one page to the next.

● Then say: *Now let's continue reading the book and talk about growing some more. Ahora, continuemos leyendo el libro y hablando un poco más acerca de crecer.*

Listen for Understanding As you reread, continue to track the print. Point to pictures of adults as you come to them in the story.

● Say: *These people are grown-ups. Do grown-ups keep growing like children? Why are some people little even though they are grown? Estas personas son adultos. ¿Los adultos siguen creciendo como los niños? ¿Por qué algunas personas son bajas de estatura cuando son adultos?*

Respond to the Story Have children describe changes in the growing cycle. Ask: *When do most people stop growing? How can people change after they stop growing? ¿Cuándo deja de crecer la mayoría de la gente? ¿Cómo puede cambiar la gente después de que deja de crecer?*

💡 **TIP** Point out to children that even though people stop growing in their late teens, they can still learn new things as grown-ups.

ELL Invite children to share family names in their home language, including names for mother, father, baby, child, teen, grandmother, and grandfather. For additional suggestions on how to meet the needs of children at the Beginning, Intermediate, Advanced, and Advanced-High levels of English proficiency, see pages 184–187.

Learn About Letters and Sounds

✓ **Can children identify sounds and letters /h/h and /y/y?**

Review Letters and Sounds /h/, /y/ Display *ABC Picture Cards* for *Hh* and *Yy*.

● Chant the following as you point to *Hh* on the card: *I see a letter. A letter I see. I see an h, say the sound with me: /h/, /h/. Veo una letra. Veo una h. Digan el sonido conmigo: /h/, /h/.* Have children say the sound as they trace first the upper case letter and then the lower case letter in the air. Repeat with *Yy*.

● Have partners take turns writing the upper case and lower case form of each letter on paper.

I'm Growing!
¡Estoy creciendo!

large group | 15 minutes

Math Time

Observe and Investigate

 Can children name shapes?

I Spy Name the shape of something in the classroom and have children guess what it is.

- Here are some shape guidelines: circles are perfectly round; triangles have three sides; equilateral triangles have three sides with all the same angles; isosceles triangles have three sides with two sides and angles the same; right triangles have three sides with one right angle; parallelograms have four sides with opposite sides the same length; squares have four sides all the same length with all right angles; and rhombuses have four sides all the same length.

- Note that this can be played during transitions, while waiting, and other downtime. If you do not have a certain shape, such as a parallelogram, to "spy" in your classroom, strategically place Patten Block shapes or other flat manipulatives around the room.

Online Math Activity

Children can complete Piece Puzzler 1 and Piece Puzzler 2 during computer time or Center Time.

large group | 15 minutes

✗✗✗ Social and Emotional Development

Making Good Choices

 Do children appreciate their own abilities and understand how their actions affect others?

Trying New Things Revisit the *Making Good Choices Flip Chart, page 27,* "Trying New Things."

- Display the Dog Puppet. Say: ***Tell the puppet what the children are doing and how they feel about themselves as they are doing it.*** *Cuéntenle al títere lo que están haciendo los niños y cómo se sienten al hacerlo.* Provide each child a turn.

- Remind children to notice what they can do during Center Time and to be proud of their own accomplishments. Explain that when they work well, they also help others around them.

ELL Provide sentence frames for children to use during the conversation with the puppet: ***The children play a game of _____. They feel good because _____.***

Making Good Choices Flip Chart, p. 27

 **Learning Goals**

Social and Emotional Development
- Child identifies self by categories (such as gender, age, family member, cultural group).
- Child describes personal interests and competencies positively (such as, "I can hop.").

Mathematics
- Child recognizes, names, describes, matches, compares, sorts common two-dimensional shapes (such as circle, square, rectangle, triangle, rhombus).

Vocabulary

circle	círculo	proud	orgulloso
rhombus	rombo	square	cuadrado
triangle	triángulo		
parallelogram	paralelogramo		

Differentiated Instruction

✋ **Extra Support**

Observe and Investigate

If...children have difficulty identifying shapes, **then...**display Pattern Block pieces and review the names of shapes with them.

⭐ **Enrichment**

Observe and Investigate

Challenge children to give "I Spy" clues, naming the shape of something in the classroom and having other children guess what it is.

Focus Question
How do people grow and change?
¿Cómo crece y cambia la gente?

Learning Goals

Language and Communication
• Child exhibits an understanding of instructional terms used in the classroom.

Mathematics
• Child creates two-dimensional shapes; recreates two-dimensional shapes from memory.
• Child manipulates (flips, rotates) and combines shapes.

Vocabulary

circle	círculo	triangle	triángulo
puzzle	rompecabezas	rhombus	rombo
solve	resolver	square	cuadrado
parallelogram	paralelogramo		

Differentiated Instruction

 Extra Support
Observe and Investigate
If...children need help making Pattern Block Puzzles, **then...**use your simplest puzzles, or use a pencil to draw lines within puzzles to guide children.

★ **Enrichment**
Observe and Investigate
Challenge children to do the hardest puzzles on their own, or have children solve one puzzle as many ways as they can.

Math Time

large group — 20 minutes

Language and Communication Skills Use shape names while modeling how to solve a puzzle, and encourage children to use the names as they work on puzzles themselves.

Oral Language and Academic Vocabulary

✓ **Can children identify shape names?**

Talk About Puzzles Remind children that they began doing puzzles on Day 1. They will continue to do more puzzles today. Ask: *What do you like about doing puzzles?* *¿Qué les gusta de armar rompecabezas?*

• Display *Math and Science Flip Chart* page 50 and have children name the shapes they used to complete Pattern Block Puzzle 1.

Observe and Investigate

✓ **Can children recreate patterns?**

Pattern Block Puzzles Have children work in small groups.

• Make copies of the Pattern Block Puzzles from the Flip Chart.

• Children choose and complete Pattern Block Puzzles. Make a big deal when new puzzles are introduced, as it motivates children.

• As necessary, help children recognize that they can flip or turn pattern blocks to make them fit the puzzle.

• For reinforcement, suggest children make their own unique puzzles using actual blocks, and then trace what they created to "see" the puzzle.

• Explain that as children work on puzzles, they will get better and better at doing them. As they grow, they will be able to do even harder puzzles.

TIP Tell children that they will have another chance to work with Pattern Block Puzzles in a few days.

ELL Place children in groups with English proficient learners so that they can hear shape words and puzzle-solving strategies being discussed in English.

Math and Science Flip Chart, p. 50

Center Time

▶ **Center Rotation** Center Time includes teacher-guided activities and independent activities. Refer to the **Learning Centers** on pages 100–101 for independent activity ideas.

 small group   30 minutes

Library and Listening Center

Center Tip

 Track children's listening skills and retention of information.

Materials drawing paper, crayons or washable markers

How Are We the Same? Tell children that they will draw and write about ways they and their families are like the boy and his family in *I'm Growing!*

- Display the Big Book *I'm Growing!* Then play the story CD and have children follow along as they listen.

- Have children draw to show one way that they are like the boy and one thing that his family does that their family does, too.

- Have children share and describe their pictures.

Center Tip

If...children need additional exposure to the Big Book before they draw, **then...**play the CD once more or have small groups go back to the Big Book to look through the illustrations.

Purposeful Play

 Observe children describing themselves and their abilities.

Children choose an open center for free playtime. Encourage children to take pride in their accomplishments by taking turns acting out things that they can do now that they couldn't do last year.

Let's Say Good-Bye

 large group   15 minutes

 Read Aloud Revisit the story, "Growing Up Dream"/"El sueño de crecer" for your afternoon Read Aloud. Remind children to listen for information about growing and changing.

 Home Connection Refer to the Home Connections activities listed in the Resources and Materials chart on page 97. Remind children to tell families about the Big Book *I'm Growing!* Sing the "Good-Bye Song" as the children prepare to leave.

✓ **Learning Goals**

Social and Emotional Development
• Child identifies self by categories (such as gender, age, family member, cultural group).

Emergent Literacy: Reading
• Child describes, relates to, and uses details and information from books read aloud.

Emergent Literacy: Writing
• Child uses scribbles, shapes, pictures, symbols, and letters to represent language.

Writing

Recap the day. Have children discuss what they learned about growing today. Create a list on chart paper as children dictate their responses. Then read aloud the list and have children write to complete a sentence frame:
I learned _____. *Hoy aprendí _____.*

Focus Question

How do people grow and change?
¿Cómo crece y cambia la gente?

Learning Goals

Social and Emotional Development
• Child identifies self by categories (such as gender, age, family member, cultural group).

• Child describes personal interests and competencies positively (such as, "I can hop.").

Language and Communication
• Child names and describes actual or pictured people, places, things, actions, attributes, and events.

• Child speaks in complete sentences of four or more words including a subject, verb, and object.

Vocabulary

book	libro	glasses	lentes
grandparent	abuelos	hair	cabello
old	mayor	teach	enseñar

Differentiated Instruction

 Extra Support

Phonological Awareness
If...children have difficulty telling whether or not two words have the same end sound, **then**...have children identify end sounds in individual words: *cat, big, nap, bed, brain, neck.*

 Enrichment

Phonological Awareness
Challenge children to tell partners two words that end with the same sound, and have the partner name the end sound.

Let's Start the Day

Opening Routines and Transition Tips
For **Opening Routines** and **Transition Tips** turn to pages 178–181 and visit DLMExpressOnline.com for more ideas.

 Read **"Miguel's Birthday"/**"El cumpleaños de Miguel" from the *Teacher's Treasure Book,* page 174, for your morning Read Aloud.

Language Time

large group — 15 minutes

Social and Emotional Development Identify specifics and compliment children's progress as they continue to learn about growing and changing.

Oral Language and Vocabulary

Can children describe why older family members are important?

Learn from Family Members Talk about the value of older family members. Ask: *What can an older family member teach you about your family? What stories might an older family member tell you?* ¿Qué puede enseñarles un miembro más grande de la familia acerca de su propia familia? ¿Qué cuentos o historias les podría contar una persona mayor? Explain that older family members often remember stories and important information that other family members might not know.

● Display *Oral Language Development Card 58.* Ask: **Who is the older person in this picture? What are the grandparent and the child doing?** ¿Quién es la persona mayor en esta fotografía? ¿Qué están haciendo el abuelo y los niños? Then follow the suggestions on the back of the card.

Oral Language Development Card 58

ELL Explain to children that grandparents are the parents of their mother or father. If they wish, have them share the names they use for their grandparents.

Phonological Awareness

Can children identify final sounds?

Recognize Final Sounds Revisit *Rhymes and Chants Flip Chart,* page 27. Remind children to listen for the end sounds in words as you chant "A Baby Grows" together. Repeat the chant with children using the movements. Ask: **Do day and way have the same end sound? What is that sound?** ¿Day y way terminan con el mismo sonido? ¿Qué sonido es ése? Repeat with other words in the chant: *walk/talk, tricycle/bicycle.* Then say: **Listen to these words. Clap if the end sound is the same:** *baby/teeth, lot/more, nap/top, me/that, brain/heart, book/neck.* Escuchen estas palabras. Den una palmada si el sonido final es el mismo: baby/teeth, lot/more, nap/top, me/that, brain/heart, book/neck.

A Baby Grows
When I was just a baby,
I drank milk every day.
But when I got some teeth,
I ate in a different way.

I crawled around the floor a lot,
And soon I learned to walk.
I said a word, and then some more.
That's how I learned to talk!

My car seat got too small for me.
I learned to ride a tricycle.
And after several years on that,
I learned to ride my bicycle!

Rhymes and Chants Flip Chart, p. 27

Center Time

Center Rotation Center Time includes teacher-guided activities and independent activities. Refer to the **Learning Centers** on pages 100–101 for independent activity ideas.

 small group 60–90 minutes

Refer to the **Learning Centers** on pages 100–101 for independent activity ideas.

ABC Center

Center Tip

✔ Track children's ability to recognize and write letters *Hh* and *Yy*.

Materials *ABC Picture Cards* for *Hh* and *Yy*, index cards

Letter Teams Write upper and lower case letters *Hh, Yy,* and the previously introduced letter *Jj* on index cards. Hide the cards around the classroom before children go to the center

- Display the *ABC Picture Cards* for *Hh* and *Yy* in the center. Have children trace the letters on the cards and review the /h/ and /y/ sounds. Then have children separate into two teams.

- Challenge each team to find as many *Hh* cards as they can. Explain that children should only pick up *Hh* cards, and not other letter cards.

- After the letter hunt, have teams return to the center to count the number of *Hh* cards they found. The team with the most cards wins.

- Have children repeat to find *Yy* cards.

If...children have difficulty finding the cards you hid, **then...**give them clues: *You're getting warmer! You're getting cooler! Do you think you might find a card under that book?*

Creativity Center

Center Tip

✔ Track children's understanding of how plants, animals, and people grow.

Materials butcher paper, pictures from old magazines and catalogs, scissors, glue

"How It Grows" Collage Tell children that they will reread the *Concept Big Book 3* today. Have them get ready for the reading by making a "How It Grows" collage. Have children decide whether their collage will show plants, animals, or humans. Children can vote to determine the subject of their collage.

- Have children find and cut out pictures of their subject from old magazines and catalogs. Explain that children can show different animals, plants, or people, but the collage should show stages of growth as well as what the living thing needs to grow. Have children glue their pictures on the butcher paper and display their collage in the center.

If...children have difficulty finding the pictures they need in magazines or catalogs, **then...**invite them to draw their own pictures to add to the collage.

Learning Goals

Emergent Literacy: Reading
- Child names most upper- and lowercase letters of the alphabet.
- Child identifies the letter that stands for a given sound.

Science
- Child identifies organisms and describes their characteristics.
- Child understands and describes life cycles of plants and animals.
- Child observes, understands, and discusses the relationship of plants and animals to their environments.

Social Studies
- Child participates in voting for group decision-making.

Differentiated Instruction

 Extra Support

Creativity Center
If...children need ideas for creating their collage, **then...**display the *Concept Big Book* in the center and have them use the photographs as a guide to what they might show.

 Enrichment

Creativity Center
Challenge children to point to pictures in their collage as they describe what living things need and how they grow.

 Special Needs

Behavioral/Social/Emotional
If you see that a child is getting frustrated or upset by an activity, "redirect" him or her to something that is less stressful.

Focus Question

How do people grow and change?

¿Cómo crece y cambia la gente?

large group | 15 minutes

Read Aloud

 Can children tell how animals, plants, and humans grow and change?

Build Background Tell children that you will be rereading the *Concept Big Book 3: Growing and Changing/Creciendo y cambiando.*

- Display the book and ask: **What did we learn in this book? What kinds of things change and grow?** *¿Qué aprendimos en este libro? ¿Qué cosas cambian y crecen?*

Listen for Understanding Reread the *Concept Big Book 3,* tracking the print with your hand as you point to details in the pictures. As you read, pause to allow children to answer the questions in the text. Ask: **What do living things need as they grow?** *¿Qué necesitan los seres vivos para crecer?*

Respond to the Story Have children describe how things grow. Ask: **How do chickens grow? How do plants grow? How do human babies grow? How do caterpillars grow?** *¿Cómo crecen los pollitos? ¿Y las plantas? ¿Y los bebés? ¿Y las orugas?*

ELL Support comprehension by having children act out animals in the *Concept Big Book 3:* **Pretend you're a chick. Pop your head out of the egg. Pretend you're a mother bird. Feed your babies.** For additional suggestions on how to meet the needs of children at the Beginning, Intermediate, Advanced, or Advanced-High levels of English proficiency, see pages 184–187.

Learn About Letters and Sounds

 Can children identify sounds and letters /h/ and /y/?

Review Letters and Sounds /h/h, /y/y Have children sit in a circle to sing the "ABC Song." Tell them to stand when they sing the letters *h* and *y*. Ask: **Are h and y close together in the alphabet or are they far apart?** *¿Están cerca en el acededario la h y la y? ¿O están muy lejos una de otra?*

- Display the *ABC Big Book* and have volunteers find *Hh* and *Yy* in the book.

- Name each letter and say the sound as you trace over it in the book. Have children repeat as they trace the letters in the air.

- Give children containers of water. Have them dip their fingers in water and write the letters with water on the chalkboard as they say the letter sounds.

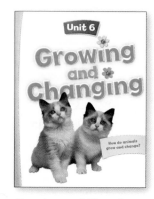

Unit 6
Growing and Changing

Growing and Changing
Creciendo y cambiando

Hh
horse

Yy
yawn

---

large group | 15 minutes

Math Time

Observe and Investigate

 Can children sort objects and describe how the groups are the same and different?

Guess My Rule Ask children to watch carefully as you sort Pattern Block shapes into piles based on something that makes them all alike.

- Tell children to silently guess your sorting rule, such as rhombuses versus all other shapes. Sort shapes one at a time, continuing until there are at least two shapes in each pile.

- Signal "shhh," and pick up a new shape. With a look of confusion, gesture to children to point quietly to which pile the shape belongs. Place the shape in its pile. Repeat this process until many shapes are sorted into each pile.

- Ask children to name your sorting rule and explain their answer.

  ELL Make sure children can name all the shapes that you use in the sorting activity, and review the shape names if needed.

large group | 15 minutes

👪 Social and Emotional Development

Making Good Choices

 Do children understand the importance of recognizing their own abilities?

Trying New Things Display *Making Good Choices Flip Chart* page 27, "Trying New Things." Review the game that the children on the chart are playing, and talk about how doing new things can make you feel proud of yourself.

- With the dog puppet, role-play other situations to model a willingness to try new things and an awareness of one's own limitations. For example, ask the puppet to clap ten times. Have the puppet clap enthusiastically and then describe what it can do: *I can clap! I can clap ten times! ¡Puedo aplaudir! ¡Puedo aplaudir diez veces!* Then ask the puppet to clap to fifty. Have the puppet politely decline: *I'm sorry. I can't count that high. Right now, I can count to 10; soon I'll be able to count to 50. Lo siento. No puedo contar hasta un número tan alto. Puedo contar hasta 10. Pronto podré contar hasta 50..* Compliment the puppet on its abilities and awareness of its limitations.

- After each role play, ask: *What can the puppet do? What can't the puppet do? Does the puppet feel proud of what it can do? ¿Qué puede hacer el títere? ¿Qué cosa no puede hacer? ¿El títere se siente orgulloso de lo que sí puede hacer?*

Building Blocks

Online Math Activity

Children can complete Piece Puzzler 1 and Piece Puzzler 2 during computer time or Center Time.

Making Good Choices Flip Chart, p. 27

 Learning Goals

Social and Emotional Development
- Child identifies self by categories (such as gender, age, family member, cultural group).
- Child describes personal interests and competencies positively (such as, "I can hop.").

Mathematics
- Child sorts objects and explains how the sorting was done.

Vocabulary

proud	orgulloso	rule	regla
rectangle	rectángulo	rhombus	rombo
parallelogram	paralelogramo		

Differentiated Instruction

 Extra Support
Observe and Investigate
If...children struggle during Guess My Rule, **then...**use simpler rules, such as squares versus circles.

Enrichment
Observe and Investigate
Draw shapes and have children guess your rule, such as shapes sorted by number of sides or angles, rectangles versus "foolers" (shapes that look just like rectangles but are not closed or parallelograms without right angles).

Accommodations for 3's
Observe and Investigate
If...children are confused by Guess My Rule, **then...**sort two familiar shapes, such as circles and squares, into two piles and have them tell what you did.

Focus Question
How do people grow and change?
¿Cómo crece y cambia la gente?

Learning Goals

Social and Emotional Development
• Child shows eagerness, curiosity, and confidence while learning new concepts and trying new things.

Language and Communication
• Child names and describes actual or pictured people, places, things, actions, attributes, and events.

Social Studies
• Child understands basic human needs for food, clothing, shelter.

• Child understands basic concepts of buying, selling, and trading.

• Child participates in voting for group decision-making.

Vocabulary

buy	comprar	clothes	ropa
cost	costar	grow	crecer
store	tienda	vote	votar

Differentiated Instruction

 Extra Support
Understand and Participate
If...children have difficulty choosing one item from all the clothing pieces shown in the Photo Library, **then...**limit their choices for the vote: *Let's vote on what we will sell in our store. Should we sell shirts, pants, or coats? Vamos a votar sobre qué venderemos en nuestra tienda. ¿Venderemos camisas, pantalones o abrigos?*

 Enrichment
Understand and Participate
Challenge children to act out the process of returning an item to the store to ask for their money back.

Social Studies Time

large group · 20 minutes

Social and Emotional Development Watch for ways that children remain focused throughout the entire activity.

Oral Language and Academic Vocabulary

✓ **Can children use the voting process to make decisions together?**

Take a Vote Remind children that as they grow, they become too big for their clothes. Ask: *What can you do when your clothes get too small? Where can you buy new clothes? ¿Qué pueden hacer cuando su ropa les queda demasiado pequeña? ¿Dónde pueden comprar ropa nueva?*

● Tell children that they will set up a clothing store in the classroom. Display pictures of clothing in the Photo Library. Have children vote on one item to sell in their store, such as shirts, pants, or coats.

Understand and Participate

✓ **Can children make good consumer choices?**

Shop for New Clothes Set up a store in the classroom with a toy cash register or cash box, counters to use as coins, and a display area.

● Give children colored construction paper and have them draw and cut out the item of clothing in different colors. Say: *We'll use counters to buy the clothes. Put a number from 1 to 10 on each one to show how much it costs. Usaremos las fichas para comprar la ropa. Pongan un número del 1 al 10 en cada prenda para mostrar cuánto cuesta.*

● Have children stock the store with their items. Then give children ten counters each and have them go shopping. Children can take turns being storeowners who take the counters as money.

● After children shop, have them report on their purchases: *What did you buy for your ten counters? How many pieces of clothing did you get? ¿Qué compraron con sus diez fichas? ¿Cuántas ropas compraron?*

TIP Set up the clothing store before the activity begins and create templates for the chosen clothing item to make it easier for children to "stock" their store.

ELL Use the Photo Library pictures and the language translation feature to teach children the names of clothing items.

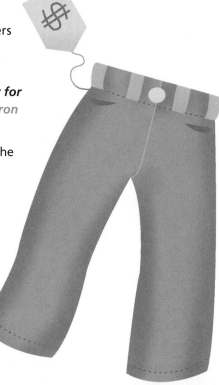
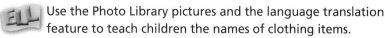

Center Time

Center Rotation Center Time includes teacher-guided activities and independent activities. Refer to the **Learning Centers** on pages 100–101 for independent activity ideas.

Construction Center

 Track children's knowledge of caterpillar and butterfly traits.

Materials green construction paper, Pattern Blocks, scissors, glue, white paper, crayons or washable markers, chenille sticks

Caterpillars and Butterflies Reinforce concepts from the *Concept Big Book* by having children make caterpillars and butterflies.

- Have children trace and cut out circles from green construction paper. Then have them overlap the circles and glue them to make a caterpillar. Encourage them to draw a face on their caterpillar.

- Have children make butterflies by coloring a sheet of paper and then folding it accordion style. Have them wrap a chenille stick around the middle to make a butterfly. Encourage children to talk about how the life cycle of caterpillars differs from the way boys and girls grow.

Center Tip

If...children struggle to create their creatures, **then...** model the steps for them or help them complete difficult steps such as gluing the circles or wrapping the chenille stick around the paper.

Purposeful Play

Observe children as they cooperate to work in groups.

Children choose an open center for free playtime. Allow children to demonstrate their knowledge and take pride in their accomplishments by using their constructions to act out the life cycle of a caterpillar. Provide stones or Shape Blocks to represent caterpillar eggs.

Let's Say Good-Bye

Read Aloud Revisit the story, "Miguel's Birthday"/"El cumpleaños de Miguel" for your afternoon Read Aloud. Remind children to listen for the names of different kinds of animals.

 Home Connection Refer to the Home Connections activities listed in the Resources and Materials chart on page 97. Remind children to tell families about the way all living things change and grow. Sing the "Good-Bye Song" as children prepare to leave.

Learning Goals

Social and Emotional Development
- Child identifies self by categories (such as gender, age, family member, cultural group).
- Child describes personal interests and competencies positively (such as, "I can hop.").

Language and Communication
- Child names and describes actual or pictured people, places, things, actions, attributes, and events.

Emergent Literacy: Writing
- Child uses scribbles, shapes, pictures, symbols, and letters to represent language.

Science
- Child identifies organisms and describes their characteristics.

Writing

Recap the day. Say: *Today we talked about how plants, animals, and people grow and change. What is one important thing you want to remember?* Hoy hablamos sobre cómo crecen y cambian las plantas, los animales y las personas. ¿Qué recuerdan sobre lo que hablamos hoy? Record answers on chart paper. Share the pen by having children write letters and words they know.

Focus Question

How do people grow and change?

¿Cómo crece y cambia la gente?

Learning Goals

Social and Emotional Development

• Child identifies self by categories (such as gender, age, family member, cultural group).

• Child describes personal interests and competencies positively (such as, "I can hop.").

Language and Communication

• Child uses oral language for a variety of purposes.

• Child speaks in complete sentences of four or more words including a subject, verb, and object.

Vocabulary

choices	decisiones	growing	crecer
learning	aprender	lie	mentir
truth	verdad		

Differentiated Instruction

 Extra Support

Phonological Awareness

If...children have difficulty generating words for their partner, **then...**supply the following words: *bag, hat, lid, hop, bell, pen.*

 Enrichment

Oral Language and Vocabulary

Challenge children to name other good choices that children their age can make.

 Special Needs

Vision Loss

If the child has peripheral vision, make sure s/he is seated so that her/his peripheral vision is optimized and that lighting is appropriate and does not cause a "glare" effect.

Let's Start the Day

 Opening Routines and Transition Tips

For **Opening Routines** and **Transition Tips** turn to pages 178–181 and visit **DLMExpressOnline.com** for more ideas.

📖 Read **"The More You Grow"/**"*Crecer y aprender*" from the *Teacher's Treasure Book,* page 116, for your morning Read Aloud.

Language Time

large group · 15 minutes

Social and Emotional Development Ask children what they should do if they don't know how to act in a situation.

Oral Language and Vocabulary

✅ Can children understand that their actions also affect other people?

Good Choices Tell children that as they've been growing, they've also been learning to make good choices. Say: ***One good choice you can make is to always tell the truth.*** *Una buena decisión es decir siempre la verdad.* Ask: ***Has anyone ever lied to you and you found out? How might someone feel if you lied to them?*** *¿Alguien alguna vez les ha mentido y ustedes se dieron cuenta? ¿Cómo se sentiría una persona si ustedes le mintieran?*

● Explain that you will read a story about a boy who doesn't tell the truth. Ask: ***How would you feel if you knew someone wasn't telling you the truth? What would you say to that person?*** *¿Cómo se sentirían si descubrieran que alguien no les dice la verdad? ¿Qué le dirían a esa persona?*

● Model responses: ***Please tell me the truth. I get confused when you lie to me. Friends don't try to hide things from each other. I would feel sad or angry. I would feel like I don't want to be their friend.*** *Por favor dime la verdad. Me siento confundido cuando me mientes. Los amigos no tratan de ocultarse cosas. Si me mientes, me sentiré triste o enojado. Sentiré que no quiero que seamos amigos.* Then have children tell what they would say.

Phonological Awareness

✅ Can children identify final sounds?

Recognize End Sounds Display the dog puppets. Have one puppet say: ***Listen to my word:*** dog. ***Can you tell me the end sound in*** dog? *Escucha esta palabra:* dog. *¿Puedes decirme el sonido final de* dog? Have the other puppet say: ***Yes!*** **Dog** ***ends with the /g/ sound. Now can you tell me the end sound in*** cat? *¡Sí!* Dog *termina con el sonido /g/. ¿Puedes decirme tú con que sonido termina* cat? **Continue in this way with other words such as** *bed, mop, doll*, and *pin*. Then have partners take turns asking each other about the end sound in words.

ELL Give children counters. Say a word sound by sound and have children put a counter in front of them for each sound: **/b/ /e/ /d/, bed.** Say the sounds again with children as they point to the counters. Have them name the last sound.

Center Time

▶ **Center Rotation** Center Time includes teacher-guided activities and independent activities. Refer to the **Learning Centers** on pages 100–101 for independent activity ideas.

Library and Listening Center

Center Tip

 Track children's ability to share their knowledge of folk tales and fairy tales.

Materials traditional folk tale and fairy tale books

Talk About Story Characters Have children look through folk tale and fairy tale books.

- Say: *Look through the books. What happens to the people in the stories? How do animals in the stories act like people?* *Hojeen los libros. ¿Qué les sucede a los personajes de estos cuentos? ¿Por qué los animales actúan como personas?*

- Encourage children to tell each other stories that include wolves, such as "Little Red Riding Hood" and "The Three Little Pigs."

- Have children discuss how real wolves grow. Prompt them to recognize that real wolves are not the sneaky or mean characters that are often shown in some fairy tales.

Center Tip

If...children have difficulty describing the growth cycle of real wolves, **then**...display the picture of baby foxes on page 20 of the *Concept Big Book*. Say: *Baby wolves need a safe place, too. Their mother takes care of them as they grow.* *Los cachorros de los lobos también necesitan un lugar seguro para vivir. Su madre los cuida mientras crecen.*

Writer's Center

 Track children's ability to write a story with a beginning, middle, and end.

Materials paper, crayons or washable markers

Write a Tale Invite children to write a fairy tale of their own.

- Say: *Write a fairy tale about a child and an animal who are friends. Remember, animals in fairy tales can talk and act like people.* *Inventen un cuento de hadas sobre un niño y un animal que son amigos. Recuerden: los animales de los cuentos de hadas pueden hablar y actuar como personas.*

- Have children draw a picture to show what happens in the beginning, in the middle, and at the end of their story. Encourage them to write about their pictures.

- Invite children to share their stories during Center Time. Have them point to the pictures as they tell what happens.

Center Tip

If...children are hesitant to share their story with others, **then**...acknowledge their efforts and invite them to tell you the story, or have them share their story with family members.

✔ Learning Goals

Language and Communication
- Child uses oral language for a variety of purposes.

Emergent Literacy: Reading
- Child enjoys and chooses reading-related activities.

Emergent Literacy: Writing
- Child experiments with and uses some writing conventions when writing or dictating.

Science
- Child identifies organisms and describes their characteristics.
- Child understands and describes life cycles of plants and animals.

Differentiated Instruction

✋ **Extra Support**
Writing Center
If...children have difficulty writing a story with a beginning, middle, and end, **then**...reread one of the folk tales or fairy tales in the center and point out the beginning, middle, and end of that story.

★ **Enrichment**
Writing Center
Challenge children to write at least one complete sentence for each picture they draw. Model complete sentences for children as needed.

Accommodations for 3's
Writing Center
If...children struggle to write a story with sequenced events, **then**...have them draw a picture of a person and an animal that are friends, and have them tell about it.

Focus Question
How do people grow and change?
¿Cómo crece y cambia la gente?

Circle Time

Literacy Time

📖 Read Aloud

✓ **Can children relate to the lesson in a folk tale?**

Build Background Tell children that you will be reading story about a boy who lives in the country.

- Ask: **What kinds of animals live in the country?** *¿Qué tipos de animales viven en el campo?* Explain that people in the country often raise sheep. Say: **People who take care of sheep in the fields are called shepherds.** *A las personas que cuidan las ovejas en los campos se las llama pastores.*

Listen for Enjoyment Read aloud *Teacher's Treasure Book*, page 235, "The Boy Who Cried Wolf"/"El niño y el lobo"

- Tell children to pay attention to the way the boy acts.

- Ask: **What does the boy do that upsets people? How do they teach him a lesson?** *¿Qué hace el niño que enfada a la gente? ¿Qué lección le dan estas personas al niño?*

Respond to the Story Have children tell what the boy does after the people teach him a lesson. Ask: **How would you feel afterwards if you were the boy? Would you lie again?** *¿Cómo se sentirían ustedes si fueran ese niño? ¿Volverían a mentir?*

💡 **TIP** As you read, emphasize the father's feelings about lying by shaking your head in disapproval as you read his words "Lying is not right" in a stern voice.

ELL Pause during the story to let children act out events. Say: **Let's yell, "Wolf! Wolf!" together. Let's laugh like the boy might laugh.** Model actions.

Learn About Letters and Sounds

✓ **Can children identify sounds and letters /h/h and /y/y?**

Review Letters and Sounds /h/h, /y/y Display the *ABC Picture Cards* for *Hh* and *Yy*. Point to each letter. **What is the name of this letter? What is the sound?** *¿Cómo se llama esta letra? ¿Qué sonido tiene?*

- Say: **H** *is for hand.* *La H está en hand.* **Put up your hand.** **Y** *is for yo-yo.* *La Y está en yo-yo.* **Pretend to play with a yo-yo.** **H** *is for head.* **Touch your head.** **Y** *is for yes.* *La Y está en yes.* **Shake your head yes.**

- Have children recite *hand, yo-yo, head,* and *yes* one word at a time. Ask: **What sound do you hear at the beginning of the word?** *¿Qué sonido escuchan al principio de cada palabra?*

- Have children trace *Hh* and *Yy* in the air as they say the sounds: /h/, /y/.

Teacher's Treasure Book

Math Time

Observe and Investigate

 Can children identify the missing number in a counting sequence?

What's the Missing Card? Tell children that they will figure out which number their partner has hidden.

- Have children work together to put Counting Cards 1–5 in numerical order.

- While one child shuts his or her eyes, the other hides a card.

- After the card is hidden, that child tells the other to look and then asks which card is missing.

- Once a child figures out the missing card, he or she should explain how he or she knew.

ELL Help familiarize children with number words *one* to *five* by having them count in rhythm with you as you clap or snap for each word. For additional suggestions on how to meet the needs of children at the Beginning, Intermediate, Advanced, and Advanced-High levels of English proficiency, see pages 184–187.

☆☆☆ Social and Emotional Development

Making Good Choices

 Can children appreciate their own abilities and recognize their limitations?

Trying New Things Display the Dog Puppets and a wooden puzzle or Pattern Blocks.

- Tell children that the puppets are solving puzzles together. Model a dialogue between the puppets. For example, Puppet 1: *I like to solve puzzles. I'm good at doing it! Let's do this new puzzle together.* *Me encanta resolver rompecabezas. ¡Soy muy bueno para armarlos! Hagamos juntos este nuevo rompecabezas.*
Puppet 2: *I like to do puzzles, too. I can't do puzzles with a lot of pieces yet. But I'll try this new one with you. I know I can learn as I try new things!* *A mí también me gusta armar rompecabezas. Pero todavía no puedo resolver los rompecabezas de muchas piezas. De todos modos, intentaré hacerlo contigo. ¡Sé que puedo aprender mientras intento hacer nuevas cosas!*

- Ask: *What can the puppets do? How do they feel about what they can do? ¿Qué pueden hacer los títeres? ¿Cómo se sienten con respecto a lo que pueden hacer?*

- Remind children that they should be proud of what they can do well and try new things whenever they get a chance.

Online Math Activity

Children can complete Piece Puzzler 1 during computer time or Center Time.

 Learning Goals

Social and Emotional Development
- Child identifies self by categories (such as gender, age, family member, cultural group).
- Child describes personal interests and competencies positively (such as, "I can hop.").

Mathematics
- Child demonstrates that the numerical counting sequence is always the same.

Vocabulary

missing	faltante	solve	resolver
proud	orgulloso	puzzle	rompecabezas
numerical order	orden númerico		

Differentiated Instruction

✋ Extra Support

Observe and Investigate

If...children struggle with the activity, count each card with them; use fewer cards; provide a list of numerals for reference; or use the dog puppet to model a counting strategy.

⭐ Enrichment

Observe and Investigate

Use more cards for the activity, or have the child who hides the card close the gap between cards before the other child guesses.

Focus Question
How do people grow and change?
¿Cómo crece y cambia la gente?

Learning Goals

Language and Communication
• Child demonstrates an understanding of oral language by responding appropriately.

Mathematics
• Child recognizes, names, describes, matches, compares, sorts common two-dimensional shapes (such as circle, square, rectangle, triangle, rhombus).

• Child manipulates (flips, rotates) and combines shapes.

• Child identifies, duplicates, and creates simple patterns.

Vocabulary

line	línea	match	coincidir
shape	figura	symmetry	simetría

Differentiated Instruction

 Extra Support

Observe and Investigate

If...children have difficulty understanding rotational symmetry, **then...**have them focus on line symmetry and create patterns with halves that match when folded in half.

Enrichment

Observe and Investigate

Challenge partners to create symmetrical patterns with Pattern Blocks and trade them to find the symmetry in each other's designs.

Dramatic Play Time

  large group 20 minutes

Language and Communication Skills As children create their designs, ask questions about symmetry as appropriate to the group.

Oral Language and Academic Vocabulary

✓ **Can children understand the concept of symmetry?**

Talk About Symmetry Draw a symmetrical shape on paper, such as a heart, and place a mirror along the symmetry line. Have children look at the shape. What do they notice? Point out that the two sides of the shape match each other. Cut out the shape and fold it in half to reinforce the concept. Explain that the shape has *symmetry*.

Observe and Investigate

✓ **Can children identify shapes and patterns with symmetry?**

Use Pattern Blocks Display *Math and Science Flip Chart*, page 50. Point out the symmetrical Pattern Block Puzzles and move your hand along the line of symmetry that divides each puzzle into two equal parts in each puzzle. Have children create the puzzles with blocks.

● Then have children make their own designs by tracing Pattern Blocks. Watch what they do with the blocks. Children are naturally attracted to symmetrical designs. Discussing their designs is a wonderful starting point for learning more about symmetry.

● Children's patterns may have line symmetry (folded shape halves fit on each other), rotational symmetry (a shape can be turned and fit on itself, like a parallelogram), or both types of symmetry.

TIP You may wish to point out and discuss the symmetry in children's designs without using the terms *line symmetry* and *rotational symmetry*.

ELL Point out to Spanish speaking children the similarity between the word *symmetry* in English and *simetría* in their own language.

Math and Science Flip Chart, p. 50

Building Blocks

Online Math Activity

Children can complete Piece Puzzler 2 during computer time or Center Time.

Center Time

 small group   30 minutes

Learning Goals

Language and Communication
• Child speaks in complete sentences of four or more words including a subject, verb, and object.

Emergent Literacy: Writing
• Child experiments with and uses some writing conventions when writing or dictating.

Mathematics
• Child manipulates (flips, rotates) and combines shapes.

Math and Science Center

✓ **Track children's ability to create a symmetrical figure.**

Materials paper, crayons or washable markers, scissors, Big Book *I'm Growing!*

Line Symmetry Display the picture on page 5 of the Big Book *I'm Growing!* Hold your hand to indicate a line of symmetry on the boy to demonstrate that his body is the same on both sides.

● Show children how to fold a sheet of paper in half and draw half of a body along the fold. Have children unfold their paper to see a whole body shape that is symmetrical.

● Then have children draw facial features on the body, such as eyes, a nose, and a mouth. Provide a large mirror and have children use it to view the symmetry in their own faces.

Center Tip

If...children have difficulty drawing half of a body along the paper fold, **then**...provide a template for tracing and show them where to place it.

Writing

Recap the day. Ask: **What lesson did you learn from the story "The Boy Who Cried Wolf"?** *¿Qué lección aprendieron del cuento "El niño y el lobo"?* Have children draw and write about the lesson they learned. If needed, help them write words dictated to you.

Purposeful Play

✓ **Observe children demonstrating concepts from the story.**

Children choose an open center for free playtime. Encourage them to think about how a person's actions can affect others as they act out the story "The Boy Who Cried Wolf."

Let's Say Good-Bye

 large group   15 minutes

 Read Aloud Revisit the story, "The More You Grow"/*"Crecer y aprender"* for your afternoon Read Aloud. Ask children to tell what they like best about this story.

 Home Connection Refer to the Home Connections activities listed in the Resources and Materials chart on page 97. Remind children to retell the story "The Boy Who Cried Wolf" to their families. Sing the "Good-Bye Song" as children prepare to leave.

DAY 5

Focus Question

How do people grow and change?

¿Cómo crece y cambia la gente?

✓ Learning Goals

Social and Emotional Development
• Child identifies self by categories (such as gender, age, family member, cultural group).
• Child describes personal interests and competencies positively (such as, "I can hop.").

Language and Communication
• Child names and describes actual or pictured people, places, things, actions, attributes, and events.
• Child speaks in complete sentences of four or more words including a subject, verb, and object.

Vocabulary

baby	pequeño	change	cambiar
grow	crecer	grown-up	adulto
people	personas		

Differentiated Instruction

 Extra Support

Oral Language and Vocabulary
If...children have difficulty describing what they can do now and what they might do as an adult, **then...**invite them to act out their responses.

 Enrichment

Oral Language and Vocabulary
Invite partners to play a game about the human body in the Photo Library. To play, click on Game Time! Then select the Human Body category and play the "Select the Correct Picture" game.

Let's Start the Day

> **Opening Routines and Transition Tips**
> For **Opening Routines** and **Transition Tips** turn to pages 178–181 and visit **DLMExpressOnline.com** for more ideas.

 Read **"Keiko's Good Thinking"/**"*Keiko resuelve un problema*" from the *Teacher's Treasure Book,* page 169, for your morning Read Aloud.

Language Time

large group 15 minutes

 **Social and Emotional Development** Acknowledge children's efforts this week and compliment their eagerness to try new things.

Oral Language and Vocabulary

✓ **Can children describe how people change as they grow?**

Same and Different Talk with children about their work this week. Say: ***This week we learned how people grow and change. How do children change as they grow?*** *Esta semana aprendimos cómo crece y cambia la gente. ¿Cómo cambian los niños a medida que crecen?*

● Display *Rhymes and Chants Flip Chart,* page 27. Chant "A Baby Grows" with children as you perform the movements with them. Ask: ***What can you do now that you couldn't do when you were a baby? What do you think you will be able to do when you are a grown-up?*** *¿Qué pueden hacer ahora que no podían hacer cuando eran pequeños? ¿Qué creen que serán capaces de hacer cuando sean adultos?*

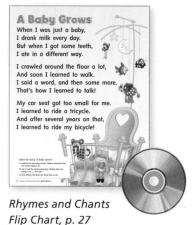

A Baby Grows

When I was just a baby,
I drank milk every day.
But when I got some teeth,
I ate in a different way.

I crawled around the floor a lot,
And soon I learned to walk.
I said a word, and then some more.
That's how I learned to talk!

My car seat got too small for me.
I learned to ride a tricycle.
And after several years on that,
I learned to ride my bicycle!

Rhymes and Chants Flip Chart, p. 27

Phonological Awareness

✓ **Can children identify final sounds?**

Recognize Final Sounds Chant "A Baby Grows" with children once more. Point to the crib in the picture. Say: ***Let's say the word*** crib ***together:*** crib. ***What is the end sound in the word*** crib? ***What other word in the chant ends with the /b/ sound?*** *Digamos juntos la palabra* crib: crib. *¿Qué sonido escuchan al final de la palabra* crib? *¿Qué otra palabra del poema termina con /b/?* Repeat with the words *walk/talk* and *day/way*.

ELL Have three children stand in line to make a "living" word. Have the first child say /kr/, the second child say /i/, and the third child say /b/. Then have them repeat their sounds faster. ***When I put the sounds together I get the word*** crib. ***What is the word? What is the last sound in*** crib? (Point to the child saying the /b/ sound.) Repeat with other words.

Center Time

▶ **Center Rotation** Center Time includes teacher-guided activities and independent activities. Refer to the **Learning Centers** on pages 100–101 for independent activity ideas.

 small group 60–90 minutes

Creativity Center

 Track children's knowledge of their own abilities and limitations.

Materials Big Book *I'm Growing!*, poster board, crayons or washable markers

Try a New Game Display the picture of children on page 22 of the Big Book *I'm Growing!*/*¡Estoy creciendo!* Have children discuss what kind of game the children in the picture might be playing.

- Tell children to think of a new game for the classroom. Explain that the game may include a ball if they wish. The game should be something that everyone in class can play.

- Have children work together to make rules for their game. They can draw on poster board to show how the game is played and then write below their drawing.

- Have children try their new game in the classroom.

Center Tip

If...children need more space to play their game, **then...** invite them to play the game on the playground at recess.

Pretend and Learn Center

 Track children's ability to describe themselves accurately.

Materials Big Book *I'm Growing!*, poster board paper, crayons or washable markers, scissors, glue or tape

New Clothes Point out the boy on page 5 of the Big Book *I'm Growing!* and read his words aloud.

- Invite children to draw a figure of a child on poster board. Tell them to draw their own face and hair on the figure but no other details. Have them cut out their figures.

- Have children draw and cut out paper clothes for the figure. Tell them to first draw clothes that are too small and place them on the figure as they say: **Look at me! I'm growing. My clothes don't fit.** *¡Mírenme! Estoy creciendo. Mi ropa ya no me queda.*

- Then have children make clothes that fit and tape or glue them on the figure. Prompt them to tell what they would say about having new clothes.

Center Tip

If...children are familiar with paper dolls, **then...**have them create tabs on items of clothing and use the tabs to attach the clothing to the figure.

Learning Goals

Social and Emotional Development
- Child identifies self by categories (such as gender, age, family member, cultural group).
- Child describes personal interests and competencies positively (such as, "I can hop.").

Emergent Literacy: Writing
- Child experiments with and uses some writing conventions when writing or dictating.

Science
- Child identifies organisms and describes their characteristics.

Differentiated Instruction

Extra Support
Pretend and Learn Center
If...children have difficulty creating the figure or the clothes, **then...**have them draw pictures of themselves in clothes that are too small and pictures of themselves in clothes that fit.

Enrichment
Creativity Center
Challenge children to make a book that describes their new game and add it to the classroom library.

Accommodations for 3's
Creativity Center
If...children have difficulty describing their ideas for a new game, **then...**have them act out their ideas for the group.

How do people grow and change?

¿Cómo crece y cambia la gente?

Circle Time

Literacy Time

large group · 15 minutes

 Learning Goals

Emergent Literacy: Reading
• Child names most upper- and lowercase letters of the alphabet.
• Child identifies the letter that stands for a given sound.
• Child describes, relates to, and uses details and information from books read aloud.

Mathematics
• Child compares the length, height, weight, volume (capacity), area of people or objects.

Science
• Child identifies organisms and describes their characteristics.
• Child understands and describes life cycles of plants and animals.

Vocabulary

bigger	más grande	growing	crecer
heavier	más pesado	older	mayor
taller	más alto		

 Differentiated Instruction

 Extra Support

Learn About Letters and Sounds
If...children have difficulty writing the letters *Hh* and *Yy*, **then...**use pencil to lightly draw the letters on paper, and have children trace over the letters with crayons.

Enrichment

Learn About Letters and Sounds
Challenge children to name and write other words that begin with the sounds /h/ and /y/.

Special Needs

Speech and Language Delays
Use simple sentences and ask the child to tell you what you just said.

📖 Read Aloud

✓ **Can children describe ways that people grow?**

Build Background Tell children that you will be rereading the book *I'm Growing!/¡Estoy creciendo!* Display the Big Book. Point to the title.

● Ask: *Which of the children on the cover tells this story? What does he say about growing? ¿Cuál de los niños de la portada cuenta este cuento? ¿Qué dice ese niño acerca de crecer?*

Listen for Understanding Reread the book to review how people grow and change. Discuss with children one way people change is they gain weight as they grow. Have children compare how much they weigh now to how much they weighed when they were a baby. Ask children how much they think they will weigh when they get older.

● As you read, encourage children to chime in with words that they remember.

● Pause often to allow children to relate to the pictures: *"I have a lot of baby pictures, too." "I'm losing some of my teeth, too." "My hair looks a lot like Louie's hair!"*

Respond and Connect Have children connect their new learning to their daily lives. Ask: *How will you keep changing as you grow? ¿Cómo seguirán cambiando ustedes a medida que crezcan?*

TIP Make sure children understand that everyone in class will grow at different rates, and that staying healthy and eating nutritious foods will help them grow.

Learn About Letters and Sounds

✓ **Can children identify sounds and letters /h/h and /y/y?**

Review Letters and Sounds /h/h, /y/y Display *ABC Picture Cards* for *Hh* and *Yy*. Say the name of each letter and its sound as you point to it.

● Ask children to trace each letter in the air as they say the sound.

● Have children write each letter on paper as they say the letter sound.

● Display pictures for *yellow, hands, head, yo-yo, yogurt,* and *horse,* from the Photo Library. Have children say each word with you, identify the beginning sound, and name the letter that stands for the sound.

ELL As you access pictures from the Photo Library, have children listen to the names of the pictures in English. Then have them listen to the words in their home language.

I'm Growing!
¡Estoy creciendo!

Hh — horse
Yy — yawn

Math Time

Observe and Investigate

✓ **Can children recreate patterns?**

Pattern Block Puzzles This activity is a variation of the activity introduced on Day 2.

● Display *Math and Science Flip Chart,* page 50. Have children choose and complete Pattern Block Puzzles.

● Make a big deal when puzzles are completed, as it motivates children.

● For reinforcement, suggest children make their own unique puzzles using actual blocks, and then trace what they created to "see" the puzzle.

ELL Help children expand their vocabulary by pairing them with proficient partners who have a good grasp of mathematical terms. For additional suggestions on how to meet the needs of children at the Beginning, Intermediate, Advanced, and Advanced-High levels of English proficiency, see pages 184–187.

Math and Science Flip Chart, p. 50

Building Blocks

Online Math Activity

Children can complete Piece Puzzler 1 and Piece Puzzler 2 during computer time or Center Time.

✗✗✗ Social and Emotional Development

Making Good Choices

✓ **Do children understand the importance of trying new things?**

Trying New Things Display *Making Good Choices Flip Chart* page 27, "Trying New Things."

● Point to the flip chart illustration. Say: ***The children are trying their best as they play a new game. What did we learn about trying our best when we do things? How does trying new things make you feel?*** *Los niños están intentando hacer todo lo posible mientras juegan un nuevo juego. ¿Qué aprendimos sobre intentar hacer todo lo posible cuando hacemos algo? ¿Cómo se sienten al intentar cosas nuevas?*

● Display a new activity for children to try, such as a new board game or a new Pattern Block puzzle to solve. Say: ***Let's do this new activity together. Try your best even if it seems hard. I'll start and show you how to do it.*** *Hagamos juntos esta nueva actividad. Intenten hacer todo lo posible aun si les parece difícil. Empezaré yo y les mostraré cómo hacerlo.* After the activity, praise children for their accomplishments and encourage them to tell how they feel about their abilities.

Making Good Choices Flip Chart, p. 27

✓ Learning Goals

Social and Emotional Development

• Child identifies self by categories (such as gender, age, family member, cultural group).

• Child describes personal interests and competencies positively (such as, "I can hop.").

Mathematics

• Child creates two-dimensional shapes; recreates two-dimensional shapes from memory.

Vocabulary

block	bloque	pattern	patrón
puzzle	rompecabezas	shape	figura
trace	calcar		

Differentiated Instruction

✋ **Extra Support**

Observe and Investigate

If...children struggle to make their own unique puzzles, **then...**create a puzzle with blocks for them and have them trace the blocks on paper to "see" the puzzle.

⭐ **Enrichment**

Observe and Investigate

Challenge children to show one of the puzzles they created and then play "teacher" by explaining to the group how to use blocks to recreate it.

Dramatic Play Time

large group · 20 minutes

✓ Learning Goals

Social and Emotional Development
• Child identifies self by categories (such as gender, age, family member, cultural group).
• Child describes personal interests and competencies positively (such as, "I can hop.").

Language and Communication
• Child uses newly learned vocabulary daily in multiple contexts.

Science
• Child identifies organisms and describes their characteristics.
• Child understands and describes life cycles of plants and animals.
• Child recognizes and selects healthy foods.

Fine Arts
• Child expresses ideas, emotions, and moods through individual and collaborative dramatic play.

Vocabulary

babies	bebé	birthday	cumpleaños
children	niños	grandmother	abuela
parents	padres	teens	adolescentes

Differentiated Instruction

 Extra Support

Explore and Express
If...children have difficulty dramatizing a large family scene, **then...**have them break into smaller groups and act out a family party with fewer family members.

 Enrichment

Explore and Express
Challenge children to speak in complete sentences and to ask other family member appropriate questions: *How are you feeling today, Grandmother? May I give the baby a cookie, Mother? ¿Cómo te sientes hoy, abuela? ¿Puedo darle una galleta al bebé, mami?*

Social and Emotional Development Skills Support self-concept skills by encouraging children to do as much preparation for the dramatic play as they can independently. You may also wish to encourage children to work in pairs to prepare. Praise their efforts.

Oral Language and Academic Vocabulary

✓ **Can children name family members at all stages of life?**

Name Family Members Display the picture of the family party on pages 18–19 in the Big Book *I'm Growing!/¡Estoy creciendo!* Say: **This family is celebrating a birthday. Whose birthday is it?** *Esta familia está festejando un cumpleaños. ¿De quién es el cumpleaños?*

• Point out the grandmother and discuss her characteristics, such as gray hair. **Who else is in the family? Point to the babies. How do you know they are babies? Do you see children? Teens? Parents? How can you tell?** *¿Quién más es de la familia? ¿Cómo saben que son bebés? ¿Ven niños, adolescentes y padres? ¿Cómo pueden saber quién es quién?*

Explore and Express

✓ **Can children portray family members at different stages of life?**

A Family Birthday Invite children to act out a family birthday party for a grandmother or grandfather. Have them draw pictures of presents and party food. Suggest that they include some nutritious food choices.

• Have children choose roles for the dramatic play. Say: **Choose who you will be at the party. Play older people and younger people. Play babies, children, teens, and parents. Choose someone to be the grandmother or grandfather.** *Escojan quiénes van a estar en la fiesta. Representen personas mayores y personas jóvenes. Actúen como bebes, niños, adolescentes y padres. ¿Quién quiere ser la abuela o el abuelo?* **Explain that children will switch roles later.**

• Have children act out their family party. Encourage them to stay in character during the play, and remind them to sing "Happy Birthday" to the birthday person. Then have them switch roles and dramatize the party scene again.

TIP Encourage children to discuss how the people at the party are related. Are some brothers and sisters, aunts and uncles, or cousins?

ELL Children should have the opportunity to practice language skills in conversations. Make sure they are not assigned the role of babies just because of a limited English vocabulary.

Center Time

> **Center Rotation** Center Time includes teacher-guided activities and independent activities. Refer to the **Learning Centers** on pages 100–101 for independent activity ideas.

Writer's Center

☑ **Track children's ability to recall and describe events.**

Materials paper, crayons or washable markers

Thank-You Notes Have children pretend they are the grandmother or grandfather at the birthday party they acted out. Have them write a note to thank the other family members for the party.

- Show children how to fold a sheet of drawing paper in half to make a card. On the front of the card, have them draw a picture that shows a scene from the party.

- Tell children to complete the thank-you note on the inside of the card. Provide a sentence frame to complete: ***Thank you for*** _____. *Gracias por* _____

- Encourage children to think of a real person they would like to thank. Have them write a thank you note to that person.

Center Tip

If...children have difficulty writing the thank-you note, **then...**print the sentence frame on the card for them and have them draw or write words to complete it.

Writing

Recap the day and week. Ask: *Tell me one new thing you learned this week about the way people change as they grow. Mencionen alguna cosa nueva que hayan aprendido esta semana sobre la manera en que la gente cambia a medida que crece.* Record answers on chart paper. Share the pen by having children write their names next to their responses.

Purposeful Play

☑ **Observe children describing experiences.**

Children choose an open center for free playtime. Encourage pride in accomplishments by suggesting that children share and read aloud the thank-you notes they wrote.

Let's Say Good-Bye

 Read Aloud Revisit the story, "Keiko's Good Thinking"/"Keiko resuelve un problema" for your afternoon Read Aloud. Remind children to listen carefully to check their understanding of the story.

 Home Connection Refer to the Home Connections activities listed in the Resources and Materials chart on page 97. Remind children to tell families what they learned about how people change and grow. Sing the "Good-Bye Song" as children prepare to leave.

Week 4

Focus Question

How do living things grow and change?

¿Cómo crecen y cambian los seres vivos?

This week children will compare and contrast the growth stages of plants, animals, and people. They will count living things, observe seed sprouts, build habitat models, role play caring for living things, and demonstrate and describe how living things move differently as they grow.

Unit 6 Growing and Changing
Week 4
Learning Goals

Social and Emotional Development	DAY 1	2	3	4	5
Child demonstrates initiative in independent activities; makes independent choices.	✓	✓	✓	✓	✓

Language and Communication	1	2	3	4	5
Child demonstrates an understanding of oral language by responding appropriately.		✓	✓	✓	
Child follows two- and three-step oral directions.				✓	✓
Child begins and ends conversations appropriately.					✓
Child follows basic rules for conversations (taking turns, staying on topic, listening actively).				✓	
Child uses appropriate nonverbal skills during conversations (making eye contact; using facial expressions).			✓		
Child names and describes actual or pictured people, places, things, actions, attributes, and events.	✓	✓	✓	✓	✓
Child understands or knows the meaning of many thousands of words, many more than he or she uses.	✓				
Child uses newly learned vocabulary daily in multiple contexts.			✓	✓	
Child builds English listening and speaking vocabulary for common objects and phrases. (ELL)	✓				

Emergent Literacy: Reading	1	2	3	4	5
Child enjoys and chooses reading-related activities.				✓	
Child names most upper- and lowercase letters of the alphabet.	✓	✓	✓	✓	✓
Child identifies the letter that stands for a given sound.	✓	✓	✓	✓	✓
Child produces the most common sound for a given letter.				✓	
Child retells or reenacts poems and stories in sequence.		✓		✓	
Child asks and answers questions about books read aloud (such as, "Who?" "What?" "Where?").	✓	✓		✓	✓

Emergent Literacy: Writing	1	2	3	4	5
Child participates in free drawing and writing activities to deliver information.			✓		
Child uses scribbles, shapes, pictures, symbols, and letters to represent language.			✓		✓

Mathematics	DAY 1	2	3	4	5
Child understands that objects, or parts thereof, can be counted.				✓	
Child recites number words in sequence from one to thirty.		✓			
Child recognizes and names numerals 0 through 9.				✓	
Child uses concrete objects or makes a verbal word problem to add up to 5 objects.	✓	✓	✓	✓	✓
Child measures passage of time using standard or non-standard tools.			✓		

Science	1	2	3	4	5
Child identifies organisms and describes their characteristics.	✓	✓	✓		✓
Child understands and describes life cycles of plants and animals.	✓		✓		✓
Child follows basic health and safety rules.	✓				

Social Studies	1	2	3	4	5
Child identifies common events and routines.			✓		

Fine Arts	1	2	3	4	5
Child uses and experiments with a variety of art materials and tools in various art activities.			✓		
Child participates in a variety of music activities (such as listening, singing, finger plays, musical games, performances).					✓

Physical Development	1	2	3	4	5
Child coordinates body movements in a variety of locomotive activities (such as walking, jumping, running, hopping, skipping, climbing).					✓

Materials and Resources

	DAY 1	DAY 2	DAY 3	DAY 4	DAY 5
Program Materials	• Teacher's Treasure Book • Oral Language Development Card 59 • Rhymes and Chants Flip Chart • Making Good Choices Flip Chart • Math and Science Flip Chart • Home Connections Resource Guide • Book: *I'm Growing!* • ABC Picture Cards: *Hh, Jj, Yy* • Building Blocks Online Math Activities	• Teacher's Treasure Book • Making Good Choices Flip Chart • Dog Puppets • ABC Picture Cards: *Hh, Jj, Yy* • Alphabet/Letter Tiles • Two-Color Counters • Book: *My Garden* • ABC Big Book • Farm Animal Counters • Math and Science Flip Chart • Building Blocks Online Math Activities	• Teacher's Treasure Book • Oral Language Development Card 60 • Rhymes and Chants Flip Chart • Making Good Choices Flip Chart • Concept Big Book 3: *Growing and Changing* • ABC Picture Cards: *Hh, Jj, Yy* • ABC Big Book • Two-Color Counters • Building Blocks Online Math Activities	• Teacher's Treasure Book • Math and Science Flip Chart • Dog Puppets • ABC Picture Cards: *Hh, Jj, Yy* • ABC Big Book • Two-Color Counters • Numeral Cards 1–8 • Farm Animal Counters • Building Blocks Online Math Activities	• Teacher's Treasure Book • Rhymes and Chants Flip Chart • Making Good Choices Flip Chart • Home Connections Resource Guide • ABC Picture Cards: *Hh, Jj, Yy* • Alphabet/Letter Tiles • Book: *My Garden* • Two-Color Counters • Building Blocks Online Math Activities
Other Materials	• books about how animals grow • drawing paper • crayons, scissors • various seeds • paper towels • sandwich bags • paste or glue • yarn	• small box for Letter Bingo • cardboard square for each child for Bingo • large pieces of poster board • paints, crayons	• drawing paper • crayons, scissors • mural paper • assorted seeds • paint, glue • class calendar • blocks • clay • construction paper	• folk tale and fairy tale books	• drawing paper • crayons, markers • masking tape for Hopscotch Review grid • small toy dinosaurs • cardboard circles • drum or other musical instrument • blocks, clay, scissors • construction paper • animal toys
Home Connection	Encourage children to tell their families about how animals and plants grow and change. Send home the following materials: Weekly Family Letter, Home Connections Resource Guide, pp. 59–60.	Encourage children to tell their families about living things need to grow and change. Remind children to tell their families how they learned to add using Farm Animal Counters.	Encourage children to tell their families about how living things grow and change over time. Remind children to tell their families how a calendar helps us keep track of passing time.	Encourage children to tell their families about how animals grow and change over time. Send home Storybook 18, Home Connections Resource Guide, pp. 149–150 (English), and 151–152 (Spanish).	Encourage children to tell their families about the ways living things grow and change. Remind children to tell their families about the many things they are able to do now that they were not able to do before.

Assessment

As you observe children throughout the week, you may fill out an Anecdotal Observational Record Form to document an individual's progress toward a goal or signs indicating the need for developmental or medical evaluation. You may also choose to select work for each child's portfolio. The Anecdotal Observational Record Form and Weekly Assessment rubrics are available in the assessment section of DLMExpressOnline.com.

More Literature Suggestions

- **Red Sings from Treetops: A Year in Colors** by Joyce Sidman
- **Babies Can't Eat Kimchee** by Nancy Patz
- **Is It a Living Thing?** by Bobbie Kalman
- **What's Alive?** by Kathleen Weidner Zoehfeld
- **From the Garden, A Counting Book About Growing Food** by Michael Dahl

- **El ciclo de vida de la mariposa** por Bobbie Kalman
- **El viejo reloj** por Fernando Alfonso
- **Leo, el retoño tardío** por Robert Kraus
- **El animal más grande del mundo** por Allan Fowler
- **Oli el elefante** por Burny Bos

Week 4

Daily Planner

	DAY 1	DAY 2
Let's Start the Day **Language Time** *large group*	**Opening Routines** p. 140 **Morning Read Aloud** p. 140 **Oral Language and Vocabulary** p. 140 Polliwogs and Frogs **Phonological Awareness** p. 140 Recognize Same Final Sounds	**Opening Routines** p. 146 **Morning Read Aloud** p. 146 **Oral Language and Vocabulary** p. 146 Different Kinds of Plants **Phonological Awareness** p. 146 Recognize Same Final Sounds
Center Time *small group*	**Focus On:** **Library and Listening Center** p. 141 **Pretend and Learn Center** p. 141	**Focus On:** **ABC Center** p. 147 **Creativity Center** p. 147
Circle Time **Literacy Time** *large group*	**Read Aloud** *My Garden/Mi jardín* p. 142 **Learn About Letters and Sounds:** *Jj, Hh, Yy* p. 142	**Read Aloud** *My Garden/Mi jardín* p. 148 **Learn About Letters and Sounds:** *Jj, Hh, Yy* p. 148
Math Time *large group*	**Finger Word Problems** p. 143	**Five Little Monkeys** p. 149
Social and Emotional Development *large group*	**Figuring Things Out** p. 143	**Being Helpful** p. 149
Content Connection *large group*	**Science:** **Oral Language and Academic Vocabulary** p. 144 Talking About How an Oak Tree Grows **Observe and Investigate** p. 144 How Seeds Change and Grow	**Math:** **Oral Language and Academic Vocabulary** p. 150 Animal Scenes **Observe and Investigate** p. 150 Adding Things Together
Center Time *small group*	**Focus On:** **Math and Science Center** p. 145 **Purposeful Play** p. 145	**Focus On:** **Math and Science Center** p. 151 **Purposeful Play** p. 151
Let's Say Good-Bye *large group*	**Read Aloud** p. 145 **Writing** p. 145 **Home Connection** p. 145	**Read Aloud** p. 151 **Writing** p. 151 **Home Connection** p. 151

DAY 3

Opening Routines p. 152
Morning Read Aloud p. 152
Oral Language and Vocabulary
p. 152 Parts of a Plant
Phonological Awareness
p. 152 Recognize Same
Final Sounds

Focus On:
Writer's Center p. 153
Creativity Center p. 153

Read Aloud
*Growing and Changing/Creciendo y
cambiando* p. 154
Learn About Letters and Sounds:
/j/, /h/, and /y/ p. 154

Snapshots (Adding) p. 155

Solving Problems p. 155

Social Studies:
Oral Language and Academic Vocabulary
p. 156 Talk About Calendars and Time
Understand and Participate
p. 156 Living Things Change Over Time

Focus On:
Construction Center p. 157
Purposeful Play p. 157

Read Aloud p. 157
Writing p. 157
Home Connection p. 157

DAY 4

Opening Routines p. 158
Morning Read Aloud p. 158
Oral Language and Vocabulary
p. 158 Story Characters with Problems
Phonological Awareness
p. 158 Recognize Same Final Sounds

Focus On:
Library and Listening Center p. 159
Pretend and Learn Center p. 159

Read Aloud
The Half-Chicken/Medio Pollito
p. 160
Learn About Letters and Sounds:
Jj, Hh, Yy p. 160

How Many Now? p. 161

Being Helpful p. 161

Math:
**Oral Language and Academic
Vocabulary** p. 162
Talk About Numerals
Observe and Investigate
p. 162 Finger Word Problems

Focus On:
Math and Science Center p. 163
Purposeful Play p. 163

Read Aloud p. 163
Writing p. 163
Home Connection p. 163

DAY 5

Opening Routines p. 164
Morning Read Aloud p. 164
Oral Language and Vocabulary
p. 164 Living Things Change
Phonological Awareness
p. 164 Recognize Same Final Sounds

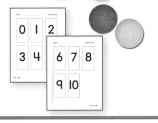

Focus On:
Writer's Center p. 165
ABC Center p. 165

Read Aloud
My Garden/Mi jardín p. 166
Learn About Letters and Sounds:
Hopscotch Review p. 166

Dinosaur Shop (Adding) p. 167

Being Helpful p. 167

Outdoor Play Time:
Oral Language and Academic Vocabulary
p. 168 Growing and Changing
Explore Movement p. 168 Moving Quickly

Focus On:
Construction Center p. 169
Purposeful Play p. 169

Read Aloud p. 169
Writing p. 169
Home Connection p. 169

Week 4

Learning Centers

Math and Science Center

What Plants Need
Children draw a plant and glue four lines of yarn outward from the drawing. They paste a picture that shows what plants need at the end of each line of yarn. See p. 145.

Adding Animals
Children take turns putting animal counters on a paper and asking how many there are altogether. A partner gives the answer. See p. 151.

Word Problems
Partners make up word problems for adding using sets of animal counters on a Farm Places Scene. See p. 163.

Let's Weigh It
Children weigh fruits, vegetables, and other objects on a balance scale. They compare the weights to learn which item weighs more.

ABC Center

Letter Bingo
Children use Bingo cards with the letters *J, j, H, h, Y, y* written randomly in the squares. See p. 147.

Matching Letters
Children use Alphabet/Letter Tiles to match upper case and lower case forms of *Jj, Hh, Yy* as they chant the sound of each letter. See p. 165.

Disappearing Letters
Children dip a paintbrush in water and "write" the letters *Jj, Hh, Yy* on the chalkboard. Before each letter disappears, children say the sound the letter represents.

Creativity Center

Plant Puzzles
Children create puzzles by drawing a picture of a tree and cutting it into four or five pieces. Partners exchange and assemble each other's puzzles. See p. 147.

Collage of Seeds
Children create a design using a variety of plant seeds. They glue their seeds in interesting shapes or use different seeds to represent the different parts of a tree or flower. See p. 153.

Leaf Mobiles
Children color leaf cutouts and attach them to a hanger with yarn to make leaf mobiles.

Animals and Their Habitats
Children create a matching game by drawing animals and habitats on large cards, such as: *bee/hive, bear/cave, bird/nest, fish/pond*.

Library and Listening Center

Browsing Animal Books
Children browse through animal books to select a baby and an adult animal to draw. They fold a sheet of drawing paper and draw a baby animal on the left side and an adult animal on the right side.
See p. 141.

Browsing Stories and Tales
Partners browse through folk tale and fairy tale books to find story characters with problems to solve. Children discuss whether a character solved the problem in a good way and whether there were other solutions to the problem. See p. 159.

Jungle Life
Partners look through books about jungle animals. Children make a "picture list" of three or four animals they learn about and tell what they eat and how they care for their young.

Construction Center

Build a Forest
Children use blocks to build a forest and clay to make forest animals. They draw pictures of trees and seedlings, lean them against the blocks, and talk about how they grow and change. See p. 157.

Build a Pond Habitat
Children use blocks and other materials to build a pond habitat that includes plants, such as water lilies, grass, and trees, and animals, such as ducks, frogs, and fish.
See p. 169.

Build an Animal Park
Children construct an animal park with blocks and other materials, including stuffed animals or plastic animal models. The builders may wish to take others on "tours" of their park.

Writer's Center

Matching Final Sounds
Children are assigned a word that ends with /d/, /g/, /k/, or /n/. They draw a picture of the word, write a label, and underline the final letter in the word. See p. 153.

Then and Now
Children create a two-part drawing that shows something they could do when they were a baby and something they are able to do today. See p. 165.

Learn Something New
Children draw a picture of something they would like to learn how to do soon. They complete a sentence frame by writing or dictating it: *I want to learn how to _____.*

Pretend and Learn Center

Follow the Mom
Children play a variation of "Follow the Leader." The child who is "Mom" chooses an animal and pantomimes the way that animal moves. The other children are "babies" and follow by moving in a similar way, but more slowly. Children take turns being Mom. See p. 141.

Act Out Stories
Children form groups to act out "Jack and the Beanstalk" or "The Ugly Duckling." They decide which characters they will play, practice their parts, and perform for the class. See p. 159.

Animal Mystery
A child places a picture of a familiar animal in a box. The other children try to figure out what animal it is by asking yes/no questions about what it looks like, where it lives, and what it eats.

Sing a Song
Children make up new verses for the song, "The Wheels on the Bus." For example: *The frog by the lake goes hop, hop, hop...*

DAY 1

Let's Start the Day

Focus Question

How do living things grow and change?

¿Cómo crecen y cambian los seres vivos?

✓ Learning Goals

Social and Emotional Development
• Child demonstrates initiative in independent activities; makes independent choices.

Language and Communication
• Child understands or knows the meaning of many thousands of words, many more than he or she uses.

Vocabulary

back legs	patas traseras	frog	rana
pond	estanque	tail	cola
swim	nadar		
polliwog/tadpole	renacuajo		

Differentiated Instruction

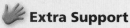 **Extra Support**

Phonological Awareness

If...children have difficulty recognizing same ending sounds, **then...**give additional practice with these word pairs and their ending sounds: *may, say; by, fly; bee, see.*

⭐ **Enrichment**

Phonological Awareness

Challenge children to suggest other words that end with the same sound as *grow, show,* and *now, how.*

Accommodations for 3's

Phonological Awareness

If...children have difficulty recognizing words that end with the same sound, **then...**show two pictures of objects, such as a *dog* and *log,* and ask: **Do dog and log end with the sound /g/?**
¿Terminan dog y log con el sonido /g/?

▶ **Opening Routines and Transition Tips**
For **Opening Routines** and **Transition Tips** turn to pages 178–181 and visit DLMExpressOnline.com for more ideas.

📖 Read **"The Caterpillar"/**"La oruga" from the Teacher's Treasure Book, page 89, for your morning Read Aloud.

Language Time

🕐 large group 15 minutes

👫 **Social and Emotional Development** Remind children that it is fun to learn new things. Ask children what they should do if they find that a new thing is confusing for them. Allow discussion.

Oral Language and Vocabulary

✓ **Can children use words that tell about frogs and where they live?**

Polliwogs and Frogs Talk about familiar animals, such as dogs and cats—how they start their life as babies and then grow up over time. Ask: **What do we call a baby dog?**
¿Cómo se llama la cría de un perro?

● Display *Oral Language Development Card 59*. Name the animals (polliwogs/tadpoles, frog) Point out the tadpoles' tails and the frog's back legs. Then follow the suggestions on the back of the card.

Oral Language Development Card 59

Phonological Awareness

✓ **Can children identify words that end with the same sound?**

Recognize Same Final Sounds Display *Rhymes and Chants Flip Chart*, page 28. Tell children to listen carefully to the ending sounds in words. Remind them that rhyming words end with the same sound.

Sing "What Will I Be?" to the tune of *Frere Jacques*. Guide children to recognize the ending sounds in *be, see.*

ELL Use the *Rhymes and Chants Flip Chart* to talk about the words *sapling, tree, bear,* and *cub.* Use this sentence frame: *A [sapling, cub] is little. A [tree, bear] is big.* Have children repeat while pointing to the pictures.

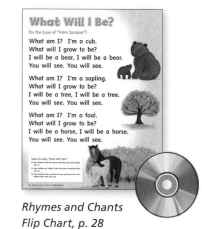

Rhymes and Chants Flip Chart, p. 28

Center Time

Center Rotation Center Time includes teacher-guided activities and independent activities. Refer to the **Learning Centers** on pages 138–139 for independent activity ideas.

 small group 60–90 minutes

Library and Listening Center

Center Tip

✓ Track the use of words that describe baby animals and their adult counterparts as children share drawings.

Materials books about how animals grow, drawing paper, crayons

Browsing Animal Books Have children browse through books to select a baby and an adult animal to draw.

● Have children fold a large piece of drawing paper in half. On the left side, have them draw a picture of a baby animal, such as a fawn. On the right side, they should draw the adult animal, a deer.

● Ask: *How are the two animals alike? How are they different?*
¿En qué se parecen los dos animales? ¿En qué se diferencian?

● Have children share their drawings and tell whether the baby has a special name.

If...children have difficulty recalling the name of a baby animal, **then...**offer them a clue by saying a word that has the same final sound (e.g., *tub/cub* or *pick/chick.*)

Pretend and Learn Center

Center Tip

✓ Look for examples of children solving problems and figuring out what to do. Compliment them on their efforts.

Follow the Mom Have children use what they have learned about animals and their babies to move in a variety of ways.

● Have children play "Follow the Mom," a variation of "Follow the Leader." The child who is Mom pantomimes the way that animal moves. The rest of the children, the babies, follow the Mom by moving in a similar way, but more slowly, as babies would.

● Give several children a turn to be Mom and lead. As children play the game, ask: *What is the mom called? What are her babies called?*
¿Cómo se llama la mamá? ¿Cómo se llaman sus bebés? Encourage children to role-play animals, such as cat/kittens; horse/colts; bear/cubs; pig/piglets; hen/chicks; cow/calves.

If...children have difficulty coming up with movements to pantomime, **then...**show them a picture or offer a suggestion.

✓ Learning Goals

Social and Emotional Development
• Child demonstrates initiative in independent activities; makes independent choices.

Language and Communication
• Child understands or knows the meaning of many thousands of words, many more than he or she uses.

Differentiated Instruction

 Extra Support
Library and Listening Center
If...children have difficulty drawing pictures of baby and adult animals, **then...**have them cut and paste pictures from magazines.

 Enrichment
Library and Listening Center
Have children label their pictures.

 Special Needs
Delayed Motor Development
Change the child's position often, so he or she does not become uncomfortable.

Focus Question
How do living things grow and change?
¿Cómo crecen y cambian los seres vivos?

Circle Time

Literacy Time

large group   15 minutes

Read Aloud

✓ **Can children retell parts of a story?**

Build Background Tell children that you will be reading a book about a girl whose grandfather takes care of a big garden.

- Ask: *What kinds of plants grow in a garden? What do plants need in order to grow? ¿Qué tipo de plantas hay en un jardín? ¿Qué necesitan las plantas para crecer?*

Listen for Enjoyment Display the cover of Big Book, "My Garden"/*"Mi jardín,"* and read the title. Conduct a picture walk.

- Browse through the pages. Name the different plants that Maria's grandfather shows Maria and her friends.

- Say: *Maria's grandfather explains to Maria and her friends how plants and flowers grow. What does he tell them? El abuelo les explica a María y a sus amigas cómo crecen las plantas y las flores. ¿Qué les dice?*

Respond to the Story Have children talk about the different kinds of plants in the garden. Ask: *How do plants grow? ¿Cómo crecen las plantas?*

TIP Have children use the pictures in the Big Book to retell the story. Ask: *What is Maria's grandfather telling the children on this page? ¿Qué les dice el abuelo a los niños en esta página?*

ELL As you leaf through the *book,* point to four or five different kinds of flowers and trees and name them. Have children say the names several times with you. Then point to each picture again to see whether children can say their names independently.

Learn About Letters and Sounds

✓ **Can children identify the sounds /j/, /h/, and /y/, spelled *Jj*, *Hh*, and *Yy*?**

Review Letters *Jj*, *Hh*, *Yy* Use the ABC Picture Cards to review the letters. Point to the jump rope on the ABC Picture Card for *Jj*. Say: *The word* jump rope *begins with the letter* j. *The letter* j *makes the sound /j/. What sound does the letter* j *make? La palabra* jump rope *empieza con la letra j. La letra j tiene el sonido /j/. ¿Qué sonido tiene la letra j.*

- Point to the upper case and lower case *Jj*, trace them on the card, and then write the letters on the chalkboard. Have children use a paintbrush dipped in water to "write" their own upper case and lower case *Jj* on the chalkboard.

- Repeat for the letters *Hh* and *Yy*. Point out how upper case and lower case *Yy* are similar.

My Garden
Mi jardín

jump rope
yawn

Learning Goals

Emergent Literacy: Reading
- Child names most upper- and lowercase letters of the alphabet.
- Child identifies the letter that stands for a given sound.
- Child asks and answers questions about books read aloud (such as "Who?" "What?" "Where?").

Science
- Child identifies organisms and describes their characteristics.
- Child understands and describes life cycles of plants and animals.

Vocabulary

bloom	florecer	flowers	flores
garden	jardín	gardener	jardinero
plants	plantas	roots	raíces
gardenias	gardenias		
greenhouse	invernadero		

Differentiated Instruction

✋ Extra Support
Learn About Letters and Sounds
If...children have difficulty "writing" the letters *Jj*, *Hh*, *Yy* with a wet paintbrush,
then...have them dip their finger in water and trace letters that you have written on the chalkboard.

⭐ Enrichment
Learn About Letters and Sounds
Challenge children to find words and names that begin with *Jj*, *Hh*, and *Yy* around the classroom. Have them choose a word or name and use Alphabet/Letter Tiles to build it.

Math Time

Observe and Investigate

☑ **Can children add up to 5 objects?**

Finger Word Problems Tell children that today they will solve adding problems with their fingers. They should place their hands in their laps between each problem.

- Tell children that you want to buy 3 packs of rose seeds and 2 packs of daisy seeds. Ask: *How many packs of seeds is that altogether? ¿Cuántas cajas de semillas hay en total?* Guide children in showing 3 fingers on one hand and 2 fingers on the other, and ask: *How many is that altogether? ¿Cuántos son en total?*

- Ask children how they got their answer, and repeat with other problems. For example: *There is 1 frog swimming in a lake. Then 3 more frogs jump in. How many frogs are in the lake altogether? Hay 1 rana nadando en un lago. Luego 3 ranas más saltaron adentro. ¿Cuántas ranas hay en el lago?*

ELL Give children many opportunities to respond to questions about adding classroom objects throughout the day, for example: *There are 2 books on the table. Let's add 2 more. How many books are there altogether?* For additional suggestions on how to meet the needs of children at the Beginning, Intermediate, Advanced, and Advanced-High levels of English proficiency, see pages 184–187.

⚝⚝⚝ Social and Emotional Development

Making Good Choices

☑ **Do children show initiative and persistence in trying new activities and figuring things out?**

Figuring Things Out Discuss how sometimes we have to work hard to learn new things. Display the *Making Good Choices Flip Chart,* page 28. Point to the girl who is working on the puzzle.

- Ask: *Do you think the girl will complete the puzzle? How can you tell? ¿Piensan que la niña completará el rompecabezas? ¿Cómo lo saben?*

- Then discuss how it feels when you try something new on your own. Ask: *How might you feel at first? What is likely to happen if you keep working at something? ¿Cómo se sentirían al principio? ¿Qué pasaría si siguieran trabajando?*

Making Good Choices Flip Chart, p. 28

Building Blocks

Online Math Activity

Introduce Pizza Pizzazz 4: Count Hidden Pepperoni, where children are shown a pizza with pepperoni, the pizza box top is closed, one or more topping is added, and children have to make a twin pizza with that many toppings.

Building Blocks

Online Math Activity

Children can complete Pizza Pizzazz 4 during computer time or Center Time.

Learning Goals

Social and Emotional Development
• Child demonstrates initiative in independent activities; makes independent choices.

Mathematics
• Child uses concrete objects or makes a verbal word problem to add up to 5 objects.

Vocabulary

adding	sumar	problems	problemas
solve	resolver	together	juntos

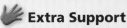

Differentiated Instruction

✋ **Extra Support**
Observe and Investigate
If...children struggle with adding up to 5 objects, **then...**focus on adding up to 4 objects before progressing further.

⭐ **Enrichment**
Observe and Investigate
Children who have mastered adding up to 5 objects can practice adding up to 7 objects.

Accommodations for 3's
Observe and Investigate
If...children struggle with adding up to 5 objects, **then...**have them add up to 3 objects.

How do living things grow and change?

¿Cómo crecen y cambian los seres vivos?

 Learning Goals

Social and Emotional Development
• Child demonstrates initiative in independent activities; makes independent choices.

Language and Communication
• Child names and describes actual or pictured people, places, things, actions, attributes, and events.

• Child builds English listening and speaking vocabulary for common objects and phrases. (ELL**)**

Science
• Child identifies organisms and describes their characteristics.

• Child understands and describes life cycles of plants and animal**s.**

• Child follows basic health and safety rules.

Vocabulary

acorn	bellota	oak tree	roble
sunflower	girasol	seedling	plántula
lima bean	frijol de lima		

Differentiated Instruction

 Extra Support

Observe and Investigate
If...children have difficulty following directions for the activity with seeds,
then...model each step for them.

Enrichment

Observe and Investigate
Challenge children to use the terms *observe* and *magnify* when discussing their observations of the seeds.

 Special Needs

Hearing Impairments
If the child depends on sign language to communicate, learn signs, especially their name sign, so he or she can feel like part of the class in class discussions.

Science Time

 large group   20 minutes

Personal Safety Skills Model how to properly hold the hand lens as children examine seeds. Make sure they wash their hands with soap and water after the activity.

Oral Language and Academic Vocabulary

Can children identify and describe the steps that show how an oak tree grows?

Talking About How an Oak Tree Grows Point to the acorn on the *Math and Science Flip Chart*. If possible, have an acorn on hand to show children. Say: *This is an acorn. An acorn is a seed from an oak tree.* *Ésta es una bellota. Es la semilla de un roble.*

● Explain that an oak tree grows from an acorn. Point to the picture of the seedling. Say: *This is an oak tree seedling. It is a young oak tree or a baby oak tree.* *Ésta es la plántula de un árbol de roble. Es un roble joven o un árbol de roble bebé.*

● Discuss the other steps in the diagram. Point out that the steps are in a circle because they continue on and on.

ELL Make sure children understand the words *acorn, seedling,* and *oak tree.* Say: *Point to the seedling. Point to the acorns on the ground. Point to the acorns on the oak tree.* Have children repeat the words and phrases back to you in English.

Observe and Investigate

Can children observe seeds and describe how they sprout over time?

How Seeds Change and Grow Give children seeds, such as sunflower or lima bean seeds. (You may want to soak the lima beans overnight.) Have children look closely at the seeds, using the hand lenses, and describe what they see.

● Have partners fold a strip of paper towel and moisten it without soaking it. Then have them place it in a plastic sandwich bag.

● Say: *Now let's put a few seeds on the paper towel strip*. *Ahora, vamos a poner algunas semillas en la tira de papel.* Then have children close the bags and put them in the Science Center. Have children observe what happens to the seeds over time.

TIP Tell children to use the hand lenses to observe the seeds each day.

Math and Science Flip Chart, p. 51

Center Time

▶ **Center Rotation** Center Time includes teacher-guided activities and independent activities. Refer to the **Learning Centers** on pages 138–139 for independent activity ideas.

small group   30 minutes

Refer to the **Learning Centers** on pages 138–139 for independent activity ideas.

Learning Goals

Social and Emotional Development
• Child demonstrates initiative in independent activities; makes independent choices.

Language and Communication
• Child names and describes actual or pictured people, places, things, actions, attributes, and events.

Science
• Child identifies organisms and describes their characteristics.

Math and Science Center

✓ **Have children identify what plants need in order to live and grow.**

Materials picture books about plants, large sheets of paper, yarn, crayons, scissors, paste

What Plants Need Have groups of four children work together. Have each group choose a plant to draw on a large sheet of paper. Say: *We are going to draw a picture of a plant and then show what a plant needs to live and grow. Vamos a dibujar una planta y mostrar lo que necesita para vivir y crecer.*

• Tell children to stretch four pre-cut lines of yarn outward from their drawing of a plant and glue them to the paper.

• Be sure children understand that plants need soil, sunlight, air, and water to grow. Have them draw pictures that represent these four things and attach them to the ends of the yarn.

Center Tip

If...children need help thinking of pictures that represent what plants need, **then...**suggest they draw rain or a watering can to represent water and wavy blue lines to represent air.

Writing

Recap the day. Have children discuss plants and animals they learned about. Ask: *How do oak trees change and grow over time? ¿Cómo cambian y crecen los robles con el tiempo?* Record their answers. Read them back as you track the print, and emphasize the correspondence between speech and print.

Purposeful Play

✓ **Observe children taking turns and solving problems in creative ways.**

Children choose an open center for free playtime. Encourage creative thinking and problem-solving skills by suggesting they take turns pretending to be seeds that are ready to sprout.

Let's Say Good-Bye

large group   15 minutes

 Read Aloud Revisit the story, "The Caterpillar,"/"La oruga" for your afternoon Read Aloud. Remind children to listen for words with the sounds /j/, /h/, and /y/.

 Home Connection Refer to the Home Connections activities listed in the Resources and Materials chart on page 135. Remind children to tell families about how animals and plants grow and change. Sing the "Good-Bye Song"/"Hora de ir casa" as children prepare to leave.

DAY 2

Let's Start the Day

Focus Question
How do living things grow and change?
¿Cómo crecen y cambian los seres vivos?

> **Opening Routines and Transition Tips**
> For **Opening Routines** and **Transition Tips** turn to pages 178–181 and visit **DLMExpressOnline.com** for more ideas.
>
> Read **"Puppy, the Seedlings, and Me"**/"Todos crecemos" from the *Teacher's Treasure Book,* page 115, for your morning Read Aloud.

Learning Goals

Social and Emotional Development
• Child demonstrates initiative in independent activities; makes independent choices.

Language and Communication
• Child names and describes actual or pictured people, places, things, actions, attributes, and events.

Vocabulary

cherry tree	cerezo	daisies	margaritas
gardenias	gardenias	roots	raíces
roses	rosas		
water lilies	lirios acuáticos		

Differentiated Instruction

 Extra Support
Oral Language and Vocabulary
If...children have difficulty thinking of specific plants that grow in their neighborhood, **then...** ask them where in their neighborhood they might see trees, bushes, or flowers.

 Enrichment
Oral Language and Vocabulary
Ask children to name different kinds of plants that we eat, such as carrots, tomatoes, zucchini, lettuce, grapes, and corn.

 Special Needs
Behavioral Social/Emotional
Learn to read the child's body language. When s/he appears to be getting frustrated or agitated, change the task or set up a "calm-down" place in your room.

Language Time

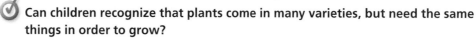 large group • 15 minutes

Social and Emotional Development Encourage children to actively participate and contribute to the discussion about plants.

Oral Language and Vocabulary

✓ **Can children recognize that plants come in many varieties, but need the same things in order to grow?**

Different Kinds of Plants Have children talk about plants they are familiar with. Ask: *What kinds of plants do you have at home? What kinds of plants grow in your neighborhood? ¿Qué tipos de plantas tienen en casa? ¿Qué tipos de plantas crecen en su vecindario?*

● As children name plants, say: *Some plants have flowers that come in pretty colors. Algunas plantas tienen flores de colores hermosos.* Encourage children to name flowering plants, such as roses, daisies, and gardenias.

● Ask: *What do all plants need in order to grow? What happens if they do not get the things they need? ¿Qué necesitan todas las plantas para crecer? ¿Qué sucede si no reciben las cosas que necesitan?*

ELL Display plant photos from the Photo Library. Choose plants, such as carrot, grass, rose, sunflower, water lily, and tomato. Then ask children to tell you what color each plant is.

Phonological Awareness

✓ **Can children identify words that end with the same sound?**

Recognize Same Final Sounds Display the Dog Puppets. Tell children that each puppet will say a word. If the words end with the same sound, children should raise their hands high. If the words do not end with the same sound, they should keep their hands in their lap.

Have the puppets say these words, emphasizing the final sounds: *rose/nose, sun/hat, big/rug, stop/cap, tree/my, hot/dot, leaf/pick, seed/hide.*

Center Time

▶ **Center Rotation** Center Time includes teacher-guided activities and independent activities. Refer to the **Learning Centers** on pages 138–139 for independent activity ideas.

 small group 60–90 minutes

ABC Center

☑ **Review the letters and sounds for Jj, Hh, and Yy.**

Materials Alphabet Letter Tiles for *J, j, H, h, Y, y*; Two-Color Counters; a small box or can; a cardboard square for each child, divided into nine small squares with the letters J, j, H, h, Y, y written randomly in the squares.

Letter Bingo Place the Alphabet Tiles in a box or can. Give each child a card.

- Choose an Alphabet Tile from the box. Ask: ***What is the name of this letter? What sound does the letter make?*** *¿Cuál es el nombre de esta letra? ¿Cuál es su sonido?*

- Have children say the name of the letter and identify its sound. Then have them find it on their cards, and cover it with a counter.

- The first child to cover a row across or down wins the game. Play several times.

Center Tip

If...children have difficulty distinguishing between upper case and lower case letters on their cards, **then...**display the ABC Picture Cards for Jj, Hh, and Yy, and review the upper case and lower case forms.

Creativity Center

☑ **Listen for words children use to describe plants and their parts as they put plant puzzles together.**

Materials large pieces of posterboard, paints or crayons

Plant Puzzles Tell children that they will make plant puzzles to share with classmates.

- Distribute a large piece of posterboard to each child. Have children draw or paint a picture of a flower or tree on the poster board. Say: ***Be sure to show all the parts of your plant clearly.*** *Asegúrense de mostrar claramente todas las partes de su planta.*

- Then help children cut their pictures into four or five pieces. Put the pieces in envelopes with children's names so that they can exchange and assemble each other's plant puzzles.

Center Tip

If...children do not know what kind of plant to draw, **then...**provide them with simple drawings that they can use as a reference.

 ### Learning Goals

Emergent Literacy: Reading
- Child names most upper- and lowercase letters of the alphabet.
- Child identifies the letter that stands for a given sound.

Science
- Child identifies organisms and describes their characteristics.

Differentiated Instruction

 #### Extra Support
ABC Center

If...children have difficulty remembering the sound of a letter, **then...**have them echo the sound after you say it.

Enrichment
ABC Center

Challenge children to name words that begin with the sounds /j/, /h/, and /y/.

Accommodations for 3's
ABC Center

If...children have difficulty finding a letter from among the other letters, **then...**play the game with only two letters at a time, such as *Jj* and *Hh*, using cards that have only six squares.

Circle Time

Literacy Time

large group | 15 minutes

 Read Aloud

✓ **Can children retell parts of a story?**

Build Background Tell children they will listen once again to a story about four friends who visit a garden.

● Ask: *How do people take care of a garden? What do they do to help their plants grow? ¿Cómo se cuida un jardín? ¿Qué se hacen para ayudar a las plantas a crecer?*

Listen for Understanding Display the cover of Big Book, "My Garden"/"*Mi jardín*" and read the title.

● Turn to page 2 of the story. Remind children that words are read from left to right. Say: *When there is more than one line on a page, we read the lines from top to bottom. Cuando hay más de una línea en una página, leemos las líneas de arriba hacia abajo.* Track the text as you read the lines on page 2.

● Say: *Listen carefully as I read the story, so that you will be able to remember and retell parts of the story. Escuchen cuidadosamente mientras leo el cuento para recordar y volver a contar algunas partes.*

Respond to the Story Have children retell the part of the story when Maria's grandfather explains how plants grow.

TIP Have children point to pictures in the book as they retell parts of the story.

ELL As you read "My Garden," point to specific illustrations, and ask questions, such as: *What kind of flower is this? Is this an apple tree or a cherry tree?* Have children answer the questions with complete sentences. For additional suggestions on how to meet the needs of children at the Beginning, Intermediate, Advanced, and Advanced-High levels of English proficiency, see pages 184–187.

Learn About Letters and Sounds

✓ **Can children identify the sounds /j/, /h/, and /y/, spelled *Jj*, *Hh*, and *Yy*?**

Review Letters *Jj*, *Hh*, *Yy* Sing the "ABC Song" with children as you turn the pages of the *ABC Big Book*. Stop when you come to a letter that is being reviewed. For *Hh*, review the target words horse, hand, and hammer. Say: *These words begin with the letter h and the sound /h/. Estas palabras empiezan con la letra h y el sonido /h/.* Ask: *What sound do you hear at the beginning of horse, hand, and hammer? What letter stands for the sound /h/? ¿Qué sonido escuchan al principio de las palabras horse, hand y hammer? ¿Qué letra tiene el sonido /h/?*

● Model how to write upper case and lower case *Hh* on the chalkboard. Have children "write" upper case and lower case *Hh* on a partner's back with their finger. Repeat the same process to review the letters *Jj* and *Yy*. Ask children to say the sound of the letter as they "write" it on their partner's back.

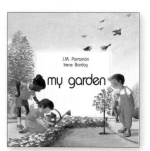

My Garden
Mi jardín

ABC Big Book

Emergent Literacy: Reading
• Child names most upper- and lowercase letters of the alphabet.
• Child identifies the letter that stands for a given sound.
• Child retells or reenacts poems and stories in sequence.
• Child asks and answers questions about books read aloud (such as, "Who?" "What?" "Where?").

Vocabulary

apple	manzano	cherry	cerezo
gardener	jardinero	pear	peral
transplant	trasplantar		

Differentiated Instruction

 Extra Support
Learn About Letters and Sounds
If...children have difficulty writing the letters *Jj*, *Hh*, *Yy*, **then...**have them use clay to form the letters and then trace them with their finger.

 Enrichment
Learn About Letters and Sounds
Have children hunt for words that begin with *Jj*, *Hh*, and *Yy* in classroom books. Have children flag the words with sticky notes and try to read them independently. Help them read any words they are not sure of.

 Special Needs
Cognitive Challenges
Model positive interactions such as sharing a toy or participating in a game or discussion.

large group | 15 minutes

Math Time

Observe and Investigate

 Can children count back from 5?

Five Little Monkeys Have children show all 5 fingers (the monkeys) on one hand. As each monkey falls off the bed, children fold a finger to show fewer fingers. Use the following words and actions.

- Say: *Five little monkeys jumping on the bed; one fell off and bumped his head.* (Lightly tap your head.) *Sobre la cama saltan cinco monitos./Uno se cae y se golpea el coquito.*

- Counting backward, repeat the above lines for numerals 4, 3, and 2. For 1 monkey, say: *One little monkey jumping on the bed; he fell off and bumped his head.* (Lightly tap your head.) *We called for the doctor, and the doctor said,* La mamá llama al doctor, y el doctor le dice así: (Pretend you are holding a phone to your ear.) *"That's what you get for jumping on the bed!"* "¡Saque ya mismo esos monitos de ahí!"

ELL To make sure children understand the humor of this finger play, pantomime what the monkeys do and why the doctor is called.

Social and Emotional Development

Making Good Choices

 Do children show a desire to figure things out on their own?

Being Helpful Revisit the *Making Good Choices Flip Chart,* page 28, "How Do I Solve Problems?"

- Display the Dog Puppet. Say: *Tell the puppet about the girl who is trying to figure out how to finish the puzzle. Tell the dog what she should do.* Cuéntenle al perrito sobre la niña que está intentando descubrir cómo terminar el rompecabezas. Díganle qué debería hacer la niña.

- Provide each child a turn to tell the puppet about a way to figure out the puzzle. For example, she could keep trying to put different pieces in the puzzle until she finds the right piece. Or, she could use the puzzle picture as a clue for what piece belongs.

- Remind children that when they do something on their own, they shouldn't give up. They should keep trying.

Online Math Activity

Introduce Dinosaur Shop 3: Add Dinosaurs (1-5), where children hear two orders for different dinosaurs to be put in one box and click the correct numeral to tell the sum of that box.

large group | 15 minutes

Making Good Choices Flip Chart, p. 28

Learning Goals

Social and Emotional Development
- Child demonstrates initiative in independent activities; makes independent choices.

Mathematics
- Child recites number words in sequence from one to thirty.

Vocabulary

count   contar

count back   contar hacia atrás

Differentiated Instruction

 Extra Support

Observe and Investigate

If...children struggle with counting back from 5, **then...**have them count back from 3.

Enrichment

Observe and Investigate

Have children do the finger play, starting with 7 monkeys and counting back.

Learning Goals

Language and Communication
• Child demonstrates an understanding of oral language by responding appropriately.

Mathematics
• Child uses concrete objects or makes a verbal word problem to add up to 5 objects.

Vocabulary

altogether	total	amounts	cantidades
count	contar	counters	fichas

Differentiated Instruction

Extra Support
Oral Language and Academic Vocabulary
If...children struggle to add numbers up to 5,
then...use only those pictures on the Flip Chart that add up to 4 or fewer.

Enrichment
Oral Language and Academic Vocabulary
Challenge children to add numbers up to 7 or 8, using Counters or blocks.

Math Time

large group | 20 minutes

Language and Communication Skills Monitor that children are responding physically and verbally as you give directions.

Oral Language and Academic Vocabulary

 Can children add up to 5 objects?

Animal Scenes Model the activity for children with the *Math and Science Flip Chart*, page 52 and the Farm Animals Counters. Set the chart on the floor or on a table.

● Put 3 horse counters on the chart and count them with children. Then add 2 sheep counters and count them. Ask: *How many animals are there altogether? ¿Cuántos animales hay en total?* Point to the counters, and allow time for children to figure it out. Then count all the animals together.

● Give each child a piece of paper and two types of Farm Animal Counters—up to three of each. Have children put counters of one type on their paper. Ask: *How many animals do you have altogether? ¿Cuántos animales tienen en total?* Discuss the different amounts children created.

Observe and Investigate

 **Can children add up to 5 objects?**

Adding Things Together Display the *Math and Science Flip Chart,* "Adding Things Together." Have children talk about all the things they see on the chart—plants, animals, and people.

● Say: *First, we are going to find the big pumpkins and put a sticky note next to them. Primero, vamos a encontrar las calabazas grandes y a pegar una nota junto a ellas.* Ask a volunteer to do it. Then say: *Let's count the big pumpkins together—1, 2. Vamos a contar todos juntos las calabazas grandes: 1, 2.*

● Ask another child to place a sticky note next to the small pumpkins. Say: *Now let's count the small pumpkins—1, 2. Ahora, vamos a contar las calabazas pequeñas: 1, 2.* Ask: *How many pumpkins are there altogether? ¿Cuántas calabazas hay en total?* Allow time for children to figure it out. Then count all the pumpkins together.

● Repeat for each object: birds, trees, people, squirrels, and dogs.

TIP Encourage children to point to each object as they count it.

ELL After each set of objects is identified, be sure to repeat the name of the objects as you point to them, for example: *Let's count the cherry trees together—1, 2, 3.*

Math and Science Flip Chart, p. 52

Center Time

small group   30 minutes

Center Rotation Center Time includes teacher-guided activities and independent activities. Refer to the **Learning Centers** on pages 138–139 for independent activity ideas.

 Learning Goals

Social and Emotional Development
• Child demonstrates initiative in independent activities; makes independent choices.

Language and Communication
• Child names and describes actual or pictured people, places, things, actions, attributes, and events.

Mathematics
• Child uses concrete objects or makes a verbal word problem to add up to 5 objects.

Math and Science Center

Center Tip

☑ **Observe children as they add numbers up to 5, or more.**

Materials Farm Animal Counters, paper

Adding Animals Have children work in pairs. One partner places two kinds of Farm Animal Counters on a piece of paper. Tell children not to place more than three counters of each kind to start. He or she asks the partner: *How many animals are there altogether? ¿Cuántos animales hay en total?*

• The partner counts aloud and gives the answer in a complete sentence, for example: *There are four animals altogether. En total hay cuatro animales.* Have partners take turns setting up the counters.

If...children have difficulty adding up to 5, **then**...have them practice with no more than two counters of each kind.

Writing

Recap the day. Have children talk about taking care of a garden. Ask: *If you were a gardener, how would you take care of your plants? Si fueran jardineros, ¿cómo cuidarían sus plantas?* Ask them to draw a picture that shows what they would do to help their plants grow.

Purposeful Play

☑ **Observe children's creativity and problem-solving skills as they role-play an interview.**

Children choose an open center for free playtime. Suggest that partners work together to role-play an interview. One child pretends to be a TV interviewer. The other child pretends to be a plant or an animal. The interviewer asks the plant or animal questions about its life, such as: *How do you get water? Who are your friends? How do you spend your day? ¿Cómo obtienes el agua? ¿Quiénes son tus amigos? ¿Cómo pasas tu día?*

Let's Say Good-Bye

large group   15 minutes

 Read Aloud Revisit the story, "Puppy, the Seedlings, and Me,"/"Todos crecemos" for your afternoon Read Aloud. Remind children to listen to learn more about what living things need to grow.

 Home Connection Refer to the Home Connections activities listed in the Resources and Materials chart on page 135. Remind children to tell families about what living things need to grow and change. Sing the "Good-Bye Song" as children prepare to leave.

DAY 3

Let's Start the Day

Focus Question

How do living things grow and change?
¿Cómo crecen y cambian los seres vivos?

▶ **Opening Routines and Transition Tips**
For **Opening Routines** and **Transition Tips** turn to pages 178–181 and visit DLMExpressOnline.com for more ideas.

📖 Read **"Jack and the Beanstalk"**/*"Jaime y los frijoles mágicos"* from the *Teacher's Treasure Book*, page 230, for your morning Read Aloud.

✓ Learning Goals

Social and Emotional Development
• Child demonstrates initiative in independent activities; makes independent choices.

Language and Communication
• Child uses appropriate nonverbal skills during conversations (making eye contact; using facial expressions).

• Child uses newly learned vocabulary daily in multiple contexts.

Vocabulary

pick	recoger	shell	cáscara
ripe	maduro	stem	tallo
seed	semilla		
pumpkin patch	huerto de calabazas		

Differentiated Instruction

✋ Extra Support

Phonological Awareness
If...children have difficulty recognizing words that end with the same sound, **then...**have them repeat the final sound they hear at the end of these word pairs: *mess/pass; hen/pen; sit/late; home/same.*

★ Enrichment

Phonological Awareness
Challenge children to find objects in the classroom whose names end with the same sound, but do not rhyme.

Accommodations for 3's

Phonological Awareness
If...children have difficulty recognizing words that end with the same sound, **then...**focus only on rhyming words.

Language Time

large group   15 minutes

Social and Emotional Development Encourage children to ask questions when they hear something they do not understand. Recognize children for raising their hand to ask a question.

Oral Language and Vocabulary

✓ **Can children use words that name the parts of a plant?**

Parts of a Plant Talk about plants that contain seeds, such as apples, tomatoes, and sunflowers. Ask: **What happens if you plant the seeds?** *¿Qué sucede si plantan semillas?*

● Display *Oral Language Development Card 60*. Have children name the plant they see (pumpkin). Point out the picture of the pumpkin seed. Then follow the suggestions on the back of the card.

Oral Language Development Card 60

Phonological Awareness

✓ **Can children identify words that end with the same sound?**

Recognize Same Final Sounds Revisit *Rhymes and Chants Flip Chart*, page 28. Remind children that words such as *be* and *see* end with the same sound and rhyme. Have children join in as you sing "What Will I Be?" to the tune of *Frere Jacques*. Ask: **Which words end with the same sound and rhyme?** *¿Qué palabras terminan con el mismo sonido y riman?* Then point to the words "cub" and "bear" and read them. Ask: **Do these words rhyme?** *¿Riman estas dos palabras?*

ELL Use the *Rhymes and Chants Flip Chart* to revisit words that tell about living things: *sapling, bear,* and *cub.* Ask children to say the words and point to their pictures.

Rhymes and Chants Flip Chart, p. 28

Center Time

> **Center Rotation** Center Time includes teacher-guided activities and independent activities. Refer to the **Learning Centers** on pages 138–139 for independent activity ideas.

small group 60–90 minutes

Refer to the **Learning Centers** on pages 138–139 for independent activity ideas.

Writer's Center

	Center Tip

 Track children's ability to identify words that end with the same sound.

Materials drawing paper, crayons

Matching Final Sounds Assign one of the following words to each child. Note that there are four groups of words that focus on final sounds /d/, /g/, /k/, and /n/. Make sure an equal or nearly equal number of children are assigned to each group. /d/: *cloud, read, seed, toad, bed*; /g/: *bug, dog, hug, pig, flag*; /k/: *book, duck, truck, sock, chick*; /n/: *rain, sun, run, moon, man*.

- Tell children to draw a picture of their word and think about its ending sound.

- Encourage children to label their pictures, and assist them as necessary. Ask them to draw a line under the last letter of the word.

- Have the four groups gather in the four corners of the classroom. Ask children to hold up their pictures and say their words.

Center Tip

If...children need help drawing their pictures, **then...**provide photos and illustrations for them to use as references.

 Learning Goals

Emergent Literacy: Writing
- Child participates in free drawing and writing activities to deliver information.

Fine Arts
- Child uses and experiments with a variety of art materials and tools in various art activities.

Differentiated Instruction

 Extra Support
Writer's Center
If...children have difficulty hearing final sounds, **then...**say the word several times, emphasizing the final sound, and then repeat the sound in isolation.

Enrichment
Writer's Center
Challenge children to draw and label a picture of another word they can add to their group.

Accommodations for 3's
Writer's Center
If...children have difficulty writing letters for a label, **then...**write the word for them and just have them underline the final letter.

Creativity Center

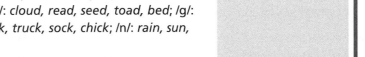 **Track children's ability to identify and describe different kinds of seeds.**

Materials mural paper or other heavy paper, assorted seeds, paint, glue

Collage of Seeds Tell children that they will use a variety of seeds to create a special design.

- Have children glue their seeds in interesting shapes and swirls. They may also want to represent a particular plant, such as a tree or flower, using one kind of seed to show each part of the plant.

- After children have completed the collage, ask each child to talk about the plant he or she created and tell what seeds were used.

Center Tip

If...children have difficulty remembering the parts of a tree or flower, **then...**display photos and illustrations to use as a reference.

Focus Question

How do living things grow and change?

¿Cómo crecen y cambian los seres vivos?

Learning Goals

Language and Communication
• Child demonstrates an understanding of oral language by responding appropriately.

Emergent Literacy: Reading
• Child names most upper- and lowercase letters of the alphabet.
• Child identifies the letter that stands for a given sound.

Science
• Child identifies organisms and describes their characteristics.
• Child understands and describes life cycles of plants and animals.

Vocabulary

butterfly	mariposa	caterpillar	oruga
chicken	pollito	colt	potro
egg	huevo	pupa	crisálida
hatches	rompe el cascarón		

Differentiated Instruction

 Extra Support

Read Aloud

If...children have difficulty retelling information from the *Concept Big Book*, **then...**break the question down into its parts by asking: **What happens to the caterpillar after it hatches? What happens when it is inside its shell-like covering?** *¿Qué le pasa a la oruga después de que sale del huevo? ¿Qué le pasa cuando está dentro de su envoltura en forma de caparazón?*

⭐ **Enrichment**

Read Aloud

Challenge children to remember and describe how a tadpole becomes a frog.

 Special Needs

Speech and Language Delays

If you do not understand what the child is saying, ask the child to repeat what s/he said once, and then try asking questions to help you understand what s/he is asking or saying.

Literacy Time

large group · 15 minutes

📖 Read Aloud

✓ **Can children retell information they learned from a book?**

Build Background Tell children that you will read more information about how living things grow and change.

● Ask: **What does a kitten grow up to be? What does a seed grow up to be?** *¿Qué será un gatito cuando crezca? ¿Qué será una semilla cuando crezca?*

Listen for Understanding Display *Concept Big Book*: 3, "Growing and Changing"/"Creciendo y cambiando" and read the title.

● Read pages 26–28. Point to the labels in the photographs and read them after reading the main text. Ask: **How does a caterpillar change? What does it finally become?** *¿Cómo cambia una oruga? ¿En qué se convertirá?*

● Review *Sequence Cards* "Metamorphosis" and "The Life Span." Have volunteers each take one card and place themselves in sequential order according to the card they are holding.

Respond to the Story Point to the babies on page 28, and ask: **Which baby will grow up to be a girl? Which baby will grow up to be a horse? What other animal babies can you name?** *¿Qué bebé se convertirá en una niña? ¿Qué cría crecerá para convertirse en un caballo? ¿Que otra cría de animal pueden nombrar?*

 TIP Remind children that they can learn information from the text, photos, and labels.

ELL As you browse through the *Concept Big Book*, encourage children to point to the photos and name things they know.

Learn About Letters and Sounds

✓ **Can children identify the sounds /j/, /h/, and /y/ spelled *Jj*, *Hh*, and *Yy*?**

Review the Letters *Jj*, *Hh*, *Yy* Sing the "ABC Song" with children as you page through the *ABC Big Book*, stopping when you get to each target letter. Review the pictures for each letter and the sound each letter makes: /j/, /h/, and /y/.

● Model how to write the upper case and lower case letters *Hh*, using the *ABC Picture Card*. Have children trace the letters with their finger.

● While one child is tracing, the other children can be writing the letter in the air or on a piece of carpet, using their finger. Have them say /h/ each time they write the letter. Repeat for upper case and lower case letters *Jj* and *Yy*.

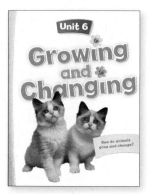

Growing and Changing
Creciendo y cambiando

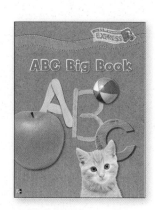

ABC Big Book

Math Time

Observe and Investigate

 Can children quickly recognize the sum of two small groups?

Snapshots (Adding) Secretly put two counters in one of your hands and one counter in the other hand. Show your closed hands to children, and then open them for two seconds, closing them immediately after.

* Ask: *How many counters did you see in each hand? ¿Cuántas fichas vieron en cada mano?* Then ask how many counters there were altogether. Open both hands, and count with children to check.

* Depending on children's ability, repeat the process with as many counters as possible. Then invite volunteers to do Snapshots with counters. This activity may also be done by partners or small groups in the Math and Science Center.

ELL During the activity, name the action you are doing—*opening* or *closing* your hand—as you do it. That way, children will associate the word with the action. Reinforce how the action is being done by using words such as *quickly* and *fast*.

Building Blocks

Online Math Activity
Children can complete Pizza Pizzazz 4 and Dinosaur Shop 3 during computer or Center Time.

☥☥☥ Social and Emotional Development

Making Good Choices

 Do children show a desire to figure things out on their own?

Solving Problems Display *Making Good Choices Flip Chart* page 28, "How Do I Solve Problems?" Review with children different things the girl can do to figure out how to complete the puzzle on her own.

* Using the Dog Puppet, role-play other situations to model how children can solve problems independently. For example, have the puppet say: *I want to draw a picture of a baby elephant with its mom, but I'm not sure what an elephant's trunk looks like. So I will look in some books about animals to find pictures of elephants. That will help me draw my own picture! Quiero hacer un dibujo de un elefante pequeño con su mamá, pero no sé cómo es la trompa de un elefante. Entonces, voy a buscar en algunos libros de animales para encontrar imágenes de elefantes. ¡Eso me ayudará a hacer mi propio dibujo!*

* After each role-play, ask: *How did the puppet solve the problem on his own? Can you think of something else the puppet could have done? What would you do? ¿Cómo resolvió el títere el problema por su cuenta? ¿Pueden pensar en otra cosa que el títere pudo haber hecho? ¿Qué harían ustedes?*

large group 15 minutes

How Do I Solve Problems?
¿Cómo resuelvo problemas?

Making Good Choices Flip Chart, p. 28

Differentiated Instruction

 Extra Support

Oral Language and Academic Vocabulary
If...children have difficulty understanding the concept of time, **then...**show them pictures of activities that take a short time, such as reading a story, and a long time, such as building a house.

 Enrichment

Oral Language and Academic Vocabulary
Have children give information about the current month, such as how many days there are and whether there are any holidays in the month.

 Special Needs

Vision Loss
Tell the child when something new is added or taken away from the classroom. Give him or her time to explore it before the other children so s/he is not afraid.

Social Studies Time

 large group   20 minutes

Oral Language and Academic Vocabulary

✓ **Can children recognize and understand time intervals?**

Talk About Calendars and Time Ask children what day it is today. Then say, for example: *You are right! Today is Wednesday. Who can tell me what day it was yesterday? What day will it be tomorrow?* *¡Tienen razón! Hoy es miércoles. ¿Quién puede decirme qué día fue ayer? ¿Qué día será mañana?* Name the days and point them out on your class calendar.

● Explain to children that a calendar helps people keep track of time. Say: *A calendar tells us what day of the week it is. It also tells us the month and year.* *Un calendario nos muestra cada día de la semana. También nos muestra el mes y el año.* Point out the name of the month, and tell children today's date.

● Explain that sometimes a day can feel like a long time. For example, you might say: *We get up in the morning and come to school. In the afternoon we do many things at home or outdoors. At night, we eat dinner and then play or read before it is time to go to bed.* *Nos levantamos en la mañana y venimos a la escuela. En la tarde hacemos muchas cosas en casa o al aire libre. Por la noche, cenamos y luego jugamos o leemos antes de ir a la cama.* Ask: *When we get up the next morning, is it the same day or is it a new day?* *Cuando nos despertamos a la mañana siguiente, ¿es el mismo día o es un nuevo día?*

Understand and Participate

✓ **Can children understand how change is related to time?**

Living Things Change Over Time Display the Concept Big Book as well as photos of animal babies and adults; human babies, children, and adults; and seedlings and adult trees.

● Explain that as time passes, everything gets older and changes—people, animals, and plants. Ask: *What are some things you can do now that you couldn't do when you were a baby? What things will you be able to do when you are older that you can't do now?* *¿Qué cosas pueden hacer ahora y no podían hacer cuando eran bebés? ¿Qué cosas podrán hacer cuando sean mayores y no pueden hacer ahora?* Give each child a turn to tell how old he/she is now and how old he/she will be on the next birthday.

● Discuss how animals and people are alike in many ways. Say: *A baby animal cannot do very much. Its mother must feed it and take care of it. As it grows up it can do more and more on its own.* *Hay muchas cosas que los animales bebé no pueden hacer. Su madre debe alimentarlos y cuidarlos. Y, a medida que crecen, pueden hacer cada vez más cosas por su cuenta.*

TIP Remind children that there are seven days in a week and have them name the days. Ask: *What is your favorite day of the week?* *¿Cuál es su día de la semana preferido?*

Center Time

▶ **Center Rotation** Center Time includes teacher-guided activities and independent activities. Refer to the **Learning Centers** on pages 138–139 for independent activity ideas.

small group — 30 minutes

Learning Goals

Social and Emotional Development
• Child demonstrates initiative in independent activities; makes independent choices.

Language and Communication
• Child names and describes actual or pictured people, places, things, actions, attributes, and events.

Emergent Literacy: Writing
• Child uses scribbles, shapes, pictures, symbols, and letters to represent language.

Social Studies
• Child identifies common events and routines.

Construction Center

✓ **Monitor children as they build a forest habitat with baby and adult animals.**

Materials blocks, clay, construction paper, crayons, scissors

Build a Forest Tell children they will use blocks to build a forest. They can show animals, plants, and people in the forest. Have children work in small groups. They can use clay to make animals, such as bears and cubs, deer and fawns.

• Children can draw pictures of trees and seedlings, cut the pictures out, and lean them against the blocks. Ask: *Do you want to include people in your forest? Perhaps a family could be hiking.* *¿Quieren incluir personas en el bosque? Tal vez pueden incluir una familia que está de excursión.*

Center Tip

If...children need help working together as a group, **then...**suggest roles for each child. For example, one child can draw pictures of trees while another makes animals from clay.

Writing

Recap the day. Have children talk about how a calendar helps us keep track of time. Ask: *What did you eat for dinner last night? What book did we read in school today? What would you like to learn about tomorrow?* *¿Qué cenaron ayer en la noche? ¿Qué libro leímos hoy en la escuela? ¿Qué les gustaría aprender mañana?* Record their answers on chart paper. Share the pen by having children write letters and words they know. Ask children to illustrate each sentence.

Purposeful Play

✓ **Observe children as they create new verses for a song.**

Children choose an open center for free playtime. Encourage creative problem-solving by asking children to make up verses about plants and animals in the forest based on the song, "The Wheels on the Bus Go Round and Round." Start children off with this suggestion: *"The bears in the forest eat lots of berries, lots of berries, lots of berries. The bears in the forest eat lots of berries—all day long!"*

Let's Say Good-Bye

large group — 15 minutes

 Read Aloud Revisit the story, "Jack and the Beanstalk,"/"Jaime y los frijoles mágicos" for your afternoon Read Aloud. Remind children to listen for the things Jack did to help the beanstalk grow.

 Home Connection Refer to the Home Connections activities listed in the Resources and Materials chart on page 135. Remind children to tell families about how living things grow and change over time. Sing the "Good-Bye Song" as children prepare to leave.

Let's Start the Day

✓ Learning Goals

Social and Emotional Development
• Child demonstrates initiative in independent activities; makes independent choices.

Language and Communication
• Child follows basic rules for conversations (making eye contact, staying on topic, listening actively).

Emergent Literacy: Reading
• Child produces the most common sound for a given letter.

Vocabulary

beginning	principio	end	final
middle	medio	problem	problema
solve	resolver		
story character	personaje de cuento		

Differentiated Instruction

✋ Extra Support

Oral Language and Vocabulary
If...children have difficulty identifying story characters with problems, **then...**read the story of "Little Red Riding Hood," and ask: *What was Little Red Riding Hood's problem? How did she solve it? ¿Cuál era el problema de Caperucita roja? ¿Cómo lo resolvió?*

⭐ Enrichment

Oral Language and Vocabulary
Challenge children to think of other ways Jack could have solved his problem in "Jack and the Beanstalk."

▶ **Opening Routines and Transition Tips**

For **Opening Routines** and **Transition Tips** turn to pages 178–181 and visit **DLMExpressOnline.com** for more ideas.

📖 Read **"The Ugly Duckling"/**"El patito feo" from the *Teacher's Treasure Book*, page 325, for your morning Read Aloud.

Language Time

 large group · 15 minutes

👫 **Social and Emotional Development** Ask children to tell you the class rules about listening and raising their hands.

Oral Language and Vocabulary

✓ Do children recognize that in many folk tales, the story character has a problem to solve?

Story Characters with Problems Talk about folk tales that children know, such as "Jack and the Beanstalk" and "The Lion and the Mouse." Say: *In these stories and in many others, the story characters have a problem to solve. En estos cuentos y en mucho otros, los personajes tienen que resolver un problema.* (Explain that *story characters* are the animals or people the story is about.)

● Ask: *What is Jack's problem in "Jack and the Beanstalk"? How does he solve his problem? ¿Qué problema tiene Jaime en "Jaime y los frijoles mágicos"? ¿Cómo lo resuelve?*

● Have children give examples of other stories in which the character has to solve a problem. Ask: *When does the story character solve the problem—at the beginning of the story or at the end of the story? How do you feel when he or she solves the problem? ¿Cuándo resuelve el personaje el problema? ¿Al principio del cuento o al final? ¿Cómo se sienten ustedes cuando el personaje resuelve el problema?*

Phonological Awareness

✓ Can children identify words that end with the same sound?

Recognize Same Final Sounds Hold one Dog Puppet and give the second one to a child. Have your puppet "say" two words, such as *leaf* and *calf*. The child's puppet must then say whether or not the words end with the same sound. Continue until each child has had a turn to use the puppet. Remind children that words that end with the same sound do not have to rhyme.

ELL Display Library Photo cards for *frog, duck, goat, moose, pig, bat, truck,* and *mouse*. Have children name each picture. Then have them match the photos whose names end with the same sound.

Center Time

▶ **Center Rotation** Center Time includes teacher-guided activities and independent activities. Refer to the **Learning Centers** on pages 138–139 for independent activity ideas.

 small group 60–90 minutes

Library and Listening Center

✓ Track children's ability to recognize that story characters often have problems to solve.

Materials a variety of familiar folk tale and fairy tale picture books

Browsing Stories and Tales Have children browse through picture books to find story characters with problems to solve.

- Say: *You know many of these stories. Look carefully at the pictures to find problems that the story characters solve.* *Ustedes conocen muchos de estos cuentos. Observen cuidadosamente las imágenes para encontrar los problemas que los personajes del cuento resolvieron.* Tell children to work in pairs and talk about what they see.

- Ask: *Do you think the story character solved the problem in a good way? Were there other ways to solve the problem?* *¿Creen que el personaje del cuento resolvió bien el problema? ¿Había otras formas de resolverlo?*

Center Tip

If...children have difficulty identifying a character's problem from the pictures, **then...**it may be helpful for them to hear the story again.

Pretend and Learn Center

✓ Track how well children can act out stories that were read aloud to them.

Act Out Stories Explain to children that they can act out two of the stories you read aloud this week, "Jack and the Beanstalk" and "The Ugly Duckling."

- Have children form groups and decide which story they would like to act out. Then have them decide which characters they will portray. Say: *Speak in a way that shows how your character feels.* *Muestren cómo se siente su personaje.*

- Encourage children to practice their stories a few times, and then act them out for the class. Remind those in the "audience" to pay attention and listen politely.

Center Tip

If...children have difficulty acting out a story, **then...** remind them of specific story details, such as how the Ugly Duckling felt when no one wanted to play with her. Or, ask questions that provide clues about story characters, such as: *How did the giant speak? How did Jack feel when he met the giant?*

 ✓ **Learning Goals**

Social and Emotional Development
- Child demonstrates initiative in independent activities; makes independent choices.

Language and Communication
- Child uses newly learned vocabulary daily in multiple contexts.

Emergent Literacy: Reading
- Child enjoys and chooses reading-related activities.
- Child retells or reenacts poems and stories in sequence.

Differentiated Instruction

✋ **Extra Support**
Pretend and Learn Center
If...children have difficulty remembering story events, **then...**ask questions about the beginning, middle, and end of the story to reinforce the sequence of events.

⭐ **Enrichment**
Pretend and Learn Center
Have children make up additional dialogue for story characters. Ask: *What happens after the story ends? What might Jack* (from "Jack and the Beanstalk") *say and do the next day? ¿Qué pasa después de que termina el cuento? ¿Qué podría decir y hacer Jaime el día siguiente?*

Accommodations for 3's
Pretend and Learn Center
If...children have difficulty acting out a story, **then...**reread one of the stories, stopping at intervals to ask: *What happens next? ¿Qué sucede después?*

How do living things grow and change?
¿Cómo crecen y cambian los seres vivos?

Circle Time

Literacy Time

Read Aloud

 Can children answer questions about a story that is read aloud?

Build Background Tell children that you will be reading a folk tale about a chicken that was different from his brothers and sisters.

● Ask: *What other story do you know about an animal that was different? What happened to the Ugly Duckling?* ¿Qué otro cuento conocen sobre un animal que era diferente? ¿Qué le sucedió al Patito feo?

Listen for Enjoyment Read aloud *Teacher's Treasure Book*, page 327, "The Half-Chicken"/"Medio Pollito."

● Tell children to listen carefully to find out what problem the half-chicken, named Medio Pollito, solves in the story.

● Ask: *Why does Medio Pollito leave home? What happens to him on the way to the king's castle?* ¿Por qué Medio Pollito se va de su casa? ¿Qué le sucede en su camino al castillo del rey?

Respond to the Story Have children tell how Medio Pollito solved his problem. Ask: *What lesson did he learn?* ¿Qué lección aprendimos?

TIP Change the tone of your voice as you read the dialogue for Medio Pollito, his mother, the cook, and the king.

ELL Talk about how the wind caused Medio Pollito to "spin" when he was on top of the roof. Explain that *spin* means the same as *turn around and around*. Have children show what it means to spin.

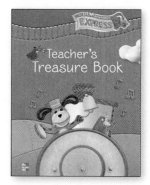

Teacher's Treasure Book

Learn About Letters and Sounds

 Can children identify the sounds /j/, /h/, and /y/ for Jj, Hh, and Yy?

Review Letters *Jj, Hh, Yy* Sing the Alphabet Song with children as you page through the *ABC Big Book*, stopping when you get to each target letter. Say the names of the pictures for each letter. Then chant the letter sound. For example: "/j/ /j/ /j/ let's jump with a jump rope" as they jump.

● Model how to write the upper case and lower case forms of each letter using the *ABC Picture Cards*. Have children trace the letters with their finger.

● While one child is tracing, the other children can be "writing" the letter in the air or on their palm with their finger. Have them say the sound of the letter each time they "write" it.

ABC Big Book

Math Time

Observe and Investigate

 Can children add up to 5 objects and match the number of objects with the numeral?

How Many Now? Give each child in the group a set of Numeral Cards from 1 to 5.

- Set out three Two-Color Counters, and say: *Let's count them together— 1, 2, 3. Vamos a contarlas todos juntos: 1, 2, 3.* Cover the counters with a cloth, and tell children to watch as you add another counter.

- Ask children to show the Numeral Card that tells how many counters there are. One child lifts the cloth to count to check their answers.

- Repeat several times, adding different combinations of sums up to 5.

☆☆☆ Social and Emotional Development

Making Good Choices

 Do children show a desire to figure things out on their own?

Being Helpful Display the Dog Puppets and show them reading a library book about plants or animals. Tell children the puppets are reading a book they haven't read before, and they have come to a part they don't understand. Model a dialogue between the puppets to show that each one can help solve the problem.

- Have one puppet use the picture on the page to figure out what he doesn't understand. Have the other puppet clarify further by relating the problem to a personal experience.

- Remind children that they should always try to figure things out and solve problems.

ELL Encourage children to read a book with a puppet so that they can "explain" to the puppet what the book is about, what the pictures show, and whether they liked the book or not.

large group 15 minutes

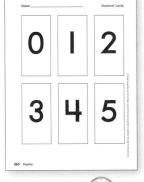

Online Math Activity panel:

Building Blocks

Online Math Activity

Children can complete Pizza Pizzazz 4 and Dinosaur Shop 3 during computer time or Center Time.

Numeral Cards:

| 0 | 1 | 2 |
| 3 | 4 | 5 |

large group 15 minutes

Focus Question
How do living things grow and change?
¿Cómo crecen y cambian los seres vivos?

Learning Goals

Language and Communication
• Child follows two- and three-step oral directions.

Mathematics
• Child uses concrete objects or makes a verbal word problem to add up to 5 objects.

Vocabulary

adding	sumar	altogether	en total
count	contar	number	número

Differentiated Instruction

 Extra Support

Observe and Investigate

If...children have difficulty during Finger Word Problems, **then...**use smaller numbers and/or help children show the correct number of fingers.

 Enrichment

Observe and Investigate

Challenge children to use numbers up to 10 or even greater. If children use numbers greater than 10, they will have to remember one number as they use their hands to show the other number.

Math Time

large group — 20 minutes

Language and Communication Skills Monitor that children are able to follow directions as they participate in both activities.

Oral Language and Academic Vocabulary

 **Can children identify numerals and match them with the corresponding number of objects?**

Talk About Numerals Display Numeral Cards, *Teacher's Treasure Book*, pages 510–511. Ask children to identify each numeral and represent it with the correct number of Two-Color Counters.

● Show Numeral Card 7. Have children display the corresponding number of counters and count to 7.

● Repeat with other Numeral Cards. (Be sure to include Numeral Cards 6 and 8.) Have children identify the numeral, display the correct number of Two-Color Counters, and count them aloud.

Observe and Investigate

Can children add up to 8 objects?

Finger Word Problems Tell children that today they will solve more difficult adding problems with their fingers. Say: *You will solve problems with numbers up to 8.* *Ustedes resolverán problemas con números hasta el 8.* Remind children to place their hands in their laps between each problem.

● Tell children that you went to the park and saw 4 children riding bikes and 3 children playing catch. Ask: *How many children did I see altogether?* *¿Cuántos niños vi en total?* Guide children in showing 4 fingers on one hand and 3 fingers on the other, and ask: *How many is that altogether?* *¿Cuántos niños hay en total?*

● Ask children how they got their answer, and repeat with other problems. For example: *In the park I saw 6 ducks swimming in the lake and 2 ducks walking on land. How many ducks did I see altogether?* *En el parque vi 6 patos nadando en el lago y 2 patos en la tierra. ¿Cuántos patos vi en total?*

● Continue with other problems, focusing on sums 5 to 8.

ELL Give children many opportunities to ask and answer the question: *How many [name of objects] are there altogether?* Also make sure that children can identify the words that name the numerals 1–10, so that language does not prevent them from learning new math concepts.

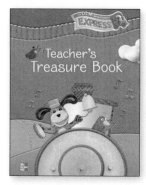

Teacher's Treasure Book

Center Time

▶ **Center Rotation** Center Time includes teacher-guided activities and independent activities. Refer to the **Learning Centers** on pages 138–139 for independent activity ideas.

   small group 30 minutes

Learning Goals

Social and Emotional Development
• Child demonstrates initiative in independent activites; makes independent choices.

Language and Communication
• Child names and describes actual or pictured people, places, things, actions, attributes, and events.

Mathematics
• Child knows that objects, or parts thereof, can be counted.

• Child uses concrete objects or makes a verbal word problem to add up to 5 objects.

Math and Science Center

✓ Track children's ability to create and solve addition problems.

Materials Farm Animal Counters, piece of paper

Word Problems Tell children that they will work with a partner to make up their own word problems for adding.

● Give partners animal counters and a piece of paper. One child chooses two sets of animals and places them on the scene, for example, 4 pigs and 2 horses. The other child makes up a word problem, for example: *4 pigs are playing a game; 2 horses come by to play with them. How many animals are there altogether?* *4 cerdos están jugando un juego; 2 caballos vienen a jugar con ellos. ¿Cuántos animales hay en total?*

● Children count the animals together to find the answer. Then partners switch roles and use different numbers of animals.

Center Tip

If...children need help making up word problems, **then...** offer suggestions for things the animals could be doing, such as *taking a walk,* *eating lunch,* or *taking a nap.*

Writing

Recap the day. Have children tell about a story character that solved a problem. *Was the story character a person or an animal? What was the problem and how did they solve it?* *¿Ese personaje del cuento era una persona o un animal? ¿Cuál era su problema y cómo lo resolvió?* Record their answers in a list. Read them aloud as you track the print, emphasizing the correspondence between speech and print.

Purposeful Play

✓ Observe children taking turns as they role-play animals caring for their young.

Children choose an open center for free playtime. Encourage cooperation skills by suggesting they take turns role-playing an animal mom taking care of her babies. Encourage children to think about how certain animals, such as kangaroos, birds, dogs, and horses, care for their young.

Let's Say Good-Bye

 large group 15 minutes

 Read Aloud Revisit the story, "The Ugly Duckling"/*"El patito feo"* for your afternoon Read Aloud. Remind children to think about how the duckling changes as they listen to the story.

 Home Connection Refer to Home Connections activities listed in the Resources and Materials chart on page 135. Remind children to tell families a story about how animals grow and change over time. Sing the "Good-Bye Song" as children prepare to leave.

DAY 5

Let's Start the Day

Focus Question

How do living things grow and change?

¿Cómo crecen y cambian los seres vivos?

 Learning Goals

Social and Emotional Development
• Child demonstrates initiative in independent activities; makes independent choices.

Language and Communication
• Child begins and ends conversations appropriately.

Fine Arts
• Child participates in a variety of music activities (such as listening, singing, finger plays, musical games, performances).

Vocabulary

bear cub   potrillito   den   guarida

seedling   brote

Differentiated Instruction

 Extra Support

Oral Language and Vocabulary
If...children have difficulty describing how living things grow and change, **then...**remind them that as people and animals grow up, they are able to do more things on their own.

Enrichment

Oral Language and Vocabulary
Challenge children to describe how a baby kangaroo changes over time.

 Special Needs

Delayed Motor Development
Allow time for the child to rest if s/he becomes tired or fatigued by a new activity.

> **Opening Routines and Transition Tips**
> For **Opening Routines** and **Transition Tips** turn to pages 178–181 and visit DLMExpressOnline.com for more ideas.
>
> Read **"Shade Trees"**/"Árbol frondoso" from the *Teacher's Treasure Book,* page 110, for your morning Read Aloud. Then read the poem a second time.

Language Time

 large group / 15 minutes

Social and Emotional Development Remind children to listen carefully as their classmates share or ask questions. Suggest that they can learn many things from each other.

Oral Language and Vocabulary

 Do children recognize that all living things change as they grow?

Living Things Change Talk about what children have learned this week about how plants, animals, and people change as they grow. Ask: **What does a tree look like when it begins to grow? How does it change over time?** *¿Cómo se ve un árbol cuando está empezando a crecer? ¿Cómo cambia con el tiempo?*

● Display *Rhymes and Chants Flip Chart,* page 28. Sing "What Will I Be?" to the tune of *Frere Jacques* with children. Ask: **What will the tiny sapling grow up to be? What will the little bear cub grow up to be?** *¿En qué se convertirá el brote cuando crezca? ¿En qué se convertirá el potrillito cuando crezca?*

Rhymes and Chants Flip Chart, p. 28

Phonological Awareness

Can children identify words that end with the same sound?

Recognize Same Final Sounds Using *Rhymes and Chants Flip Chart,* p. 28, sing "What Will I Be?" once more with children. Point to the tree in the picture. Ask: **Which word in the song rhymes with tree and ends with the same sound? Can you think of a word that rhymes with bear?** (mare, tear, wear) *¿Qué palabra de la canción rima con* tree*? ¿Qué palabra rima con* bear*?*

ELL Point to the bear cub and the adult bear in the Flip Chart illustration. Ask: **Which bear is smaller? Which bear is bigger? Which bear will grow up?** Have children answer in complete sentences. Model answers as needed. For additional suggestions on how to meet the needs of children at the Beginning, Intermediate, Advanced, and Advanced-High levels of English proficiency, see pages 184–187.

Center Time

Center Rotation Center Time includes teacher-guided activities and independent activities. Refer to the **Learning Centers** on pages 138–139 for independent activity ideas.

 small group 60–90 minutes

Writer's Center

✓ Track children's use of language to describe things they did when they were babies and things they are able to do now.

Materials drawing paper, crayons

Then and Now Have children create two-part drawings of themselves.

- Give each child a large rectangular piece of drawing paper with a line drawn down the middle to form two squares.

- On the left side of the paper, children will draw a picture of themselves as a baby. On the right side, they will draw a picture of themselves doing an activity they enjoy now. Children will label the pictures "Then" and "Now," and write their name at the top.

- When children have completed their pictures, fasten the pages together to form a class book. Create a cover with the title, *Then and Now.*

- Allow time for children to share and talk about their pictures with the class.

Center Tip

If...children do not know what to draw for their baby picture, **then...**talk about some of the things babies do, such as sleep in cribs, play in playpens, and sit in high chairs.

ABC Center

✓ Track children's ability to match upper case and lower case letters.

Materials ABC Picture Cards, Alphabet Letter Tiles, or magnetic letters; drawing paper; crayons or markers

Matching Letters Explain to children that they will match the upper case and lower case forms of the letters they reviewed this week.

- As children match the letter forms, have them chant the sound, for example: "/j/ /j/ /j/ as in *jellyfish* and *jellybeans*."

- Have children write each letter with a crayon. Encourage them to add drawings of objects whose names begin with that letter and sound.

Center Tip

If...children have difficulty writing a letter, **then...**have them trace the letter several times and then try writing it on their own.

 Learning Goals

Language and Communication
- Child names and describes actual or pictured people, places, things, actions, attributes, and events.

Emergent Literacy: Reading
- Child names most upper- and lowercase letters of the alphabet.
- Child identifies the letter that stands for a given sound.

Emergent Literacy: Writing
- Child uses scribbles, shapes, pictures, symbols, and letters to represent language.

Differentiated Instruction

 Extra Support
Writer's Center
If...children have difficulty labeling their pictures, **then...**write the words lightly in pencil, so that they may trace them.

 Enrichment
Writer's Center
Have children write a short sentence for each picture they draw, such as: "I slept a lot." and "I like to read."

Accommodations for 3's
Writer's Center
If...children have difficulty labeling their pictures, **then...**write the labels for them.

Circle Time

Learning Goals

Emergent Literacy: Reading
• Child names most upper- and lowercase letters of the alphabet.

• Child identifies the letter that stands for a given sound.

• Child asks and answers questions about books read aloud (such as "Who?" "What?" "Where?").

Science
• Child identifies organisms and describes their characteristics.

• Child understands and describes life cycles of plants and animals.

Vocabulary

apple	manzano	cherry	cerezo
gardener	jardinero	pear	peral
greenhouse	invernadero		

Differentiated Instruction

 Extra Support

Learn About Letters and Sounds
If...children have difficulty matching a word with its initial letter, **then...**have them match only sounds with letters.

 Enrichment

Learn About Letters and Sounds
Challenge children to play Word Hopscotch by writing words that begin with target letters in the hopscotch boxes. Say a word and have children hop to the word.

Literacy Time

 large group 15 minutes

📖 Read Aloud

✓ **Can children retell a story?**

Build Background Tell children that you will be rereading a story about four friends who visit a very big garden.

● Ask: *What kinds of plants did Maria and her friends see? ¿Qué tipo de plantas vieron María y sus amigos?*

Listen for Understanding Display the Big Book, *"My Garden"/"Mi jardín,"* and read the title.

● Reread pages 10–14. Ask: *What kinds of flowers grow in the garden? What kinds of trees are there? ¿Qué tipo de flores crecen en el jardín? ¿Qué tipo de árboles hay allí?*

● Reread pages 20–25. Ask: *How does a daisy seed become a daisy? Describe what happens first, next, and last. ¿Cómo una semilla de margarita se convierte en una margarita?*

Respond and Connect Point out to children that the book teaches us how plants grow and change. Ask: *If you had a garden, what kinds of plants would you grow? How would you take care of them? Si tuvieran un jardín, ¿qué tipo de plantas les gustaría cultivar? ¿Cómo las cuidarían?*

TIP Point out to children that both the text and pictures give information about plants.

ELL Provide sentence frames to help children talk about the pictures in "My Garden." Use frames such as *An apple tree has _____ and _____. There are _____ and _____ in the pond.*

Learn About Letters and Sounds

✓ **Can children identify letters with their sounds?**

Hopscotch Review Use masking tape to create a large hopscotch grid on the floor. In each box, write one of the target letters, *Jj, Hh, Yy,* as well letters from previous units *Cc, Uu, Vv, Bb, Nn.*

● Call out a sound or say a word that begins with one of the letters. A child hops to the box that contains the letters.

● Give each child at least one chance to play. Use words such as the following for *j: jacket, jar, jeans, jeep; h: hand, hair, hat, happy; y: yard, yarn, yawn, yellow; c: calendar, calf, call, cat; u: uncle, under, up, umbrella; v: vegetable, vine, vest, van; b: baby, bag, banana, bat; n: nest, nine, nut, neck.*

My Garden
Mi jardín

large group 15 minutes

Building Blocks

Online Math Activity

Children can complete Pizza Pizzazz 4 and Dinosaur Shop 3 during computer time or Center Time.

Math Time

Observe and Investigate

Can children add objects?

Materials counters, play money

Dinosaur Shop (Adding) Have children work in pairs for this activity; one is a customer, the other is a salesperson. Children should get to play each role.

- Review that one dinosaur costs one dollar. The customer orders three dinosaurs. The salesperson asks for the same amount of money, and the customer pays. After children role-play the scene, say: ***Now the salesperson counts the money and the customer counts the dinosaurs. They should each have the same number.*** ***Ahora el vendedor cuenta el dinero y el cliente cuenta los dinosaurios. Cada uno debe tener el mismo número.*** (Three dinosaurs and three dollars.)
- Have children role-play several transactions. Check to see whether children can produce ten or higher with dinosaurs and money. Check also whether they can count dinosaurs that are not arranged in a line.

ELL Make sure children understand that a *salesperson* works in a store and *sells* items. A *customer* comes into a store and *buys* items.

large group 15 minutes

Social and Emotional Development

Making Good Choices

Do children show a desire to figure things out on their own?

Being Helpful Display *Making Good Choices Flip Chart,* page 28, "How Do I Solve Problems?"

- Point to the Flip Chart illustration, and ask: ***What have we learned about figuring things out on our own?*** ***¿Qué hemos aprendido sobre averiguar algunas cosas por nuestra cuenta?***
- Place an assortment of puzzles and library books on the table. Say: ***Pretend that you are working on a puzzle, like the girl in the picture, or reading a book. Let's show what we do when we are trying to figure something out by ourselves.*** ***Imaginen que están trabajando en un rompecabezas, como la niña de la imagen, o leyendo un libro. Mostremos lo que hacemos cuando intentamos averiguar algo por nuestra cuenta.*** Encourage children to describe what is giving them difficulty and what they will do to figure it out.
- Remind children that there are many different ways to solve problems and figure things out.

Making Good Choices Flip Chart, p. 28

Learning Goals

Social and Emotional Development
- Child demonstrates initiative in independent activities; makes independent choices.

Language and Communication
- Child follows two- and three-step oral directions.

Mathematics
- Child uses concrete objects or makes a verbal word problem to add up to 5 objects.

Vocabulary

customer	cliente	dinosaur	dinosaurio
dollar	dólar	salesperson	vendedor

Differentiated Instruction

Extra Support

Observe and Investigate

If...children struggle with adding, **then...** provide fewer dinosaur counters (and less money) for them to count.

Enrichment

Observe and Investigate

Challenge children by providing more dinosaur counters (and more money) for them to count. Or, encourage them to calculate the sum before counting, either mentally or by using their fingers.

Accommodations for 3's

Observe and Investigate

If...children struggle with adding, **then...** provide fewer than five dinosaur counters (and dollars) for them to count.

Learning Goals

Social and Emotional Development
• Child demonstrates initiative in independent activities; makes independent choices.

Science
• Child identifies organisms and describes their characteristics.

Physical Development
• Child coordinates body movements in a variety of locomotive activities (such as walking, jumping, running, hopping, skipping, climbing).

Vocabulary

around	alrededor	move	moverse
quickly	rápido	run	correr
slowly	lento	space	espacio

Differentiated Instruction

 Extra Support

Explore Movement
If...children have difficulty running around the circles, **then...**hold their hand and run with them. Then let them try it on their own.

 Enrichment

Explore Movement
Have children combine movements and alternate running and skipping around the circles.

Outdoor Play Time

large group · 20 minutes

Oral Language and Academic Vocabulary

☑ **Do children recognize that running is a skill that is acquired over time?**

Growing and Changing Remind children that they have been learning that animal and human babies need adults to take care of them because they cannot do very much on their own. Say: *As you grow up, you are able to do many things with your body that you couldn't do when you were a baby. One of those things is running. A medida que crecen, son capaces de hacer con su cuerpo muchas cosas que no podían hacer cuando eran bebés. Una de estas cosas es correr.*

- Ask: *Do you like to run? How does it feel? Did anyone teach you to run, or were you just able to do it one day? ¿Les gusta correr? ¿Cómo se sienten cuando corren? ¿Alguien les enseñó a correr o simplemente fueron capaces de hacerlo un día?* Point out that as babies, we get around by crawling. When we begin walking at the age of one or two, our legs are very shaky and wobbly.

- Say: *As time passes, our body and our legs get stronger. Then we are able to walk and run without even thinking about it! Con el paso del tiempo, nuestro cuerpo y nuestras piernas se hacen más fuertes. Entonces, somos capaces de caminar y correr ¡incluso sin pensar en ello!*

- Ask children to compare the way they move now with the way they moved when they were babies. Ask: *Will you be able to run even faster as you continue to grow? Why? ¿Podrán correr todavía más rápido a medida que sigan creciendo? ¿Por qué?*

Explore Movement

☑ **Can children learn a sense of direction while running?**

Materials four cardboard circles with a 15-inch diameter, a drum or another musical instrument

Moving Quickly Take children outside to the schoolyard or playground. If possible, find a grassy area that is about 20 feet long for the running distance.

- Have the children line up on one side of the grass, while you stand at the other side. Say: *Show me how you can run to my side of the grass. I will play the drum. When I stop playing, then you have to stop, too. Muéstreme cómo pueden correr hasta donde yo estoy. Voy a tocar el tambor. Cuando deje de tocarlo, deben detenerse ustedes también.*

- Set up the cardboard circles in a line with about three feet of space between them. Have children run around the circles, first quickly, and then slowly. Ask: *How would a train move around the circles? How would an airplane fly around the circles? ¿Cómo se movería un tren alrededor de los círculos? ¿Cómo volaría un avión alrededor de los círculos?* Have children demonstrate.

- Monitor how well children are able to move. You may want to take notes, so that you can check on their progress over the next few months.

Center Time

Center Rotation Center Time includes teacher-guided activities and independent activities. Refer to the **Learning Centers** on pages 138–139 for independent activity ideas.

 small group 30 minutes

Refer to the **Learning Centers** on pages 138–139 for independent activity ideas.

Construction Center

Center Tip

✓ **Monitor children as they build a pond with ducks and frogs.**

Materials blocks, construction paper, crayons, scissors, clay, animal toys

Build a Pond Habitat Tell children that they will use blocks and other art materials to build a pond habitat with plants and animals.

- Have children work in small groups. Ask: *What will your pond look like? What animals will you put in the pond? Will there be ducks and ducklings, frogs and tadpoles, different kinds of fish? ¿Cómo es su estanque? ¿Qué animales pondrán? ¿Habrá patos y patitos, ranas y renacuajos, y diferentes tipos de peces?*

- Remind children that in "My Garden," they learned that water lilies grow in ponds. Ask: *What other kinds of plants are found in and around ponds? ¿Qué otro tipo de plantas se encuentran en el estanque y alrededor de él?*

- Have each group share their pond habitat with the class and describe the living things that grow there.

If...children need to be reminded about sharing materials and working together, **then...**suggest roles for each child in the building of the pond habitat.

Learning Goals

Social and Emotional Development
- Child demonstrates initiative in independent activities; makes independent choices.

Language and Communication
- Child names and describes actual or pictured people, places, things, actions, attributes, and events.

Science
- Child identifies organisms and describes their characteristics.
- Child understands and describes life cycles of plants and animals.

Writing

Recap the day and week. Say: *Tell me something that you learned this week about how living things grow and change. Díganme algo que hayan aprendido esta semana sobre cómo crecen y cambian los seres vivos.* Record children's answers on chart paper. Share the marker with children as you write. Have each child write his or her name beside their entry.

Purposeful Play

✓ **Observe children working cooperatively as they make up verses for a song.**

Children choose an open center for free playtime. Encourage cooperation skills by suggesting they make up new verses for "Row, Row, Row Your Boat." For example, start them off with this verse: "Row, row, row your boat gently down the stream; watch the ducklings swim and play—life is but a dream!"

Let's Say Good-Bye

 large group 15 minutes

 Read Aloud Revisit the poem, "Shade Trees"/"Árbol frondoso" for your afternoon Read Aloud. Then read the poem a second time. Remind children to listen for how trees grow and change over time.

Home Connection Refer to the Home Connections activities listed in the Resources and Materials chart on page 135. Remind children to tell families what they learned this week about the ways living things grow and change. Sing the "Good-Bye Song" as children prepare to leave.

In general, the purpose of assessing young children in the early childhood classroom is to collect information necessary to make important decisions about their developmental and educational needs. Because assessment is crucial to making informed teaching decisions, it is necessarily a vital component of *DLM Early Childhood Express.* The guidelines and forms found online allow the teacher to implement assessment necessary in the pre-kindergarten classroom.

Effective assessment is an ongoing process that always enhances opportunities for optimal growth, development, and learning. The process of determining individual developmental and educational needs tailors early childhood education practices and provides a template for setting individual and program goals.

Pre-kindergarten assessment should be authentic; that is, it should be a natural, environmental extension of the classroom. Assessments should be incorporated into classroom activities whenever possible, not completed as separate, pull-out activities in which the teacher evaluates the student one-on-one. Whenever possible, assessment should evaluate children's real knowledge in the process of completing real activities. For example, observing children as they equally distribute snacks would be a better assessment of their ability to make groups than observing an exercise in which children group counters would be.

It is also important to note that assessments should be administered over time, as environmental influences can greatly impact single outcomes. If a pre-kindergarten child is tired or ill, for example, the child may not demonstrate knowledge of a skill that has actually been mastered. It is also important to consider the length of assessment for children of this age, as attention spans are still developing and can vary greatly based on environmental influences. Most assessments should be completed within half an hour.

If possible, use multiple types of assessment for the same content area when working with pre-kindergarten children. Some children may be able to demonstrate mastery kinesthetically if they are not able to use expressive language well; others may not process auditory instruction adequately, but will be able to complete an assessment after observing someone model the task. It is vital that the assessment process should never make the child anxious or scared.

Informal Assessment

INFORMAL assessments rely heavily on observational and work-sampling techniques that continually focus on child performance, processes, and product over selected periods of time and in a variety of contexts.

ANECDOTAL assessments are written descriptions that provide a short, objective account of an event or an incident. Only the facts are reported—where, what, when, and how. Anecdotal records are especially helpful when trying to understand a child's behavior or use of skills. These recordings can be used to share the progress of individual children and to develop and individualize curriculum.

The Anecdotal Observational Record Form can be used at any time to document an individual child's progress toward a goal or signs indicating the need for developmental or medical evaluation. Observations can reflect the focused skills for the week, but are not limited to those skills. You may pair the form with video or audio recordings of the child to complete an anecdotal record.

Anecdotal Observational Record Form

CHECKLISTS are lists of skills or behaviors arranged into disciplines or developmental domains and are used to determine how a child exhibits the behaviors or skills listed. Teachers can quickly and easily observe groups of children and check the behaviors or skills each child is demonstrating at the moment.

Weekly Assessment

Weekly Assessments measure progress toward specific guidelines that are addressed in the weekly curriculum. The Performance Assessment Checklist measures progress toward the guidelines of the entire curriculum. It is intended to be used three times per year.

Performance Assessment Checklist

When using either type of checklist, it is important to remember that the skills and behaviors on the list are only guidelines. Each child is unique and has her or her own developmental timetable. It is also important to remember that the checklist only documents the presence or absence of a specific skill or behavior during the time of observation. It does not necessarily mean the skill is consistently present or lacking, though consistency may be noted when the skill has been observed over time.

PORTFOLIO assessments are collections of thoughtfully selected work samples, or artifacts, and accompanying reflections indicative of the child's learning experiences, efforts, and progress toward and/or attainment of established curriculum goals. They are an authentic, performance-based method to allow teachers to analyze progress over time. As children choose work samples for their portfolios, they become involved in their own learning and assessment and begin to develop the concept of evaluating their own work.

Although early childhood activities tend to focus on processes as opposed to products, there are numerous opportunities to collect samples of children's work. Items to collect include drawings, tracings, cuttings, attempts to print their names, and paintings. You may also include informal assessments of a child's ability to recognize letters, shapes, numbers, and rhyming words.

Formal Assessment

FORMAL assessments involve the use of standardized tests. They are administered in a prescribed manner and may require completion within a specified amount of time. Standardized tests result in scores that are usually compared to the scores of a normative group. These tests generally fall into the following categories: achievement tests, readiness tests, developmental screening tests, intelligence tests, and diagnostic tests.

Assessing Children with Special Needs

Children with special needs may require a more thorough initial assessment, more frequent on-going assessments, and continuous adaptation of activities. Assessment is essentially the first task for the teacher or caregiver in developing the individualized instruction program required for children with disabilities.

Assessing Children Who Are English Language Learners

Whenever possible, assessments should be given in both the child's first language and in English.

Focus Question

How do living things grow and change?

Everything Grows Gathering

Host an Everything Grows Gathering for Families

- Prepare for the event by placing butcher paper on a wall. Children and family members can trace their hands on the paper, sign the handprints, compare their sizes, and talk about other ways people change as they grow.

- Have children create a Guest Book for visitors to sign. During the gathering, have one or two children invite visitors to write their comments about the gathering in the Guest Book.

- Organize the classroom into four areas, focusing each area on one of the weekly themes for the unit: Animals Change, Plants Change, People Change, and Living Things Change. In each area, display the appropriate focus question and have children display examples of their completed work, such as:

  life stage sculptures

  musical instruments to "wake up" plants

  family dinner plates

  pond habitats

  writing pieces, drawings, and other creative work

- Have children show their family members around each area. Encourage them to talk about their work and answer any questions family members have. Encourage family members to also stop at the measuring chart.

- Provide nutritious "snacks for growing" that children can enjoy with their families, such as fruit kabobs and vegetable sticks with low-fat dip.

- Read aloud the Guest Book comments at the next Circle Time.

Evaluate and Inform

- ✓ Review the informal observation notes you recorded for each child during the four weeks of the unit. Identify areas in which individual children will need additional support.

- ✓ Send a summary of your observation notes home with children. Encourage parents to respond to the summary with questions or comments.

- ✓ Review dated samples of children's work in their portfolios. Copy some of these samples to send home to families along with the observation summary.

- ✓ Send home the Unit 6 My Library Book for children to read with their families.

Celebrar la unidad

Pregunta esencial

¿Cómo crecen y cambian los seres vivos?

Reunión sobre "todo crece"

Organice para los familiares una reunión sobre "todo crece"

- Prepare el evento colocando papel de estraza sobre la pared. Los niños y sus familiares pueden trazar sus manos en el papel, firmar sus contornos, comparar sus tamaños y hablar sobre algunas otras maneras en que la gente cambia a medida que crece.

- Pida a los niños que hagan un libro de invitados para que los visitantes lo firmen. Durante la reunión, haga que un niño o dos inviten a los visitantes a escribir en el libro de invitados sus comentarios acerca de la reunión.

- Organice a la clase en cuatro áreas, asignándole a cada área uno de los temas semanales de la unidad: Los animales cambian, Las plantas cambian, Las personas cambian y Los seres vivos cambian. En cada área, presente la pregunta de enfoque correspondiente y pídales a los niños que exhiban ejemplos de sus trabajos completados, como:

    esculturas de las etapas de la vida

    instrumentos musicales para "despertar" a las plantas

    platos de la comida familiar

    hábitat de estanques

    piezas de escritura, dibujos y otros trabajos creativos

- Pida a los niños que les muestren a sus familiares cada área. Anímelos a hablar sobre su trabajo y a responder las preguntas que sus familiares pudieran tener. A los familiares pídales que se detengan en la tabla de medición.

- Ofrezca nutritivos "bocadillos para crecer" para que los niños los disfruten con sus familiares, como brochetas de frutas y palitos de verduras con aderezo bajo en grasas.

- Lea en voz alta los comentarios del libro de invitados en la siguiente Hora del círculo.

Evaluar e informar

- Revise las observaciones informales que anotó para cada niño durante las cuatro semanas de la unidad. Identifique las áreas en las que cada niño podría requerir un apoyo adicional.

- Dé a los padres de los niños el resumen respectivo de sus observaciones. Insístales que respondan a este informe con preguntas o comentarios.

- Revise las muestras fechadas que hay en el portafolios de trabajo de cada niño. Haga copias de algunas de estas muestras para que las vean sus padres junto con el resumen de observaciones.

- Dé a los niños el librito de la Unidad 6 para leer con sus familias.

Appendix

About the Authors

NELL K. DUKE, ED.D., is Professor of Teacher Education and Educational Psychology and Co-Director of the Literacy Achievement Research Center at Michigan State University. Nell Duke's expertise lies in early literacy development, particularly among children living in poverty, and integrating literacy into content instruction. She is the recipient of a number of awards for her research and is co-author of several books including *Literacy and the Youngest Learner: Best Practices for Educators of Children from Birth to 5* and *Beyond Bedtime Stories: A Parent's Guide to Promoting Reading, Writing, and Other Literacy Skills From Birth to 5.*

DOUG CLEMENTS is SUNY Distinguished Professor of Education at the University of Buffalo, SUNY. Previously a preschool and kindergarten teacher, Clements currently researchs the learning and teaching of early mathematics and computer applications. He has published over 100 research studies, 8 books, 50 chapters, and 250 additional publications, including co-authoring the reports of President Bush's National Mathematics Advisory Panel and the National Research Council's book on early mathematics. He has directed twenty projects funded by the National Science Foundation and Department of Education's Institute of Education Sciences.

JULIE SARAMA Associate Professor at the University at Buffalo (SUNY), has taught high school mathematics and computer science, gifted and talented classes, and early childhood mathematics. She directs several projects funded by the National Science Foundation and the Institute of Education Sciences. Author of over 50 refereed articles, 4 books, 30 chapters, 20 computer programs, and more than 70 additional publications, she helped develop the Building Blocks and Investigations curricula and the award-winning Turtle Math. Her latest book is *Early Childhood Mathematics Education Research: Learning Trajectories for Young Children.*

WILLIAM TEALE is Professor of Education at the University of Illinois at Chicago. Author of over one hundred publications on early literacy learning, the intersection of technology and literacy education, and children's literature, he helped pioneer research in emergent literacy. Dr. Teale has worked in the area of early childhood education with schools, libraries, and other organizations across the country and internationally. He has also directed three U.S. Department of Education-funded Early Reading First projects that involve developing model preschool literacy curricula for four-year-old children from urban, low-income settings in Chicago.

Contributing Authors

Kimberly Brenneman, PhD, is an Assistant Research Professor of Psychology at Rutgers University. She is also affiliated with the Rutgers Center for Cognitive Science (RuCCS) and the National Institute for Early Education Research (NIEER). Brenneman is co-author of *Preschool Pathways to Science (PrePS): Facilitating Scientific Ways of Thinking, Talking, Doing, and Understanding* and is an educational advisor for PBS's *Sid the Science Kid* television show and website. Research interests include the development of scientific reasoning and methods to improve instructional practices that support science and mathematics learning in preschool.

Peggy Cerna is an independent Early Childhood Consultant. She was a bilingual teacher for 15 years and then served as principal of the Rosita Valley Literacy Academy, a Pre-Kindergarten through Grade 1 school in Eagle Pass, Texas. Cerna then opened Lucy Read Pre-Kindergarten Demonstration School in Austin, Texas, which had 600 Pre-Kindergarten students. During her principalship at Lucy Read, Cerna built a strong parental community with the collaboration of the University of Texas, AmeriCorps, and Austin Community College. Her passion for early literacy drove her to create book clubs where parents were taught how to read books to their children.

Dan Cieloha is an educator with more than 30 years' experience in creating, implementing, and evaluating experientially based learning materials, experiences, and environments for young children. He believes that all learners must be actively and equitably involved in constructing, evaluating, and sharing what they learn. He has spearheaded the creation and field-testing of a variety of learning materials including *You & Me: Building Social Skills in Young Children*. He is also president of the Partnership for Interactive Learning, a leading nonprofit organization dedicated to the development of children's social and thinking skills.

Paula A. Jones, M.Ed., is an Early Childhood Consultant at the state and national levels. As a former Early Childhood Director for the Lubbock Independent School District, she served as the Head Start Director and co-founded three of their four Early Childhood campuses which also became a model design and Best Practices Program for the Texas Education Agency. She was a contributing author for the first Texas Prekindergarten Guidelines, served as president for the Texas Association of Administrators and Supervisors of Programs for Young Children, and is a 2010 United Way Champions for Children Award winner.

Bobbie Sparks is a retired educator who has taught biology and middle school science as well as being the K-12 district science consultant for a suburban district. At Harris County Department of Education she served as the K-12 science consultant in Professional Development. During her career as K-12 science consultant, Sparks worked with teachers at all grade levels to revamp curriculum to meet the Texas science standards. She served on Texas state committees to develop the TEKS standards as well as committees to develop items for tests for teacher certification in science.

Opening Routines

Below are a few suggested routines to use for beginning your day with your class. You can rotate through them, or use one for a while before trying a new approach. You may wish to develop your own routines by mixing and matching ideas from the suggestions given.

1. Days of the Week

Ask children what day of the week it is. When they respond, tell them that you are going to write a sentence that tells everyone what day of the week it is. Print "Today is Monday." on the board. If you have a helper chart, have children assist you in finding the name of the day's helper. Print: "Today's helper is Miguel." Ask the helper to come forward and find the Letter Tiles or ABC Picture Cards that spell his or her name.

As the year progresses, you might want to have the helper find the letters that spell the day of the week. Eventually some children may be able to copy the entire sentence with Letter Tiles or ABC Picture Cards.

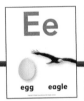

2. Calendar Search

Print "Today is _____." on the board. Ask children to help you fill in the blank. Print the day of the week in the blank. Invite children to look at the calendar to determine today's date. Write the date under the sentence that tells what day of the week it is. Invite children to clap out the syllables of both the sentence and the date.

Review the days of the week and the months of the year using the "Days of the Week Song"/"Canción de los días de la semana" and the "Months of the year"/ "Los meses del año."

Ask children what day of the week it was yesterday. When they respond, ask them what day it is today. Place a seasonal sticker on today's date. Have children follow your lead and recite "Yesterday was Monday, September 12. Today is Tuesday, September 13. Tomorrow will be Wednesday, September 14."

3. Feelings

Make happy- and sad-faced puppets for each child by cutting yellow circles from construction paper and drawing happy and sad faces on them. Laminate the faces, and glue them to tongue depressors. Cover two large coffee cans. On one can glue a happy face, and write the sentence "I feel happy today." Glue the sad face to the second can, and write the sentence "I feel sad today."

Give each child a happy- and a sad-faced puppet. Encourage children to tell how they feel today and to hold up the appropriate puppet. Encourage children to come forward and place their puppets in the can that represents their feelings. Later in the year you can add puppets to represent other emotions.

You can vary this activity by using a graph titled "How I Feel Today"/"Como me siento hoy." Have children place their puppets in the appropriate column on the graph instead of in the cans.

4. Pledge of Allegiance/ Moment of Silence

Have children locate the United States flag. Recite the Pledge of Allegiance to the U.S. flag. Then allow a minute for a moment of silence.

Discuss these activities with children, allowing them to volunteer reasons the Pledge of Allegiance is said and other places they have seen the Pledge recited.

5. Coming to Circle

Talk with children about being part of a class family. Tell children that as part of a class family they will work together, learn together, respect each other, help each other, and play together. Explain that families have rules so that jobs get done and everyone stays safe. Let children know they will learn rules for their classroom. One of those rules is how they will come together for circle. Sing "This is the Way We Come to Circle" (to the tune of "This is the Way We Wash Our Clothes").

This is the way we come to circle.
Come to circle, come to circle.
This is the way we come to circle,
So early in the morning.

This is the way we sit right down,
Sit right down, sit right down.
This is the way we sit right down,
So early in the morning.

This is the way we fold our hands,
Fold our hands, fold our hands.
This is the way we fold our hands,
So early in the morning.

Transition Tips

Sing songs or chants such as those listed below while transitioning between activities:

1. I Am Now in Pre-K

To the tune of "I'm a Little Teapot"

I am now in Pre-K,
I can learn.
I can listen. I can take a turn.
When the teacher says so,
I can play.
Choose a center and together we'll play.

2. Did You Clean Up?

To the tune of "Are You Sleeping, Are You Sleeping, Brother John?"

Did you clean up?
Did you clean up?
Please make sure.
Please make sure.
Everything is picked up.
Everything is picked up.
Please. Thank you!
Please. Thank you!

Chant: Red, Yellow, Green
Red, yellow, green
Stop, change, go
Red, yellow, green
Stop, change, go
Green says yes.
And red says no.
Yellow says everybody wait in a row.
Red, yellow, green
Stop, change, go
Red, yellow, green
Stop, change, go

3. The Five Senses Song

To the tune of "If You're Happy and You Know It"

I can see with my eyes every day (clap clap)
I can see with my eyes every day (clap clap)
I can see with my eyes
I can see with my eyes
I can see with my eyes every day (clap clap)
(Repeat with smell with my nose, hear with my ears, feel with my hands, and taste with my mouth.)

4. Eat More Vegetables

To the tune of "Row, Row, Row Your Boat"

Eat, eat, eat more,
Eat more vegetables.
Carrots, carrots, carrots, carrots
Eat more vegetables.
(Repeat with broccoli, lettuce, celery, and spinach.)

5. Circle Time

To the tune of "Here We Go 'Round the Mulberry Bush"

This is the way we come to circle
Come to circle, come to circle.
This is the way we come to circle
So early in the morning.

This is the way we sit right down,
Sit right down, sit right down.
This is the way we sit right down,
So early in the morning.

Play a short game such as one of the following to focus children's attention:

Name That Fruit!

Say: *It's red on the outside and white on the inside. It rhymes with chapel!*

Children answer, "Apple!" and then repeat twice, "Apple/Chapel."

Repeat with other fruits, such as cherry and banana.

I Spy

Use a flashlight to focus on different letters and words in the classroom. Have children identify them.

Monkey See Monkey Do

Choose one child to be the monkey leader. He or she will act out a motion such as twist, jump, clap, or raise hand, and the rest of the monkeys say the word and copy the motion.

Let's Play Pairs

Distribute one *ABC Picture Card* to each child. Draw letters from an additional set of cards. The child who has the matching letter identifies it and goes to the center of his or her choice.

That's My Friend!

Take children's name cards with their pictures from the wall and distribute making sure no one gets his or her own name. When you call a child's name, she or he has to say something positive about the child on the card and end with "That's my friend!"

Name Game

Say: *If your name begins with ____, you may choose a center.* Have the child say his or her name as he or she gets up. Repeat the child's name, emphasizing the beginning sound.

Center Management

Learning Centers provide children with additional opportunities to practice or extend each lesson's skills and concepts either individually or in small groups. The activities and materials that are explored in the centers not only promote oral language but also help develop children's social skills as they work together. The use of these Learning Centers encourage children to explore their surroundings and make their own choices.

Teacher's Role

The Learning Centers allow time for you to:

- Observe children's exploration of the centers.

- Assess children's understanding of the skills and concepts being taught.

- Provide additional support and encouragement to children who might be having difficulty with specific concepts or skills. If a child is having difficulty, model the correct approach.

Classroom Setup

The materials and activities in the centers should support what children are learning. Multiple experiences are necessary for children's comprehension. The centers should also engage them in learning by providing hands-on experiences. Every time children visit a center and practice skills or extend concepts being taught in the lessons, they are likely to broaden their understanding or discover something new.

In order to support children's learning, the materials and activities in the Learning Centers should change every week. It is important that all the children have a chance to explore every center throughout each week. Be sure they rotate to different centers and do not focus on only one activity. You might also consider adding new materials to the centers as the week progresses. This will encourage children to expand on their past work. Modify or add activities or materials based on your classroom needs.

It is crucial that children know what is expected of them in each center. To help children understand the expectation at each center, display an "I can" statement with an illustration or photograph of a student completing the activity. Discuss these expectations with children in advance, and reinforce them as needed. These discussions might include reviewing your typical classroom rules and talking about the limited number of children allowed in each center. Remind them that they may work individually or in small groups.

Library and Listening Center

Children should feel free throughout the day to explore books and other printed materials. Create a comfortable reading area in the room, and fill it with as many children's books as possible. Include a number of informational books that tell why things happen and books of rhymes, poems, and songs, as well as storybooks and simple alphabet books.

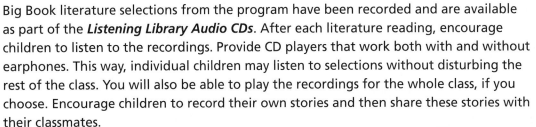

Before beginning each unit in the program, bring in books about the specific concepts or themes in a unit. Encourage children to bring in books they have enjoyed and would like to share with classmates. Even though they may not be actually reading, have children visit the area often. Here they can practice their book handling, apply their growing knowledge of print awareness, and look at pictures and talk about them. Have them read the books to you or to classmates.

Big Book literature selections from the program have been recorded and are available as part of the *Listening Library Audio CDs*. After each literature reading, encourage children to listen to the recordings. Provide CD players that work both with and without earphones. This way, individual children may listen to selections without disturbing the rest of the class. You will also be able to play the recordings for the whole class, if you choose. Encourage children to record their own stories and then share these stories with their classmates.

As you set up the Learning Centers, here are a few ideas you might want to implement in your classroom.

- Create a separate Workshop Center sign-up chart for children to use when choosing a center to explore.

- Provide an area for children who want to be alone to read or to simply reflect on the day's activities.

- Separate loud areas and quiet areas.

- Hang posters or art at eye level for the children.

- Place on shelves materials, such as books or art supplies, that are easily accessible to the children.

English Language Learners

Teaching the English Language Learner

Stages of English-Language Proficiency

An effective learning environment is an important goal of all educators. In a supportive environment, all English learners have the opportunity to participate and to learn. The materials in this guide are designed to support children while they are acquiring English, allowing them to develop English-language reading skills and the fluency they need to achieve in the core content areas as well.

This guide provides direction in supporting children in four stages of English proficiency: Beginning, Intermediate, Advanced, and Advanced-High. While children at a beginning level by definition know little English and will probably have difficulty comprehending English, by the time they progress to the intermediate or early advanced levels of English acquisition, their skills in understanding more complex language structures will have increased. These stages can be described in general terms as follows:

BEGINNING AND INTERMEDIATE Children identified at these levels of English-language proficiency demonstrate dramatic growth. During these stages, children progress from having no receptive or productive English to possessing a basic command of English. They are learning to comprehend and produce one- or two-word responses to questions, are moving to phrases and simple sentences using concrete and immediate topics, and are learning to interact in a limited fashion with text that has been taught. They progress to responding with increasing ease to more varied communication tasks using learned material, comprehending a sequence of information on familiar topics, producing basic statements and asking questions on familiar subjects, and interacting with a variety of print. Some basic errors are found in their use of English syntax and grammar.

ADVANCED Children who have reached the Advanced level of English-language proficiency have good comprehension of overall meaning and are beginning to demonstrate increased comprehension of specific details and concepts. They are learning to respond in expanded sentences, are interacting more independently with a variety of text, and in using newly acquired English vocabulary to communicate ideas orally and in writing. They demonstrate fewer errors in English grammar and syntax than at the beginning and early intermediate levels.

ADVANCED-HIGH Children who are identified at this level of English-language proficiency demonstrate consistent comprehension of meaning, including implied and nuanced meaning, and are learning the use of idiomatic and figurative language. They are increasingly able to respond using detail in compound and complex sentences and sustain conversation in English. They are able to use standard grammar with few errors and show an understanding of conventions of formal and informal usage.

It is important to provide an instructional scaffold for phonemic awareness, phonics, words structure, language structures, comprehension strategies and skills, and grammar, usage, and mechanics so that children can successfully learn to read while advancing along the continuum of English acquisition. For example, at the Beginning level, you might ask children for *yes* or *no* answers when answering questions about selection comprehension or grammar. Children at the Advanced-High level should be asked to provide answers in complete and expanded sentences. By the time children achieve an Advanced level, their knowledge of English will be more sophisticated because they are becoming more adept at comprehending English and using techniques such as making inferences or using persuasive language.

The following charts illustrate how to use sentence stems with children at each level of English-language proficiency:

Teaching Sentence Stems

- Write the sentence stems on the board, chart paper, or sentence strips. Choose stems that are appropriate for the four general levels of English proficiency.

- Model using the sentence stem(s) for the comprehension strategy or skill.

- Read each phrase as you insert the appropriate words to express an idea. Have children repeat the sentences after you. For Beginning and Intermediate children, use the stems within the questions you ask them.

Linguistic Pattern: *I predict that* _____.

Beginning	Intermediate	Advanced	Advanced-High
Simple questions about the text. Yes-or-no responses or responses that allow children to point to an object or picture.	Simple questions about the text which allow for one- or two-word responses or give children two options for a response to select from.	Questions that elicit a short response or a complete simple sentence using the linguistic pattern.	Have children make predictions on their own. Children should use the linguistic pattern and respond with a complete complex sentence.

Practicing Sentence Stems

- To give children multiple opportunities to generate the language they have just been taught, have them work in pairs or small groups and utilize cooperative learning participation strategies to facilitate this communicative practice.

- Pair children one level of proficiency above or below the other. For example, have Beginning children work with Intermediate level children.

- Use differentiated prompts to elicit the responses that incorporate the linguistic patterns and structures for the different proficiency levels. See the following sample of prompts and responses.

Beginning	Intermediate	Advanced	Advanced-High
Do you predict _____? *Yes/No*	Do you predict _____ or _____? *I predict* _____.	What do you predict _____? *I predict* _____.	Give a prediction about _____. *I predict* _____.

- Select some common cooperative learning participation strategies to teach to children. Once they have learned some language practice activities, they can move quickly into the various routines. See the examples on the next page.

English Language Learners

My Turn, Your Turn

Children work in pairs.

1. The teacher models a sentence and the whole group repeats, or echoes it.

2. One child generates an oral phrase, and the partner echoes it.

3. Partners switch and alternate roles so that each child has a chance to both generate and repeat phrases.

Talking Stick

Children work in small groups. This strategy allows every child to have an opportunity to speak several times and encourages more reflective or reticent participants to take a turn. Children can "pass" only one time.

1. The teacher charts sentence graphic organizers and linguistic patterns children will use in their responses.

2. The teacher models use of linguistic patterns from the lesson.

3. The teacher asks a question or gives a prompt, and then passes a stick, eraser, stuffed animal, or any other designated object to one child.

4. A child speaks, everyone listens, and then the child passes the object on to the person next to him or her.

5. The next child speaks, everyone listens, and the process continues until the teacher or facilitator gives a signal to return the object.

Think-Pair-Share

This strategy allows children time for processing ideas by building in sufficient wait time to process the question and frame an answer. It is an appropriate strategy to use during small- or large-group discussions or lessons, giving all children a chance to organize their thoughts and have a turn sharing their responses with a partner. It also allows for small group verbal interaction to practice language before sharing with the larger group.

1. After reading or listening to a section of text, the teacher presents a question or task. It is helpful to guide with a specific prompt, modeling the language to be used in the response.

2. Children think about their responses for a brief, designated amount of time.

3. Partners share and discuss their responses with each other.

4. An adaptation can be to have each child share his or her partner's response within a small group to promote active listening.

Teaching Vocabulary

Building the background knowledge and a context for children to learn new words is critical in helping children understand new vocabulary. Primary language can be a valuable tool for preteaching, concept development, and vocabulary. Cognates, or words similar in English counterparts, often provide an opportunity for bridging the primary language and English. Also, children who have background knowledge about a topic can more easily connect the new information they are learning with what they already know than children without a similar context from which to work. Therefore, giving children background information and encouraging them to make as many connections as possible with the new vocabulary word they encounter will help them better understand the selection they are about to read.

In addition to building background knowledge, visual displays such as pictures, graphs, charts, maps, models, or other strategies offer unambiguous access to new content. They provide a clear and parallel correspondence between the visual objects and the new vocabulary to be learned. Thus, because the correlation is clear, the negotiation of meaning is established. Additionally, this process must be constant and reciprocal between you and each child if the child is to succeed in effectively interacting with language.

Included in this guide is a routine for teaching vocabulary words. In addition to this routine, more detailed explanations of the ways to teach vocabulary are as follows:

REAL OBJECTS AND REALIA: Because of the immediate result visuals have on learning language, when explaining a word such as *car,* the best approach is simply to show a real car. As an alternative to the real object, you can show realia. Realia are toy versions of real things, such as plastic eggs to substitute for real eggs, or in this case, a toy car to signify a real car. A large, clear picture of an automobile can also work if it is absolutely recognizable.

If, however, the child has had no experience with the item in the picture, more explanation might be needed. For example, if the word you are explaining is a zoo animal such as an *ocelot,* and children are not familiar with this animal, one picture might be insufficient. They might confuse this animal with a cat or any one of the feline species. Seeing several clear pictures, then, of each individual type of common feline and comparing their similarities and differences might help clarify meaning in this particular instance. When children make a connection between their prior knowledge of the word *cat* with the new word *ocelot,* it validates their newly acquired knowledge, and thus they process learning more quickly.

PICTURES: Supplement story illustrations with visuals such as those found in the ***Photo Library CD, ABC Picture Cards,*** magazine pictures, and picture dictionaries. Videos, especially those that demonstrate an entire setting such as a farm or zoo, or videos where different animals are highlighted in the natural habitat, for instance, might be helpful. You might also wish to turn off the soundtrack to avoid a flood of language that children might not be able to understand. This way children can concentrate on the visual-word meaning correlation.

PANTOMIME: Language is learned through modeling within a communicative context. Pantomiming is one example of such a framework of communication. Some words, such as *run* and *jump,* are appropriate for pantomiming. Throughout this guide, you will find suggestions for pantomiming words like *sick* by coughing, sneezing, and holding your stomach. If children understand what you are trying to pantomime, they will more easily engage in the task of learning.

Letter Formation Guide

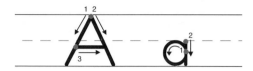

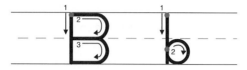

A Starting point, slanting down left
Starting point, slanting down right
Starting point, across the middle: capital *A*

a Starting point, around left all the way
Starting point, straight down,
touching the circle: small *a*

B Starting point, straight down
Starting point, around right and in
at the middle, around right and in
at the bottom: capital *B*

b Starting point, straight down, back
up, around right all the way: small *b*

C Starting point, around left to
stopping place: capital *C*

c Starting point, around left to
stopping place: small *c*

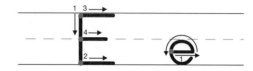

D Starting point, straight down
Starting point, around right and in
at the bottom: capital *D*

d Starting point, around left all the way
Starting point, straight down, touching
the circle: small *d*

E Starting point, straight down
Starting point, straight out
Starting point, straight out
Starting point, straight out: capital *E*

e Starting point, straight out, up and
around to the left, curving down
and around to the right: small *e*

F Starting point, straight down
Starting point, straight out
Starting point, straight out: capital *F*

f Starting point, around left and straight down
Starting point, straight across: small *f*

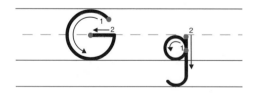

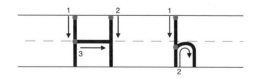

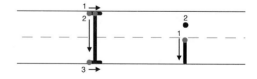

G Starting point, around left, curving up and
around
Straight in: capital *G*

g Starting point, around left all the way
Starting point, straight down, touching the
circle, around left to stopping place: small *g*

H Starting point, straight down
Starting point, straight down
Starting point, across the middle: capital *H*

h Starting point, straight down, back
up, around right, and straight down: small *h*

I Starting point, across
Starting point, straight down
Starting point, across: capital *I*

i Starting point, straight down
Dot exactly above: small *i*

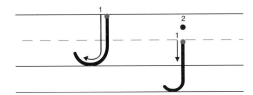

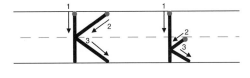

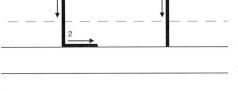

J Starting point, straight down, around left to stopping place: capital *J*

j Starting point, straight down, around left to stopping place Dot exactly above: small *j*

K Starting point, straight down Starting point, slanting down left, touching the line, slanting down right: capital *K*

k Starting point, straight down Starting point, slanting down left, touching the line, slanting down right: small *k*

L Starting point, straight down, straight out: capital *L*

l Starting point, straight down: small *l*

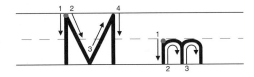

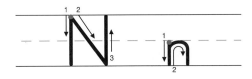

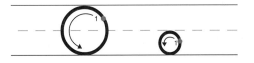

M Starting point, straight down Starting point, slanting down right to the point, slanting back up to the right, straight down: capital *M*

m Starting point, straight down, back up, around right, straight down, back up, around right, straight down: small *m*

N Starting point, straight down Starting point, slanting down right, straight back up: capital *N*

n Starting point, straight down, back up, around right, straight down: small *n*

O Starting point, around left all the way: capital *O*

o Starting point, around left all the way: small *o*

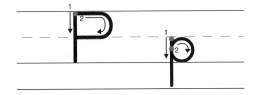

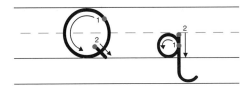

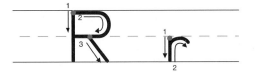

P Starting point, straight down Starting point, around right and in at the middle: capital *P*

p Starting point, straight down Starting point, around right all the way, touching the line: small *p*

Q Starting point, around left all the way Starting point, slanting down right: capital *Q*

q Starting point, around left all the way Starting point, straight down, touching the circle, curving up right to stopping place: small *q*

R Starting point, straight down Starting point, around right and in at the middle, touching the line, slanting down right: capital *R*

r Starting point, straight down, back up, curving around right to stopping place: small *r*

Letter Formation Guide

S Starting point, around left, curving right and down around right, curving left and up: capital *S*

s Starting point, around left, curving right and down around right, curving left and up to stopping place: small *s*

T Starting point, straight across
Starting point, straight down: capital *T*

t Starting point, straight down
Starting point, across short: small *t*

U Starting point, straight down, curving around right and up, straight up: capital *U*

u Starting point, straight down, curving around right and up, straight up, straight back down: small *u*

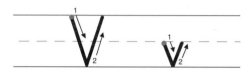

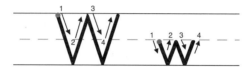

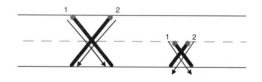

V Starting point, slanting down right, slanting up right: capital *V*

v Starting point, slanting down right, slanting up right: small *v*

W Starting point, slanting down right, slanting up right, slanting down right, slanting up right: capital *W*

W Starting point, slanting down right, slanting up right, slanting down right, slanting up right: small *w*

X Starting point, slanting down right
Starting point, slanting down left: capital *X*

X Starting point, slanting down right
Starting point, slanting down left: small *x*

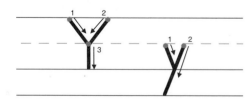

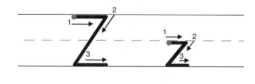

Y Starting point, slanting down right, stop
Starting point, slanting down left, stop
Starting point, straight down: capital *Y*

y Starting point, slanting down right Starting point, slanting down left, connecting the lines: small *y*

Z Starting point, straight across, slanting down left, straight across: capital *Z*

z Starting point, straight across, slanting down left, straight across: small *z*

Number Formation Guide

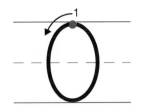

0 Starting point, curving left all the way around to starting point: *0*

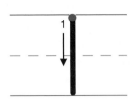

1 Starting point, straight down: *1*

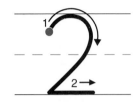

2 Starting point, around right, slanting left and straight across right: *2*

3 Starting point, around right, in at the middle, around right: *3*

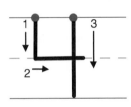

4 Starting point, straight down
Straight across right
Starting point, straight down, crossing line: *4*

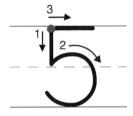

5 Starting point, straight down, curving around right and up
Starting point, straight across right: *5*

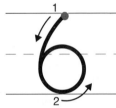

6 Starting point, slanting left, around the bottom curving up, around right and into the curve: *6*

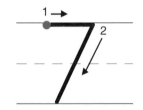

7 Starting point, straight across right, slanting down left: *7*

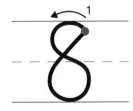

8 Starting point, curving left, curving down and around right, slanting up right to starting point: *8*

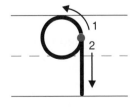

9 Starting point, curving around left all the way, straight down: *9*

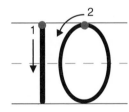

10 Starting point, straight down
Starting point, curving left all the way around to starting point: *10*

Vocabulary Development

Vocabulary development is a key part of *The DLM Early Childhood Express*. Children learn new words through exposure during reading and class discussion. They build language and vocabulary through activities using key words and phrases and by exploring selected vocabulary. After vocabulary words have been introduced, encourage children to use the words in sentences. Again, providing linguistic structures gives children a context for using new vocabulary and building oral language and gives you the opportunity to assess children's understanding of new words. For example, use sentence patterns such as the following:

- A _____ can _____.

- A _____ is a _____.
  (Use this for classification activities. *A tulip is a flower. A rabbit is an animal.*)

- The _____ is _____.
  (Use for describing. *The rabbit is soft.*)

Define words in ways children in your class can understand. When possible, show pictures of objects or actions to help clarify the meanings of words. Provide examples or comparisons to help reinforce the meanings of words and to connect new words to previously learned words. For example, say *The rabbit's FUR is soft like COTTON.* Connect words to categories. For example, say: *Pears are fruits. Are apples fruits? What else is a fruit?* Demonstrate the meaning of words when possible.

During reading, be sure children feel comfortable asking questions and sharing their reactions to what you are reading. Encourage children to share explanations, make predictions, compare and contrast ideas, sequence story events, and describe what you are reading. Encourage children's engagement by modeling reactions and responses while reading. For example, say *I like the part where _____ did _____.* or *This story is about _____.* Support children who are reluctant to speak by using linguistic structures that encourage them to talk about stories and use vocabulary words. You might use the following linguistic structures:

- This story is about _____.

- First _____.

- Next _____.

- Last _____. (Use this for retelling stories.)

- The _____ is the same as _____.

- The _____ is different from _____.

- We read about _____.

Model asking questions before, during, and after reading:

- I wonder what this story is going to be about.

- Who is _____?

- What is _____?

- What did _____ do?

- Why did _____ do _____?

- What happened first? Middle? Last?

Be sure to ask open-ended questions. Unlike questions that simply require a *yes* or *no* or one-word answer, open-ended questions encourage children to think about responses and use new vocabulary in sentences.

Throughout the day, create opportunities for children to talk to each other as they share daily experiences, discuss and explain what they are doing, and talk abut what they are learning.

Vocabulary Words by Topic

Animals

alligator/caimán
ant/horminga
anteater/oso hormiguero
bat/murciélago
bear/oso
beaver/castor
bee/abeja
beetle/escarabajo
bobcat/lince
butterfly/mariposa
camel/camello
cat/gato
chicken/gallina/pollo
chipmunk/ardilla
cow/vaca
crab/cangrejo
deer/venado/ciervo
dog/perro
dolphin/delfin
donkey/burro
dragonfly/libélula
duck/pato
eagle/águila
elephant/elefante
flamingo/flamingo
fly/mosca
fox/zorro
frog/rana
giraffe/jirafa
goat/cabra
gorilla/
grasshopper/saltamontes
hamster/hámster
hippopotamus/hipopótamo
horse/caballo
kangaroo/canguro
koala/coala

ladybug/catarina
leopard/leopardo
lion/león
llama/llama
lobster/langosta
monkey/mono
moose/alce
mosquito/mosquito
mouse/ratón
octopus/pulpo
opossum/zarigüeya
owl/búho
panda/oso panda
parakeet/periquito
peacock/pavo real
pelican/pelicano
penguin/pingüino
pig/cerdo
polar bear/oso polar
porcupine/puerco espín
rabbit/conejo
raccoon/mapache
rhinoceros/rinoceronte
robin/petirrojo
salamander/salamandra
sea horse/caballo de mar
shark/tiburón
sheep/oveja
skunk/mofeta/zorrillo
snake/serpiente
squirrel/ardilla
starfish/estrella de mar
swan/cisne
tiger/tigre
toad/sapo
turkey/pavo
turtle/tortuga
walrus/morsa

whale/ballena
zebra/cebra

Colors and Shapes

blue/azul
green/verde
red/rojo
yellow/amarillo
circle/círculo azul
diamond/diamante
oval/óvalo
rectangle/rectángulo
square/cuadrado
triangle/triángulo

Signs

deer crossing/cruce de venado
handicapped parking/
    estacionamiento para inválidos
railroad crossing/paso del tren
school crossing/cruce escolar
speed limit/limite de velocidad
stop sign/señal de alto
traffic light/semáforo
yield sign/señal de ceder el paso

Earth

beach/playa
blizzard/tormenta de nieve
cloud/nube
coral reef/arrecife de coral
desert/desierto
dry season/temporada seca
fall/otoño
fog/niebla
forest/bosque
geyser/géiser
glacier/glaciar

hail/granizo
hurricane/huracán
ice/hielo
island/isla
lake/lago
lightning/relámpago
mountain/montaña
ocean/océano
plain/llano
rain/lluvia
rain forest/selva tropical
rainy season/temporada de lluvias
rapids/rápidos
river/río
snow/nieve
spring/primavera
stream/arroyo
summer/verano
sun/sol
tornado/tornado
tundra/tundra
volcano/volcán
waterfall/cascada
wind/viento
winter/invierno

Human Body

ankle/tobillo
arm/brazo
body/cuerpo
ear/oreja
elbow/codo
eyes/ojos
feet/pies
fingers/dedos
hair/pelo
hands/manos

Vocabulary Words by Topic

head/cabeza
hearing/oído
heel/talón
hips/caderas
knee/rodilla
legs/piernas
mouth/boca
nose/nariz
sense/sentido
shoulders/hombros
sight/vista
smell/olfato
taste/gusto
teeth/dientes
toes/dedos de los pies
touch/ tacto

Plants

cactus/cactus
carrot/zanahoria
clover/trébol
cornstalk/planta de maíz
dandelion/diente de león
fern/helecho
grapevine/parra
grass/hierba
lettuce/lechuga
lilac bush/lila de monte
marigold/caléndula
moss/musgo
oak tree/árbol de roble
onion/cebolla
orange tree/naranjo
palm tree/palma
pine tree/pino
poison ivy/hiedra venenosa
rice/arroz
rose/rosa

seaweed/alga marina
sunflower/girasol
tomato/tomate
tulip/tulipán
water lily/nenúfar
wheat/trigo

Clothing

belt/cinturón
blouse/blusa
boots/botas
boy's swimsuit/traje de baño para
    niños
coat/abrigo
dress/vestido
earmuffs/orejeras
girl's swimsuit/traje de baño para
    niñas
gloves/guantes
hat/sombrero
jacket/chaqueta
jeans/pantalones vaqueros
mittens/manoplas
pajamas/pijama
pants/pantalones
raincoat/impermeable
robe/bata
scarf/bufanda
shirt/camisa
shoes/zapatos
shorts/pantalones cortos
skirt/falda
slippers/pantuflas
socks/calcetines
sweat suit/chandal
sweater/suéter
tie/corbata
vest/chaleco

Food

apples/manzanas
bacon/tocino
bagels/roscas de pan
bananas/plátanos
beans/frijoles
beef/carne
beets/betabel
blueberries/arándanos
bread/pan
broccoli/brécol
butter/mantequilla
cake/pastel
cantaloupe/cantalupo
carrots/zanahoria
cauliflower/coliflor
celery/apio
cereal/cereal
cheese/queso
cherries/cerezas
chicken/pollo
clams/almejas
cookies/galletas
corn/maíz
cottage cheese/requesón
crackers/galletas saladas
cream cheese/queso crema
cucumbers/pepinos
eggs/huevos
figs/higos
fish/pescado
grapefruit/toronja
grapes/uvas
green peppers/pimientos verdes
ham/jamón
ice-cream cone/cono de helado
jelly/gelatina
lemons/limones

lettuce/lechuga
limes/limas
macaroni/macarrones
milk/leche
mushrooms/champiñones
nuts/nueces
onions/cebollas
orange juice/jugo de naranja
oranges/naranjas
peaches/duraznos
peanut butter/crema de cacahuete
pears/peras
peas/guisantes
pie/tarta
pineapples/piñas
plums/ciruelas
pork chop/chuleta de puerco
potatoes/papas
radishes/rábanos
raisins/pasas
rice/arroz
rolls/panecillos
salad/ensalada
sausage/salchicha
shrimp/camarón
soup/sopa
spaghetti/espaguetis
squash/calabaza
strawberries/fresas
sweet potatoes/camotes
tomatoes/tomates
watermelon/sandía
yogurt/yogur

Recreation

archery/tiro el arco
badminton/bádminton
baseball/béisbol
basketball/baloncesto
biking/ciclismo
boating/paseo en bote
bowling/boliche
canoeing/piragüismo
climbing/montañismo
croquet/croquet
discus/disco
diving/buceo
fishing/pesca
football/fútbol
golf/golf
gymnastics/gimnasia
hiking/excursionismo
hockey/hockey
horseback riding/equitación
ice-skating/patinaje sobre hielo
in-line skating/patines en línea
lacrosse/lacrosse
pole-vaulting/salto con pértiga
running/atletismo
scuba diving/buceo
shot put/lanzamiento de peso
skiing/esquí
soccer/fútbol
surfing/surfing
swimming/natación
T-ball/T-ball
tennis/tenis
volleyball/voleibol
walking/caminar
waterskiing/esquí acuático
weight lifting/levantamiento

School

auditorium/auditorio
book/libro
cafeteria/cafetería
cafeteria table/mesa de cafetería
calculator/calculadora
chair/silla
chalk/tiza
chalkboard/pizarrón
chart paper/rotafolio
classroom/aula
computer/omputadora
construction paper/papel para
    construir
crayons/crayones
desk/escritorio
easel/caballete
eraser/borrador
globe/globo
glue/pegamento
gym/gimnasio
hallway/vestíbulo
janitor's room/conserjería
learning center/centro de
    aprendizaje
library/biblioteca
markers/marcadores
music room/salón de música
notebook paper/papel de cuaderno
nurse's office/enfermería
paint/pintura
paintbrush/pincel
pen/pluma
pencil/lápiz
pencil sharpener/sacapuntas
playground/patio de recreo
principal's office/oficina del
    director

ruler/regla
science room/salón de ciencias
scissors/tijeras
stairs/escaleras
stapler/grapadora
supply room/almacén
tape/cinta adhesiva

Toys

ball/pelota
balloons/globos
bike/bicicleta
blocks/cubos
clay/arcilla
coloring book/libro para colorear
doll/muñeca
doll carriage/careola de muñecas
dollhouse/casa de muñecas
farm set/juego de la granja
game/juego
grocery cart/carro de compras
hats/sombreros
in-line skates/patines
instruments/instrumentos
jump rope/cuerda para saltar
kite/cometa
magnets/imanes
marbles/canicas
puppet/títere
puzzle/rompecabezas
scooter/motoneta
skateboard/patineta
slide/tobogán
stuffed animals/peluches
tape recorder/grabadora
top/trompo
toy cars/carro de juguete
toy trucks/camión de juguete

train set/juego de tren
tricycle/triciclo
wagon/vagón
yo-yo/yó-yó

Equipment

baggage cart/carro para equipaje
baseball/béisbol
bat/baté
mitt/manopla
basketball/pelota de baloncesto
basketball net/canasta
blueprints/planos
computer/computadora
drafting tools/borradores
bow/arco
arrow/flecha
bowling ball/pelota de boliche
bowling pin/bolos de boliche
bridle/freno
saddle/silla de montar
saddle pad/montura
broom/escoba
bulldozer/aplanadora
canoe/canoa
paddle/paleta
cash register/caja registradora
computer/computadora
crane/grúa
dishwasher/lavaplatos
drill/taladro
drum/tambor
drumsticks/palillos
dryer/secadora
dustpan/recogedor
figure skates/patinaje artistico

Vocabulary Words by Topic

football/balón
shoulder pads/hombreras
football helmet/casco
goggles/gafas
golf ball/pelota de golf
golf clubs/palo de golf
tee/tee
hammer/martillo
handcuffs/esposas
badge/placa
hat/gorra
hockey stick/palo de hockey
hockey puck/disco de hockey
ice skates/patines
hoe/azadón
hose/manguera
coat/chaqueta
hat/sombrero
sprinkler/rociador
iron/plancha
ironing board/tabla de planchar
lawn mower/cortacéspedes
mail pouch/bolsa de correo
mirror/espejo
probe/sonda
pick/pico
mop/estropajo
paintbrush/brocha de pintar
piano/piano
pliers/alicates
rake/rastrillo
roller skates/patines
saw/sierra
screwdriver/desarmador
scuba tank/tanque de buceo
mask/máscara
flippers/aletas
shovel/pala

sketch pad/cuaderno para dibujo
palette/paleta
skis/esquís
ski boots/botas para esquiar
poles/palos
soccer ball/balón de fútbol
shoes/zapatos de tenis
stepladder/escalera doble
stethoscope/estetoscopio
surfboard/tabla de surf
tennis ball/pelota de tenis
tennis racket/raqueta de tenis
tractor/tractor
vacuum cleaner/aspiradora
washer/lavadora
water skis/esquís acuáticos
rope/cuerda
life jacket/chaleco salvavidas
watering can/regadera
wheelbarrow/carretilla
wrench/llave inglesa

Home

basement/sótano
bathroom/baño
bathroom sink/lavabo
bathtub/bañera
bed/cama
bedroom/recámara/habitación
blanket/cobija/manta
chair/silla
circuit breaker/cortocircuito
dresser/cómoda
electrical outlet/enchufe
end table/mesa auxiliar
fireplace/chimenea
furnace/horno
kitchen/cocina

kitchen chair/silla de cocina
kitchen sink/fregadero
kitchen table/mesa de cocina
lamp/lámpara
light switch/interruptor de la luz
living room/sala
medicine cabinet/botiquín
nightstand/mesilla de noche
pillow/almohada
refrigerator/refrigerador
shower/ducha
smoke alarm/alarma de incendios
sofa/sofá
stove/estufa
thermostat/termostato
toilet/el baño
water heater/calentador de agua

Occupations

administrative assistant/asistente
    administrativo
air traffic controller/controlador
    aéreo
airline pilot/piloto
architect/arquitecto
artist/artista
astronaut/astronauta
athlete/atleta
author/autor
ballerina/bailarina
banker/banquero
bus driver/conductor de autobús
camera operator/operador de
    cámara
carpenter/carpintero
cashier/cajero
chef/jefe de cocina
computer technician/técnico en

computación
cosmetologist/cosmetólogo
dancer/bailarín
dentist/dentista
doctor/doctor
electrician/electricista
engineer/ingeniero
farmer/granjero
firefighter/bombero
forest ranger/guardabosques
lawyer/abogado
manicurist/manicurista
musician/músico
nurse/enfermera
paramedic/paramédico
photographer/fotógrafo
police officer/policía
postal worker/empleado postal
real estate agent/corridor de
    bienes raíces
refuse collector/recolector de
    basura
reporter/reportero
school crossing guard/guarda
    escolar
server/mesero
ship captain/capitán de barco
singer/cantante
skater/patinador
teacher/maestro
truck driver/conductor de camión
veterinarian/veterinario
weaver/tejedora

Structures

adobe/casa de adobe
airplane hangar/hangar de avión
airport/aeropuerto
apartment building/edificio de
    departamentos/edificio de pisos
arena/arena
art museum/museo de arte
bakery/panadería
bank/banco
barn/granero
bridge/peunte
bus shelter/parada cubierta
city hall/ayuntamiento
clothing store/tienda de ropa
condominium/condominio
courthouse/tribunal
covered bridge/puente cubierto
dam/presa
dock/muelle
drawbridge/puente levadizo
duplex/dúplex
fire station/estación de bomberos
flower shop/floristeria
garage/garaje
gas station/gasolinera
gazebo/mirador
grain elevator/elevador de granos
grocery store/supermercado
hospital/hospital
house/casa
library/biblioteca
log cabin/cabaña de madera
marina/marina
monument/monumento
movie theater/cine
opera house/teatro de la ópera
palace/palacio

parking garage/estacionamiento
pizza shop/pizzaría
police station/estación de policía
power plant/central eléctrica
pyramid/pirámide
restaurant/restaurante
school/escuela
shelter house/albergue
shopping mall/centro comercial
skyscraper/rascacielos
stadium/estadio
swimming pool/alberca/piscina
tent/tienda
toy store/juguetería
train station/estación del tren
windmills/molino de viento

Transportation

airplane/avión
bicycle/bicicleta
bus/autobús
canoe/canoa
car/coche
four-wheel-drive vehicle/coche con
    doble tracción
helicopter/helicóptero
hot air balloon/globo de aire
    caliente
kayak/kayac
moped/ciclomotor
motor home/casa motora
motorboat/lancha motora
motorcycle/motocicleta
pickup truck/camioneta
rowboat/bote de remos
sailboat/velero
school bus/camión escolar

semitrailer truck/camión con semi-
    remolque
ship/barco
submarine/submarino
subway/metro
taxi/taxi
train/tren
van/furgoneta

Learning Trajectories for Math

Children follow natural developmental progressions in learning. Curriculum research has revealed sequences of activities that are effective in guiding children through these levels of thinking. These developmental paths are the basis for *Building Blocks* learning trajectories.

Learning Trajectories for Primary Grades Mathematics

Learning trajectories have three parts: a mathematical goal, a developmental path along which children develop to reach that goal, and a set of activities matched to each of the levels of thinking in that path that help children develop the next higher level of thinking. The **Building Blocks** learning trajectories give simple labels, descriptions, and examples of each level. Complete learning trajectories describe the goals of learning, the thinking and learning processes of children at various levels, and the learning activities in which they might engage. This document provides only the developmental levels.

The following provides the developmental levels from the first signs of development in different strands of mathematics through approximately age 8. Research shows that when teachers understand how children develop mathematics understanding, they are more effective in questioning, analyzing, and providing activities that further children's development than teachers who are unaware of the development process. Consequently, children have a much richer and more successful math experience in the primary grades.

Each of the following tables, such as "Counting," represents a main developmental progression that underlies the learning trajectory for that topic.

For some topics, there are "subtrajectories"—strands within the topic. In most cases, the names make this clear. For example, in Comparing and Ordering, some levels are "Composer" levels and others involve building a "Mental Number Line." Similarly, the related subtrajectories of "Composition" and "Decomposition" are easy to distinguish. Sometimes, for clarification, subtrajectories are indicated with a note in italics after the title. For example, Parts and Representing are subtrajectories within the Shape Trajectory.

Frequently Asked Questions (FAQ)

1. Why use learning trajectories? Learning trajectories allow teachers to build the mathematics of children—the thinking of children as it develops naturally. So, we know that all the goals and activities are within the developmental capacities of children. Finally, we know that the activities provide the mathematical building blocks for success.

2. When are children "at" a level? Children are at a certain level when most of their behaviors reflect the thinking—ideas and skills—of that level. Most levels are levels of thinking. However, some are merely "levels of attainment" and indicate a child has gained knowledge. For example, children must learn to name or write more numerals, but knowing more numerals does not require more complex thinking.

3. Can children work at more than one level at the same time? Yes, although most children work mainly at one level or in transition between two levels. Levels are not "absolute stages." They are "benchmarks" of complex growth that represent distinct ways of thinking.

4. Can children jump ahead? Yes, especially if there are separate subtopics. For example, we have combined many counting competencies into one "Counting" sequence with subtopics, such as verbal counting skills. Some children learn to count to 100 at age 6 after learning to count objects to 10 or more, some may learn that verbal skill earlier. The subtopic of verbal counting skills would still be followed.

5. How do these developmental levels support teaching and learning? The levels help teachers, as well as curriculum developers, assess, teach, and sequence activities. Through planned teaching and encouraging informal, incidental mathematics, teachers help children learn at an appropriate and deep level.

6. Should I plan to help children develop just the levels that correspond to my children's ages? No! The ages in the table are typical ages children develop these ideas. (These are rough guides only.) These are "starting levels" not goals. We have found that children who are provided high-quality mathematics experiences are capable of developing to levels one or more years beyond their peers.

Developmental Levels for Counting

The ability to count with confidence develops over the course of several years. Beginning in infancy, children show signs of understanding numbers. With instruction and number experience, most children can count fluently by age 8, with much progress in counting occurring in kindergarten and first grade. Most children follow a natural developmental progression in learning to count with recognizable stages or levels. This developmental path can be described as part of a learning trajectory.

Age Range	Level Name	Level	Description
1–2	Precounter	1	At the earliest level a child shows no verbal counting. The child may name some number words with no sequence.
1–2	Chanter	2	At this level, a child may sing-song or chant indistinguishable number words.
2	Reciter	3	At this level, the child may verbally count with separate words, but not necessarily in the correct order.
3	Reciter (10)	4	A child at this level may verbally count to 10 with some correspondence with objects. He or she may point to objects to count a few items, but then lose track.
3	Corresponder	5	At this level, a child may keep one-to-one correspondence between counting words and objects—at least for small groups of objects laid in a line. A corresponder may answer "how many" by recounting the objects.
4	Counter (Small Numbers)	6	At around 4 years of age, the child may begin to count meaningfully. He or she may accurately count objects in a line to 5 and answer the "how many" question with the last number counted. When objects are visible, and especially with small numbers, the child begins to understand cardinality (that numbers tell how many).
4	Producer (Small Numbers)	7	The next level after counting small numbers is to count out objects to 5. When asked to show four of something, for example, this child may give four objects.
4	Counter (10)	8	This child may count structured arrangements of objects to 10. He or she may be able to write or draw to represent 1–10. A child at this level may be able to tell the number just after or just before another number, but only by counting up from 1.
5	Counter and Producer— Counter to (10+)	9	Around 5 years of age, a child may begin to count out objects accurately to 10 and then beyond to 30. He or she has explicit understanding of cardinality (that numbers tell how many). The child may keep track of objects that have and have not been counted, even in different arrangements. He or she may write or draw to represent 1 to 10 and then 20 and 30, and may give the next number to 20 or 30. The child also begins to recognize errors in others' counting and is able to eliminate most errors in his or her own counting.

Age Range	Level Name	Level	Description
5	Counter Backward from 10	10	Another milestone at about age 5 is being able to count backward from 10 to 1, verbally, or when removing objects from a group.
6	Counter from N (N+1, N–1)	11	Around 6 years of age, the child may begin to count on, counting verbally and with objects from numbers other than 1. Another noticeable accomplishment is that a child may determine the number immediately before or after another number without having to start back at 1.
6	Skip Counting by 10s to 100	12	A child at this level may count by 10s to 100 or beyond with understanding.
6	Counter to 100	13	A child at this level may count by 1s to 100. He or she can make decade transitions (for example, from 29 to 30) starting at any number.
6	Counter On Using Patterns	14	At this level, a child may keep track of a few counting acts by using numerical patterns, such as tapping as he or she counts.
6	Skip Counter	15	At this level, the child can count by 5s and 2s with understanding.
6	Counter of Imagined Items	16	At this level, a child may count mental images of hidden objects to answer, for example, "how many" when 5 objects are visible and 3 are hidden.
6	Counter On Keeping Track	17	A child at this level may keep track of counting acts numerically, first with objects, then by counting counts. He or she counts up one to four more from a given number.
6	Counter of Quantitative Units	18	At this level, a child can count unusual units, such as "wholes" when shown combinations of wholes and parts. For example, when shown three whole plastic eggs and four halves, a child at this level will say there are five whole eggs.
6	Counter to 200	19	At this level, a child may count accurately to 200 and beyond, recognizing the patterns of ones, tens, and hundreds.
7	Number Conserver	20	A major milestone around age 7 is the ability to conserve number. A child who conserves number understands that a number is unchanged even if a group of objects is rearranged. For example, if there is a row of ten buttons, the child understands there are still ten without recounting, even if they are rearranged in a long row or a circle.
7	Counter Forward and Back	21	A child at this level may count in either direction and recognize that sequence of decades mirrors single-digit sequence.

Learning Trajectories for Math

Developmental Levels for Comparing and Ordering Numbers

Comparing and ordering sets is a critical skill for children as they determine whether one set is larger than another in order to make sure sets are equal and "fair." Prekindergartners can learn to use matching to compare collections or to create equivalent collections. Finding out how many more or fewer in one collection is more demanding than simply comparing two collections. The ability to compare and order sets with fluency develops over the course of several years. With instruction and number experience, most children develop foundational understanding of number relationships and place value at ages four and five. Most children follow a natural developmental progression in learning to compare and order numbers with recognizable stages or levels. This developmental path can be described as part of a learning trajectory.

Age Range	Level Name	Level	Description
2	Object Corresponder	1	At this early level, a child puts objects into one-to-one correspondence, but may not fully understand that this creates equal groups. For example, a child may know that each carton has a straw, but does not necessarily know there are the same numbers of straws and cartons.
2	Perceptual Comparer	2	At this level, a child can compare collections that are quite different in size (for example, one is at least twice the other) and know that one has more than the other. If the collections are similar, the child can compare very small collections.
3	First-Second Ordinal Counter	3	At this level the child can identify the "first" and often "second" object in a sequence.
3	Nonverbal Comparer of Similar Items	4	At this level, a child can identify that different organizations of the same number are equal and different from other sets (1–4 items). For example, a child can identify ••• and •'• as equal and different from •• or •'•.
4	Nonverbal Comparer of Dissimilar Items	5	At this level, a child can match small, equal collections of dissimilar items, such as shells and dots, and show that they are the same number.
4	Matching Comparer	6	As children progress, they begin to compare groups of 1–6 by matching. For example, a child gives one toy bone to every dog and says there are the same number of dogs and bones.

Age Range	Level Name	Level	Description
4	Knows-to-Count Comparer	7	A significant step occurs when the child begins to count collections to compare. At the early levels, children are not always accurate when a larger collection's objects are smaller in size than the objects in the smaller collection. For example, a child at this level may accurately count two equal collections, but when asked, says the collection of larger blocks has more.
4	Counting Comparer (Same Size)	8	At this level, children make accurate comparisons via counting, but only when objects are about the same size and groups are small (about 1–5 items).
5	Counting Comparer (5)	9	As children develop their ability to compare sets, they compare accurately by counting, even when a larger collection's objects are smaller. A child at this level can figure out how many more or less.
5	Ordinal Counter	10	At this level, a child identifies and uses ordinal numbers from "first" to "tenth." For example, the child can identify who is "third in line."
6	Counting Comparer (10)	11	This level can be observed when the child compares sets by counting, even when a larger collection's objects are smaller, up to 10. A child at this level can accurately count two collections of 9 items each, and says they have the same number, even if one collection has larger blocks.
6	Mental Number Line to 10	12	As children move into this level, they begin to use mental images and knowledge of number relationships to determine relative size and position. For example, a child at this level can answer which number is closer to 6, 4 or 9 without counting physical objects.
6	Serial Orderer to 61	13	At this level, the child orders lengths marked into units (1–6, then beyond). For example, given towers of cubes, this child can put them in order, 1 to 6.
7	Place Value Comparer	14	Further development is made when a child begins to compare numbers with place value understanding. For example, a child at this level can explain that "63 is more than 59 because six tens is more than five tens, even if there are more than three ones."
7	Mental Number Line to 100	15	Children demonstrate the next level when they can use mental images and knowledge of number relationships, including ones embedded in tens, to determine relative size and position. For example, when asked, "Which is closer to 45, 30 or 50?" a child at this level may say "45 is right next to 50, but 30 isn't."
8+	Mental Number Line to 1,000s	16	At about age 8, children may begin to use mental images of numbers up to 1,000 and knowledge of number relationships, including place value, to determine relative size and position. For example, when asked, "Which is closer to 3,500—2,000 or 7,000?" a child at this level may say "70 is double 35, but 20 is only fifteen from 35, so twenty hundreds, 2,000, is closer."

Developmental Levels for Recognizing Number and Subitizing (Instantly Recognizing)

The ability to recognize number values develops over the course of several years and is a foundational part of number sense. Beginning at about age two, children begin to name groups of objects. The ability to instantly know how many are in a group, called *subitizing,* begins at about age three. By age eight, with instruction and number experience, most children can identify groups of items and use place values and multiplication skills to count them. Most children follow a natural developmental progression in learning to count with recognizable stages or levels. This developmental path can be described as part of a learning trajectory.

Age Range	Level Name	Level	Description
2	Small Collection Namer	1	The first sign occurs when the child can name groups of 1 to 2, sometimes 3. For example, when shown a pair of shoes, this young child says, "two shoes."
3	Maker of Small Collections	2	At this level, a child can nonverbally make a small collection (no more than 4, usually 1 to 3) with the same number as another collection. For example, when shown a collection of 3, the child makes another collection of 3.
4	Perceptual Subitizer to 4	3	Progress is made when a child instantly recognizes collections up to 4 and verbally names the number of items. For example, when shown 4 objects briefly, the child says "4."
5	Perceptual Subitizer to 5	4	This level is the ability to instantly recognize collections up to 5 and verbally name the number of items. For example, when shown 5 objects briefly, the child says "5."
5	Conceptual Subitizer to 51	5	At this level, the child can verbally label all arrangements to about 5, when shown only briefly. For example, a child at this level might say, "I saw 2 and 2, and so I saw 4."
5	Conceptual Subitizer to 10	6	This step is when the child can verbally label most arrangements to 6 shown briefly, then up to 10, using groups. For example, a child at this level might say, "In my mind, I made 2 groups of 3 and 1 more, so 7."
6	Conceptual Subitizer to 20	7	Next, a child can verbally label structured arrangements up to 20 shown briefly, using groups. For example, the child may say, "I saw 3 fives, so 5, 10, 15."
7	Conceptual Subitizer with Place Value and Skip Counting	8	At this level, a child is able to use groups, skip counting, and place value to verbally label structured arrangements shown briefly. For example, the child may say, "I saw groups of tens and twos, so 10, 20, 30, 40, 42, 44, 46…46!"
8+	Conceptual Subitizer with Place Value and Multiplication	9	As children develop their ability to subitize, they use groups, multiplication, and place value to verbally label structured arrangements shown briefly. At this level, a child may say, "I saw groups of tens and threes, so I thought, 5 tens is 50 and 4 threes is 12, so 62 in all."

Learning Trajectories for Math

Developmental Levels for Composing (Knowing Combinations of Numbers)

Composing and decomposing are combining and separating operations that allow children to build concepts of "parts" and "wholes." Most prekindergartners can "see" that two items and one item make three items. Later, children learn to separate a group into parts in various ways and then to count to produce all of the number "partners" of a given number. Eventually children think of a number and know the different addition facts that make that number. Most children follow a natural developmental progression in learning to compose and decompose numbers with recognizable stages or levels. This developmental path can be described as part of a learning trajectory.

Age Range	Level Name	Level	Description
4	Pre-Part-Whole Recognizer	1	At the earliest levels of composing, a child only nonverbally recognizes parts and wholes. For example, when shown 4 red blocks and 2 blue blocks, a young child may intuitively appreciate that "all the blocks" includes the red and blue blocks, but when asked how many there are in all, the child may name a small number, such as 1.
5	Inexact Part-Whole Recognizer	2	A sign of development is that the child knows a whole is bigger than parts, but does not accurately quantify. For example, when shown 4 red blocks and 2 blue blocks and asked how many there are in all, the child may name a "large number," such as 5 or 10.
5	Composer to 4, then 5	3	At this level, a child knows number combinations. A child at this level quickly names parts of any whole, or the whole given the parts. For example, when shown 4, then 1 is secretly hidden, and then shown the 3 remaining, the child may quickly say "1" is hidden.
6	Composer to 7	4	The next sign of development is when a child knows number combinations to totals of 7. A child at this level quickly names parts of any whole, or the whole when given parts, and can double numbers to 10. For example, when shown 6, then 4 are secretly hidden, and then shown the 2 remaining, the child may quickly say "4" are hidden.
6	Composer to 10	5	This level is when a child knows number combinations to totals of 10. A child at this level may quickly name parts of any whole, or the whole when given parts, and can double numbers to 20. For example, this child would be able to say "9 and 9 is 18."
7	Composer with Tens and Ones	6	At this level, the child understands two-digit numbers as tens and ones, can count with dimes and pennies, and can perform two-digit addition with regrouping. For example, a child at this level may explain, "17 and 36 is like 17 and 3, which is 20, and 33, which is 53."

Developmental Levels for Adding and Subtracting

Single-digit addition and subtraction are generally characterized as "math facts." It is assumed children must memorize these facts, yet research has shown that addition and subtraction have their roots in counting, counting on, number sense, the ability to compose and decompose numbers, and place value. Research has also shown that learning methods for addition and subtraction with understanding is much more effective than rote memorization of seemingly isolated facts. Most children follow an observable developmental progression in learning to add and subtract numbers with recognizable stages or levels. This developmental path can be described as part of a learning trajectory.

Age Range	Level Name	Level	Description
1	Pre +/−	1	At the earliest level, a child shows no sign of being able to add or subtract.
3	Nonverbal +/−	2	The first sign is when a child can add and subtract very small collections nonverbally. For example, when shown 2 objects, then 1 object being hidden under a napkin, the child identifies or makes a set of 3 objects to "match."
4	Small Number +/−	3	This level is when a child can find sums for joining problems up to 3 1 2 by counting with objects. For example, when asked, "You have 2 balls and get 1 more. How many in all?" the child may count out 2, then count out 1 more, then count all 3: "1, 2, 3, 3!"
5	Find Result +/−	4	**Addition** Evidence of this level in addition is when a child can find sums for joining (you had 3 apples and get 3 more; how many do you have in all?) and part-part-whole (there are 6 girls and 5 boys on the playground; how many children were there in all?) problems by direct modeling, counting all, with objects. For example, when asked, "You have 2 red balls and 3 blue balls. How many in all?" the child may count out 2 red, then count out 3 blue, then count all 5. **Subtraction** In subtraction, a child can also solve take-away problems by separating with objects. For example, when asked, "You have 5 balls and give 2 to Tom. How many do you have left?" the child may count out 5 balls, then take away 2, and then count the remaining 3.

Age Range	Level Name	Level	Description
5	Find Change +/−	5	**Addition** At this level, a child can find the missing addend (5 + _ =7) by adding on objects. For example, when asked, "You have 5 balls and then get some more. Now you have 7 in all. How many did you get?" The child may count out 5, then count those 5 again starting at 1, then add more, counting "6, 7," then count the balls added to find the answer, 2. **Subtraction** A child can compare by matching in simple situations. For example, when asked, "Here are 6 dogs and 4 balls. If we give a ball to each dog, how many dogs will not get a ball?" a child at this level may count out 6 dogs, match 4 balls to 4 of them, then count the 2 dogs that have no ball.
5	Make It +/−	6	A significant advancement occurs when a child is able to count on. This child can add on objects to make one number into another without counting from 1. For example, when told, "This puppet has 4 balls, but she should have 6. Make it 6," the child may put up 4 fingers on one hand, immediately count up from 4 while putting up 2 fingers on the other hand, saying, "5, 6," and then count or recognize the 2 fingers.
6	Counting Strategies +/−	7	This level occurs when a child can find sums for joining (you had 8 apples and get 3 more…) and part-part-whole (6 girls and 5 boys…) problems with finger patterns or by adding on objects or counting on. For example, when asked "How much is 4 and 3 more?" the child may answer "4…5, 6, 7. 7!" Children at this level can also solve missing addend (3 + _ = 7) or compare problems by counting on. When asked, for example, "You have 6 balls. How many more would you need to have 8?" the child may say, "6, 7 [puts up first finger], 8 [puts up second finger]. 2!"
6	Part-Whole +/−	8	Further development has occurred when the child has part-whole understanding. This child can solve problems using flexible strategies and some derived facts (for example, "5 + 5 is 10, so 5 + 6 is 11"), can sometimes do start-unknown problems (_ + 6 = 11), but only by trial and error. When asked, "You had some balls. Then you get 6 more. Now you have 11 balls. How many did you start with?" this child may lay out 6, then 3, count, and get 9. The child may put 1 more, say 10, then put 1 more. The child may count up from 6 to 11, then recount the group added, and say, "5!"

Age Range	Level Name	Level	Description
6	Numbers-in-Numbers +/−	9	Evidence of this level is when a child recognizes that a number is part of a whole and can solve problems when the start is unknown (_ + 4 = 9) with counting strategies. For example, when asked, "You have some balls, then you get 4 more balls, now you have 9. How many did you have to start with?" this child may count, putting up fingers, "5, 6, 7, 8, 9." The child may then look at his or her fingers and say, "5!"
7	Deriver +/−	10	At this level, a child can use flexible strategies and derived combinations (for example, "7 + 7 is 14, so 7 + 8 is 15") to solve all types of problems. For example, when asked, "What's 7 plus 8?" this child thinks: 7 + 8 = 7 [7 + 1] = [7 +7] + 1 = 14 + 1 = 15. The child can also solve multidigit problems by incrementing or combining 10s and 1s. For example, when asked "What's 28 + 35?" this child may think: 20 + 30 = 50; + 8 = 58; 2 more is 60, and 3 more is 63. He or she can also combine 10s and 1s: 20 + 30 = 50. 8 + 5 is like 8 plus 2 and 3 more, so it is 13. 50 and 13 is 63.
8+	Problem Solver +/−	11	As children develop their addition and subtraction abilities, they can solve by using flexible strategies and many known combinations. For example, when asked, "If I have 13 and you have 9, how could we have the same number?" this child may say, "9 and 1 is 10, then 3 more makes 13. 1 and 3 is 4. I need 4 more!"
8+	Multidigit +/−	12	Further development is shown when children can use composition of 10s and all previous strategies to solve multidigit +/− problems. For example, when asked, "What's 37 − 18?" this child may say, "Take 1 ten off the 3 tens; that's 2 tens. Take 7 off the 7. That's 2 tens and 0…20. I have one more to take off. That's 19." Or, when asked, "What's 28 + 35?" this child may think, 30 + 35 would be 65. But it's 28, so it's 2 less…63.

Learning Trajectories for Math

Developmental Levels for Multiplying and Dividing

Multiplication and division build on addition and subtraction understanding and are dependent upon counting and place-value concepts. As children begin to learn to multiply, they make equal groups and count them all. They then learn skip counting and derive related products from products they know. Finding and using patterns aid in learning multiplication and division facts with understanding. Children typically follow an observable developmental progression in learning to multiply and divide numbers with recognizable stages or levels. This developmental path can be described as part of a learning trajectory.

Age Range	Level Name	Level	Description
2	Non-quantitative Sharer "Dumper"	1	Multiplication and division concepts begin very early with the problem of sharing. Early evidence of these concepts can be observed when a child dumps out blocks and gives some (not an equal number) to each person.
3	Beginning Grouper and Distributive Sharer	2	Progression to this level can be observed when a child is able to make small groups (fewer than 5). This child can share by "dealing out," but often only between 2 people, although he or she may not appreciate the numerical result. For example, to share 4 blocks, this child may give each person a block, check that each person has one, and repeat this.
4	Grouper and Distributive Sharer	3	The next level occurs when a child makes small equal groups (fewer than 6). This child can deal out equally between 2 or more recipients, but may not understand that equal quantities are produced. For example, the child may share 6 blocks by dealing out blocks to herself and a friend one at a time.
5	Concrete Modeler ×/÷	4	As children develop, they are able to solve small-number multiplying problems by grouping—making each group and counting all. At this level, a child can solve division/sharing problems with informal strategies, using concrete objects—up to 20 objects and 2 to 5 people—although the child may not understand equivalence of groups. For example, the child may distribute 20 objects by dealing out 2 blocks to each of 5 people, then 1 to each, until the blocks are gone.
6	Parts and Wholes ×/÷	5	A new level is evidenced when the child understands the inverse relation between divisor and quotient. For example, this child may understand "If you share with more people, each person gets fewer."

Age Range	Level Name	Level	Description
7	Skip Counter ×/÷	6	As children develop understanding in multiplication and division, they begin to use skip counting for multiplication and for measurement division (finding out how many groups). For example, given 20 blocks, 4 to each person, and asked how many people, the children may skip count by 4, holding up 1 finger for each count of 4. A child at this level may also use trial and error for partitive division (finding out how many in each group). For example, given 20 blocks, 5 people, and asked how many each should get, this child may give 3 to each, and then 1 more.
8+	Deriver ×/÷	7	At this level, children use strategies and derived combinations to solve multidigit problems by operating on tens and ones separately. For example, a child at this level may explain "7 × 6, five 7s is 35, so 7 more is 42."
8+	Array Quantifier	8	Further development can be observed when a child begins to work with arrays. For example, given 7 × 4 with most of 5 × 4 covered, a child at this level may say, "There are 8 in these 2 rows, and 5 rows of 4 is 20, so 28 in all."
8+	Partitive Divisor	9	This level can be observed when a child is able to figure out how many are in each group. For example, given 20 blocks, 5 people, and asked how many each should get, a child at this level may say, "4, because 5 groups of 4 is 20."
8+	Multidigit ×/÷	10	As children progress, they begin to use multiple strategies for multiplication and division, from compensating to paper-and-pencil procedures. For example, a child becoming fluent in multiplication might explain that "19 times 5 is 95, because 20 fives is 100, and 1 less five is 95."

Developmental Levels for Measuring

Measurement is one of the main real-world applications of mathematics. Counting is a type of measurement which determines how many items are in a collection. Measurement also involves assigning a number to attributes of length, area, and weight. Prekindergarten children know that mass, weight, and length exist, but they do not know how to reason about these or to accurately measure them. As children develop their understanding of measurement, they begin to use tools to measure and understand the need for standard units of measure. Children typically follow an observable developmental progression in learning to measure with recognizable stages or levels. This developmental path can be described as part of a learning trajectory.

Age Range	Level Name	Level	Description
3	Length Quantity Recognizer	1	At the earliest level, children can identify length as an attribute. For example, they might say, "I'm tall, see?"
4	Length Direct Comparer	2	In this level, children can physically align 2 objects to determine which is longer or if they are the same length. For example, they can stand 2 sticks up next to each other on a table and say, "This one's bigger."
5	Indirect Length Comparer	3	A sign of further development is when a child can compare the length of 2 objects by representing them with a third object. For example, a child might compare the length of 2 objects with a piece of string. Additional evidence of this level is that when asked to measure, the child may assign a length by guessing or moving along a length while counting (without equal-length units). For example, the child may move a finger along a line segment, saying 10, 20, 30, 31, 32.
6	Serial Orderer to 6+	4	At this level, a child can order lengths, marked in 1 to 6 units. For example, given towers of cubes, a child at this level may put them in order, 1 to 6.
6	End-to-End Length Measurer	5	At this level, the child can lay units end-to-end, although he or she may not see the need for equal-length units. For example, a child might lay 9-inch cubes in a line beside a book to measure how long it is.
7	Length Unit Iterater	6	A significant change occurs when a child iterates a single unit to measure. He or she sees the need for identical units. The child uses rulers with help.
7	Length Unit Relater	7	At this level, a child can relate size and number of units. For example, the child may explain, "If you measure with centimeters instead of inches, you'll need more of them because each one is smaller."
8+	Length Measurer	8	As a child develops measurement ability, they begin to measure, knowing the need for identical units, the relationships between different units, partitions of unit, and the zero point on rulers. At this level, the child also begins to estimate. The children may explain, "I used a meterstick 3 times, then there was a little left over. So, I lined it up from 0 and found 14 centimeters. So, it's 3 meters, 14 centimeters in all."
8+	Conceptual Ruler Measurer	9	Further development in measurement is evidenced when a child possesses an "internal" measurement tool. At this level, the child mentally moves along an object, segmenting it, and counting the segments. This child also uses arithmetic to measure and estimates with accuracy. For example, a child at this level may explain, "I imagine one meterstick after another along the edge of the room. That's how I estimated the room's length to be 9 meters."

Learning Trajectories for Math

Developmental Levels for Recognizing Geometric Shapes

Geometric shapes can be used to represent and understand objects. Analyzing, comparing, and classifying shapes help create new knowledge of shapes and their relationships. Shapes can be decomposed or composed into other shapes. Through their everyday activities, children build both intuitive and explicit knowledge of geometric figures. Most children can recognize and name basic two-dimensional shapes at four years of age. However, young children can learn richer concepts about shape if they have varied examples and nonexamples of shape, discussions about shapes and their characteristics, a wide variety of shape classes, and interesting tasks. Children typically follow an observable developmental progression in learning about shapes with recognizable stages or levels. This developmental path can be described as part of a learning trajectory.

Age Range	Level Name	Level	Description
2	Shape Matcher— Identical	1	The earliest sign of understanding shape is when a child can match basic shapes (circle, square, typical triangle) with the same size and orientation.
2	Shape Matcher— Sizes	2	A sign of development is when a child can match basic shapes with different sizes.
2	Shape Matcher— Orientations	3	This level of development is when a child can match basic shapes with different orientations.
3	Shape Recognizer— Typical	4	A sign of development is when a child can recognize and name a prototypical circle, square, and, less often, a typical triangle. For example, the child names this a square. □ Some children may name different sizes, shapes, and orientations of rectangles, but also accept some shapes that look rectangular but are not rectangles. Children name these shapes "rectangles" (including the nonrectangular parallelogram).
3	Shape Matcher— More Shapes	5	As children develop understanding of shape, they can match a wider variety of shapes with the same size and orientation.
3	Shape Matcher— Sizes and Orientations	6	The child matches a wider variety of shapes with different sizes and orientations.
3	Shape Matcher— Combinations	7	The child matches combinations of shapes to each other.
4	Shape Recognizer— Circles, Squares, and Triangles	8	This sign of development is when a child can recognize some nonprototypical squares and triangles and may recognize some rectangles, but usually not rhombi (diamonds). Often, the child does not differentiate sides/corners. The child at this level may name these as triangles.
4	Constructor of Shapes from Parts— Looks Like *Representing*	9	A significant sign of development is when a child represents a shape by making a shape "look like" a goal shape. For example, when asked to make a triangle with sticks, the child may create the following: △ .

Age Range	Level Name	Level	Description
5	Shape Recognizer— All Rectangles	10	As children develop understanding of shape, they recognize more rectangle sizes, shapes, and orientations of rectangles. For example, a child at this level may correctly name these shapes "rectangles."
5	Side Recognizer *Parts*	11	A sign of development is when a child recognizes parts of shapes and identifies sides as distinct geometric objects. For example, when asked what this shape is, the child may say it is a quadrilateral (or has 4 sides) after counting and running a finger along the length of each side.
5	Angle Recognizer *Parts*	12	At this level, a child can recognize angles as separate geometric objects. For example, when asked, "Why is this a triangle," the child may say, "It has three angles" and count them, pointing clearly to each vertex (point at the corner).
5	Shape Recognizer— More Shapes	13	As children develop, they are able to recognize most basic shapes and prototypical examples of other shapes, such as hexagon, rhombus (diamond), and trapezoid. For example, a child can correctly identify and name all the following shapes:
6	Shape Identifier	14	At this level, the child can name most common shapes, including rhombi, without making mistakes such as calling ovals circles. A child at this level implicitly recognizes right angles, so distinguishes between a rectangle and a parallelogram without right angles. A child may correctly name all the following shapes:
6	Angle Matcher *Parts*	15	A sign of development is when the child can match angles concretely. For example, given several triangles, the child may find two with the same angles by laying the angles on top of one another.

Age Range	Level Name	Level	Description
7	Parts of Shapes Identifier	16	At this level, the child can identify shapes in terms of their components. For example, the child may say, "No matter how skinny it looks, that's a triangle because it has 3 sides and 3 angles."
7	Constructor of Shapes from Parts—Exact Representing	17	A significant step is when the child can represent a shape with completely correct construction, based on knowledge of components and relationships. For example, when asked to make a triangle with sticks, the child may create the following:
8	Shape Class Identifier	18	As children develop, they begin to use class membership (for example, to sort) not explicitly based on properties. For example, a child at this level may say, "I put the triangles over here, and the quadrilaterals, including squares, rectangles, rhombi, and trapezoids, over there."
8	Shape Property Identifier	19	At this level, a child can use properties explicitly. For example, a child may say, "I put the shapes with opposite sides that are parallel over here, and those with 4 sides but not both pairs of sides parallel over there."
8	Angle Size Comparer	20	The next sign of development is when a child can separate and compare angle sizes. For example, the child may say, "I put all the shapes that have right angles here, and all the ones that have bigger or smaller angles over there."
8	Angle Measurer	21	A significant step in development is when a child can use a protractor to measure angles.
8	Property Class Identifier	22	The next sign of development is when a child can use class membership for shapes (for example, to sort or consider shapes "similar") explicitly based on properties, including angle measure. For example, the child may say, "I put the equilateral triangles over here, and the right triangles over here."
8	Angle Synthesizer	23	As children develop understanding of shape, they can combine various meanings of angle (turn, corner, slant). For example, a child at this level could explain, "This ramp is at a 45° angle to the ground."

Learning Trajectories for Math

Developmental Levels for Composing Geometric Shapes

Children move through levels in the composition and decomposition of two-dimensional figures. Very young children cannot compose shapes but then gain ability to combine shapes into pictures, synthesize combinations of shapes into new shapes, and eventually substitute and build different kinds of shapes. Children typically follow an observable developmental progression in learning to compose shapes with recognizable stages or levels. This developmental path can be described as part of a learning trajectory.

Age Range	Level Name	Level	Description
2	Pre-Composer	1	The earliest sign of development is when a child can manipulate shapes as individuals, but is unable to combine them to compose a larger shape.
3	Pre-Decomposer	2	At this level, a child can decompose shapes, but only by trial and error.
4	Piece Assembler	3	Around age 4, a child can begin to make pictures in which each shape represents a unique role (for example, one shape for each body part) and shapes touch. A child at this level can fill simple outline puzzles using trial and error.
5	Picture Maker	4	As children develop, they are able to put several shapes together to make one part of a picture (for example, 2 shapes for 1 arm). A child at this level uses trial and error and does not anticipate creation of the new geometric shape. The children can choose shapes using "general shape" or side length, and fill "easy" outline puzzles that suggest the placement of each shape (but note that the child is trying to put a square in the puzzle where its right angles will not fit).
5	Simple Decomposer	5	A significant step occurs when the child is able to decompose ("take apart" into smaller shapes) simple shapes that have obvious clues as to their decomposition.

Age Range	Level Name	Level	Description
5	Shape Composer	6	A sign of development is when a child composes shapes with anticipation ("I know what will fit!"). A child at this level chooses shapes using angles as well as side lengths. Rotation and flipping are used intentionally to select and place shapes.
6	Substitution Composer	7	A sign of development is when a child is able to make new shapes out of smaller shapes and uses trial and error to substitute groups of shapes for other shapes in order to create new shapes in different ways. For example, the child can substitute shapes to fill outline puzzles in different ways.
6	Shape Decomposer (with Help)	8	As children develop, they can decompose shapes by using imagery that is suggested and supported by the task or environment.
7	Shape Composite Repeater	9	This level is demonstrated when the child can construct and duplicate units of units (shapes made from other shapes) intentionally, and understands each as being both multiple, small shapes and one larger shape. For example, the child may continue a pattern of shapes that leads to tiling.
7	Shape Decomposer with Imagery	10	A significant sign of development is when a child is able to decompose shapes flexibly by using independently generated imagery.
8	Shape Composer—Units of Units	11	Children demonstrate further understanding when they are able to build and apply units of units (shapes made from other shapes). For example, in constructing spatial patterns, the child can extend patterning activity to create a tiling with a new unit shape—a unit of unit shapes that he or she recognizes and consciously constructs. For example, the child may build Ts out of 4 squares, use 4 Ts to build squares, and use squares to tile a rectangle.
8	Shape Decomposer — Units of Units	12	As children develop understanding of shape, they can decompose shapes flexibly by using independently generated imagery and planned decompositions of shapes that themselves are decompositions.

Developmental Levels for Comparing Geometric Shapes

As early as four years of age, children can create and use strategies, such as moving shapes to compare their parts or to place one on top of the other, for judging whether two figures are the same shape. From Pre-K to Grade 2, they can develop sophisticated and accurate mathematical procedures for comparing geometric shapes. Children typically follow an observable developmental progression in learning about how shapes are the same and different with recognizable stages or levels. This developmental path can be described as part of a learning trajectory.

Age Range	Level Name	Level	Description
3	"Same Thing" Comparer	1	The first sign of understanding is when the child can compare real-world objects. For example, the children may say two pictures of houses are the same or different.
4	"Similar" Comparer	2	This sign of development occurs when the child judges two shapes to be the same if they are more visually similar than different. For example, the child may say, "These are the same. They are pointy at the top."
4	Part Comparer	3	At this level, a child can say that two shapes are the same after matching one side on each. For example, a child may say, "These are the same" (matching the two sides).
4	Some Attributes Comparer	4	As children develop, they look for differences in attributes, but may examine only part of a shape. For example, a child at this level may say, "These are the same" (indicating the top halves of the shapes are similar by laying them on top of each other).
5	Most Attributes Comparer	5	At this level, the child looks for differences in attributes, examining full shapes, but may ignore some spatial relationships. For example, a child may say, "These are the same."
7	Congruence Determiner	6	A sign of development is when a child determines congruence by comparing all attributes and all spatial relationships. For example, a child at this level may say that two shapes are the same shape and the same size after comparing every one of their sides and angles.
7	Congruence Superposer	7	As children develop understanding, they can move and place objects on top of each other to determine congruence. For example, a child at this level may say that two shapes are the same shape and the same size after laying them on top of each other.
8+	Congruence Representer	8	Continued development is evidenced as children refer to geometric properties and explain with transformations. For example, a child at this level may say, "These must be congruent because they have equal sides, all square corners, and I can move them on top of each other exactly."

Developmental Levels for Spatial Sense and Motions

Infants and toddlers spend a great deal of time learning about the properties and relations of objects in space. Very young children know and use the shape of their environment in navigation activities. With guidance they can learn to "mathematize" this knowledge. They can learn about direction, perspective, distance, symbolization, location, and coordinates. Children typically follow an observable developmental progression in developing spatial sense with recognizable stages or levels. This developmental path can be described as part of a learning trajectory.

Age Range	Level Name	Level	Description
4	Simple Turner	1	An early sign of spatial sense is when a child mentally turns an object to perform easy tasks. For example, given a shape with the top marked with color, the child may correctly identify which of three shapes it would look like if it were turned "like this" (90 degree turn demonstrated), before physically moving the shape.
5	Beginning Slider, Flipper, Turner	2	This sign of development occurs when a child can use the correct motions, but is not always accurate in direction and amount. For example, a child at this level may know a shape has to be flipped to match another shape, but flips it in the wrong direction.
6	Slider, Flipper, Turner	3	As children develop spatial sense, they can perform slides and flips, often only horizontal and vertical, by using manipulatives. For example, a child at this level may perform turns of 45, 90, and 180 degrees. For example, a child knows a shape must be turned 90 degrees to the right to fit into a puzzle.
7	Diagonal Mover	4	A sign of development is when a child can perform diagonal slides and flips. For example, children at this level may know a shape must be turned or flipped over an oblique line (45 degree orientation) to fit into a puzzle.
8	Mental Mover	5	Further signs of development occur when a child can predict results of moving shapes using mental images. A child at this level may say, "If you turned this 120 degrees, it would be just like this one."

Learning Trajectories for Math

Developmental Levels for Patterning and Early Algebra

Algebra begins with a search for patterns. Identifying patterns helps bring order, cohesion, and predictability to seemingly unorganized situations and allows one to make generalizations beyond the information directly available. The recognition and analysis of patterns are important components of young children's intellectual development because they provide a foundation for the development of algebraic thinking. Although prekindergarten children engage in pattern-related activities and recognize patterns in their everyday environment, research has revealed that an abstract understanding of patterns develops gradually during the early childhood years. Children typically follow an observable developmental progression in learning about patterns with recognizable stages or levels. This developmental path can be described as part of a learning trajectory.

Age Range	Level Name	Level	Description
2	Pre-Patterner	1	A child at the earliest level does not recognize patterns. For example, a child may name a striped shirt with no repeating unit a "pattern."
3	Pattern Recognizer	2	At this level, the child can recognize a simple pattern. For example, a child at this level may say, "I'm wearing a pattern" about a shirt with black and white stripes.
4	Pattern Fixer	3	At this level the child fills in missing elements of a pattern, first with ABABAB patterns. When given items in a row with an item missing, such as ABAB_BAB, the child identifies and fills in the missing element (A).
4	Pattern Duplicator AB	4	A sign of development is when the child can duplicate an ABABAB pattern, although the children may have to work alongside the model pattern. For example, given objects in a row, ABABAB, the child may make his or her own ABABAB row in a different location.
4	Pattern Extender AB	5	At this level the child extends AB repeating patterns. For example, given items in a row—ABABAB—the child adds ABAB to the end of the row.
4	Pattern Duplicator	6	At this level, the child is able to duplicate simple patterns (not just alongside the model pattern). For example, given objects in a row, ABBABBABB, the child may make his or her own ABBABBABB row in a different location.
5	Pattern Extender	7	A sign of development is when the child can extend simple patterns. For example, given objects in a row, ABBABBABB, he or she may add ABBABB to the end of the row.
7	Pattern Unit Recognizer	8	At this level, a child can identify the smallest unit of a pattern. For example, given objects in a row with one missing, ABBAB_ABB, he or she may identify and fill in the missing element.

Developmental Levels for Classifying and Analyzing Data

Data analysis contains one big idea: classifying, organizing, representing, and using information to ask and answer questions. The developmental continuum for data analysis includes growth in classifying and counting to sort objects and quantify their groups. Children eventually become capable of simultaneously classifying and counting; for example, counting the number of colors in a group of objects. Children typically follow an observable developmental progression in learning about patterns with recognizable stages or levels. This developmental path can be described as part of a learning trajectory.

Age Range	Level Name	Level	Description
2	Similarity Recognizer	1	The first sign that a child can classify is when he or she recognizes, intuitively, two or more objects as "similar" in some way. For example, "that's another doggie."
2	Informal Sorter	2	A sign of development is when a child places objects that are alike in some attribute together, but switches criteria and may use functional relationships as the basis for sorting. A child at this level might stack blocks of the same shape or put a cup with its saucer.
3	Attribute Identifier	3	The next level is when the child names attributes of objects and places objects together with a given attribute, but cannot then move to sorting by a new rule. For example, the child may say, "These are both red."
4	Attribute Sorter	4	At the next level the child sorts objects according to given attributes, forming categories, but may switch attributes during the sorting. A child at this stage can switch rules for sorting if guided. For example, the child might start putting red beads on a string, but switches to spheres of different colors.
5	Consistent Sorter	5	A sign of development is when the child can sort consistently by a given attribute. For example, the child might put several identical blocks together.
6	Exhaustive Sorter	6	At the next level, the child can sort consistently and exhaustively by an attribute, given or created. This child can use terms "some" and "all" meaningfully. For example, a child at this stage would be able to find all the attribute blocks of a certain size and color.

Age Range	Level Name	Level	Description
6	Multiple Attribute Sorter	7	A sign of development is when the child can sort consistently and exhaustively by more than one attribute, sequentially. For example, a child at this level can put all the attribute blocks together by color, then by shape.
7	Classifier and Counter	8	At the next level, the child is capable of simultaneously classifying and counting. For example, the child counts the number of colors in a group of objects.
7	List Grapher	9	In the early stage of graphing, the child graphs by simply listing all cases. For example, the child may list each child in the class and each child's response to a question.
8+	Multiple Attribute Classifier	10	A sign of development is when the child can intentionally sort according to multiple attributes, naming and relating the attributes. This child understands that objects could belong to more than one group. For example, the child can complete a two-dimensional classification matrix or form subgroups within groups.
8+	Classifying Grapher	11	At the next level the child can graph by classifying data (e.g., responses) and represent it according to categories. For example, the child can take a survey, classify the responses, and graph the result.
8+	Classifier	12	A sign of development is when the child creates complete, conscious classifications logically connected to a specific property. For example, a child at this level gives a definition of a class in terms of a more general class and one or more specific differences and begins to understand the inclusion relation.
8+	Hierarchical Classifier	13	At the next level, the child can perform hierarchical classifications. For example, the child recognizes that all squares are rectangles, but not all rectangles are squares.
8+	Data Representer	14	Signs of development are when the child organizes and displays data through both simple numerical summaries such as counts, tables, and tallies, and graphical displays, including picture graphs, line plots, and bar graphs. At this level the child creates graphs and tables, compares parts of the data, makes statements about the data as a whole, and determines whether the graphs answer the questions posed initially.